U.S. WOMEN'S HISTORY

U.S. WOMEN'S HISTORY

Untangling the Threads of Sisterhood

EDITED BY LESLIE BROWN, JACQUELINE CASTLEDINE, AND ANNE VALK

FOREWORD BY DEBORAH GRAY WHITE

RUTGERS UNIVERSITY PRESS

New Brunswick, New Jersey, and London

Library of Congress Cataloging-in-Publication Data
Names: Brown, Leslie, 1954– editor. | Castledine, Jacqueline Ann, editor. | Valk,
Anne M., 1964– editor.
Title: U.S. women's history : untangling the threads of sisterhood / edited by Leslie
Brown, Jacqueline Castledine, and Anne Valk ; foreword by Deborah Gray White.
Description: New Brunswick, New Jersey : Rutgers University Press, [2016] |
Includes bibliographical references and index.
Identifiers: LCCN 2016015541| ISBN 9780813575841 (hardcover : alk. paper) | ISBN
9780813575834 (pbk. : alk. paper) | ISBN 9780813575858 (e-book : epub) | ISBN
9780813575865 (e-book : web pdf)
Subjects: LCSH: Women—United States—History. | African American women—
United States—History.
Classification: LCC HQ1410 .U177 2016 | DDC 305.40973—dc23
LC record available at https://lccn.loc.gov/2016015541

A British Cataloging-in-Publication record for this book is available from the British
Library.

www.rutgersuniversitypress.org

Manufactured in the United States of America

To Nancy A. Hewitt—teacher, mentor, scholar, and friend—and to Leslie Brown, her first Ph.D. student, who left us too soon

CONTENTS

4   The Maid and Mr. Charlie: Rosa Parks and the
     Struggle for Black Women's Bodily Integrity   67
     DANIELLE L. MCGUIRE

5   Cold War History as Women's History   83
     JACQUELINE CASTLEDINE

6   "I'm Gonna Get You": Black Womanhood and
     Jim Crow Justice in the Post–Civil Rights South   98
     CHRISTINA GREENE

PART THREE: RETHINKING FEMINISM

7   Gender Expression in Antebellum America: 127
     Accessing the Privileges and Freedoms of
     White Men
     JEN MANION

8   When a "Sister" Is a Mother: Maternal   147
     Thinking and Feminist Action, 1967–1980
     ANDREA ESTEPA

9   Contested Geography: The Campaign against   166
     Pornography and the Battle for Urban Space
     in Minneapolis
     KIRSTEN DELEGARD

10   Remembering Together: Take Back the   186
     Night and the Public Memory of Feminism
     ANNE VALK

     Selected Bibliography   207
     Notes on Contributors   213
     Index   219

FOREWORD

When Nancy Hewitt and I began our careers as historians we could assign just about every book written in women's history and still not feel we were overtaxing our students, at least not our graduate students. For a few years in the 1980s we could teach women cross-culturally and internationally and know we were current and keeping up with the historiography. But not so slowly things changed. *U.S. Women's History: Untangling the Threads of Sisterhood* embodies that change and helps us chart it as well.

It's hard to envision an era when the field was relatively closed to women's history and the women who wrote it; but it was not that long ago that lay people, history buffs, and professional historians thought that only white men (and perhaps their minority surrogates) were worthy of investigation and faculty positions. No one would have thought that a comparison of Irish immigrant and African American domestics was a topic worthy of historical study, or that antebellum women cross-dressers could make for riveting history. If they thought about Rosa Parks at all they would have been satisfied with the characterization of her as the "mother of the civil rights movement" and horrified that anyone, much less a professional historian, would dare suggest that she was probably the survivor of sexual violence; "Take Back the Night" would live on ahistorically as something that was just a good idea, and most would not be able to comprehend why a women's historian could find reason to query the cold reception of women's history in Russia, for they themselves would have had the same reaction.

We would not be where *Untangling the Threads* takes us without visionary historians like Nancy, who at once inserted women into the historical narrative and interpreted their presence as well. Nancy's first book, *Women's Activism and Social Change: Rochester, New York, 1822–1872*, pushed the envelope, so to speak. Rather than lumping all of the white women reformers in Rochester into the undifferentiated category of white women reformers, Nancy's story dealt with the ever so elusive category of class (elusive because of the mediating identity category of race). Her second monograph,

Southern Discomfort: Women's Activism in Tampa, Florida, 1880s–1920s, which dealt with Cuban, African American, African Caribbean, and Italian women in Tampa, pushed the envelope even more by showing us that not only did race, class, and gender matter, but immigrant status, color, labor, and geography mattered as well. This rich history of a "border" city was a model for writing what has become known as intersectional history. *Untangling the Threads* bears the imprint of Nancy's works, and models their depth and expansiveness. It demonstrates how far we have come from the days when everything about women's history could be taught in just one course and shows us how variegated women's history is.

Untangling the Threads is also indicative of the power and influence that one historian can have. For anyone who doubts the importance of a smart, thoughtful, dedicated, unselfish mentor, this collection stands as an antidote to that doubt. The contributors to this volume were all mentored by Nancy and this surely helps account for its richness and range. All the identity variables are represented in this volume. Intersectionality is here, at its best. It's not just about white women or rich women or beautiful women, but together the essays tell us about the history of American women who were white, Black, brown, immigrant, rich, poor, middle class, southern, midwestern, northern, liberal, conservative, mothers, and feminists. In presenting women in all their diversity, the chapters showcase Nancy Hewitt's deep commitment not only to the inclusion of everyone who made and makes America, but to the younger historians whose ideas and dreams she validated, often when no one else would.

As many questions as *Untangling the Threads* answers, as much as it tells us about how far we have come in including those previously excluded from the historical narrative, it still leaves some troubling concerns: Once the threads of sisterhood are untangled will *only* threads be left, and is that enough? It might not be the province of historians to wonder about the effects that diversity, such as that presented here, has on future organizing. Our job is to uncloak and unravel the past. We generally leave it to sociologists, political scientists, community organizers, and activists to make sense of our findings, to formulate policy, and to originate social movements. Still, I wonder if historians have a greater role to play in shaping contemporary issues, and I am concerned that in our focus on difference we might be missing what we women do have in common and thus overlook chances for bonding and organizing across difference. I wonder if it is not time to reconsider the uses of intersectionality and consider how and if it can be used not only as a tool for analysis but also for political organizing. Now that we know what separates us, is it not time for historians to join the conversation about how to bridge difference in contemporary America? In this year of presidential politics, when there is a real possibility that Hillary Clinton will be our next president, this concern hits me as particularly salient. Perhaps because there is so much talk about erecting walls to exclude people, I wonder if we intersectional women's historians are not enablers. I wonder whether our focus on difference breaks down or erects walls that prevent effective political coalition. Will women's historians be part of the problem or the solution, and which side of the debate is difference on? Is it possible to use this history to bridge difference for women's common good, or are we just predictors and foreboders of disaster? Nancy showed us how Rochester women of different classes worked differently for the common cause of women's rights; can we do the same for other periods and chart a course for the future benefit of American women?

These are particular idiosyncratic concerns of mine, but they do not obscure my sense of the importance of *Untangling the Threads*, or of the importance of Nancy Hewitt to the historical profession. For fifteen years Nancy was my colleague at Rutgers University and the essays presented here are those that were presented at the 2013 conference entitled "Solidarity and Social Justice: Recasting Histories of Sex, Class, and Race in America," which honored Nancy and her years of service to Rutgers, and the endless hours she spent mentoring students at Duke and Rutgers. She has since retired from Rutgers, and with utmost sincerity I can testify that I miss her. Just as she gave 100 percent to her graduate students, she gave the same to the Rutgers history department. I appreciated the fact that she did not pull punches. She was as honest in collegiality as she was with her research. I so valued her intelligence, her advice, and her integrity. *U.S. Women's History: Untangling the Threads of Sisterhood* is a wonderful collection and the perfect way to honor this original thinker and amazing path-breaking historian.

Deborah Gray White
March 2016

PREFACE
A Feminist Way of Being—
Celebrating Nancy A. Hewitt

I had the pleasure to speak about Nancy Hewitt—historian, activist, teacher, mentor—at a celebration upon her retirement from Rutgers University in 2013. I have known her since we were both at Duke some decades ago and, like so many others, I have benefited not only from her work but also from her kindness and support. I especially remember Nancy's encouraging me to be a part of the women's history group made up of historians from the colleges in the area—and that connection was very important for me, a perennial outlier in academia. As I thought about Nancy for my talk, what came to my mind was the phrase "feminist way of being"; a way she had of not only writing about the world but also consciously making choices—often unconventional ones—about the kind of life she wanted to lead. The following pages highlight just a fraction of the writing and living that moved her colleagues, students, and family to pay tribute to her.

> It was the Vietnam War that turned me into a history major and it was the women's liberation movement that inspired me to get a PhD in women's history, so it was not surprising that history and politics, teaching and activism, seemed fused to me as it has been for so many of us who came of age in the sixties and seventies.
>
> —Nancy Hewitt[1]

Nancy grew up in a working-class family in Spencerport, New York, eleven miles outside of Rochester. In 1969, a year following a flurry of labor strikes by women, the assassination of Martin Luther King Jr., and the Tet Offensive that marked the height of the U.S. involvement in Vietnam, Hewitt got a scholarship to Smith College. Her husband Steven told me she did well academically there but felt out of place among the "Julie Nixon type" of young women at a time of cultural and political upheaval in the country. So, Hewitt returned to upstate New York where she enrolled at SUNY Brockport, and worked day and night shifts at Eastman Kodak, Scrantom's Book and Stationery Store, and Dunkin' Donuts—the latter of which found her donning a pink-and-white waitress's uniform and, in her own words, smelling perpetually of jelly, sugar, and honey glaze.

This period also found her reading everything she could about the burgeoning feminist movement and ringing doorbells for the antiwar presidential candidate George McGovern. These years were the beginning of a political and personal metamorphosis. Nancy, the self-described small-town honor student cheerleader, was becoming an antiwar radical feminist and reflected on the transformation in herself as well as others who became radicalized, and those who did not.

After graduating from SUNY in 1974, Nancy was torn between going to graduate school and becoming a full-time activist. She chose the latter—it was the seventies after all—and backpacked to Berkeley to work as an intern for the Women's Herstory Archives (WHA) only to find her idealism tested. Working conditions at the WHA were worse than those at Dunkin' Donuts! So Nancy did what any emerging feminist would do: she helped organize the other interns—then promptly got fired. But it was okay because the experience of digging and reading through the archives had already set the stage for her "falling in love" with Emma Goldman, the feminist anarchist and a pioneer advocate of birth control.

Voraciously absorbing Goldman's two-volume autobiography, *Living My Life*, Hewitt found a figure who had constructed, then followed, a path of personal and political radicalism out of the turmoil that she had experienced in the Baltic and within her own family in the Jewish ghetto of Russia (now modern Lithuania). After escaping an arranged marriage by immigrating to the United States, Goldman settled in Rochester, where the activist formed her views on the place of community within the framework of an internationalist ideology of social justice. Nancy characterized this relationship as "The Emma Thread": activism that "embeds a global vision of change in communal and communitarian values." The idea would lead Hewitt to become a social historian who believed that community study was the most effective way of exploring "the larger trajectory of ordinary people's lives." For Nancy, Rochester now belonged more to the Jewish émigré Goldman than to its other famous feminist resident, Susan B. Anthony.

Furthermore, in Berkeley Nancy found "a special energy and comfort in the all-female spaces that were now a part of my daily life." The diverse circles of women in her Berkeley community exposed Hewitt to "how race, class, and ideology shaped different conceptions of equality and liberation." This idea was affirmed through her reading about women's movements in China, Vietnam, and Cuba, which showed her how women had gained a semblance of equality by struggling alongside men against authoritarian regimes. As she wrote, "global and local perspectives, sisterhood and dif-ference, lesbian separatism and social networks that included men seemed deeply intertwined, each incomplete without its counterpart."

Hewitt returned back home from California to an ailing brother and a dad who needed her attention. While back in Rochester, she helped found a feminist newspaper, worked again at the stationery store, and compiled—in a time before computer searches—a catalogue of every book on anarchism she could find at the University of Rochester library.

Nine months later, Hewitt entered the next phase of her life when she received an acceptance letter from the University of Pennsylvania history department. She was one of three students admitted into the PhD program; and the one student who felt that the others knew so much more than she did. It was the historian Carroll Smith-Rosenberg who "worked to gently but firmly transform me from a feminist polemicist into a women's histo-rian," albeit a radical one. Nancy joined the local chapter of the Mid-Atlantic Radical Historians Organization, where she and her fellow students debated Karl Marx and Michel Foucault, organized protests, exchanged ideas about teaching—and drank plenty of beer.

When *historian* Hewitt revisited the archives at the University of Roch-ester, she examined the rich harvest of antebellum women activists who sought to transform society. Among them was Amy Post, a Quaker aboli-tionist and women's rights advocate, whose political views were matched by her own feminist way of being. Post refused to consume slave-produced goods, socialized with those who were not white, provided a refuge for escaped slaves, wives who were abused, and itinerant activists—and donned a mean set of bloomers.

Just as importantly for Hewitt's own worldview, Post also had a com-munitarian vision that included the rights of the Seneca Indians as well as issues like land reform. Moreover, Post, like Nancy, and for that matter Goldman, was shaken—in a good way—when she left her relatively iso-lated Rochester community for urban, heterogeneous, New York City with its class, ethnic, racial, and religious differences and conflicts. In Amy Post, Nancy found Goldman's foremother and maybe in certain ways, her own.

The general study of Rochester antebellum activists, which materialized into her first book, *Women's Activism and Social Change*, confirmed something else as well. The insight that Nancy had gained in Berkeley helped her to recognize how women's class locations fomented different views of what constituted emancipation and equality. As a review in *Contemporary Sociology* noted, Hewitt's study distinguished "three networks of women's activism: women from the wealthiest Rochester families who sought to ameliorate the lives of the poor; those from upwardly mobile families who, influenced by evangelical revivalism, campaigned to eradicate such social ills as slavery, vice, and intemperance; and those who combined limited economic resources with an agrarian Quaker tradition of communalism and religious democracy to advocate full racial and sexual equality."[2] No wonder the *American Historical Review* called *Women and Social Change* a "model for future community studies."[3]

Nancy further developed that model when she went to teach at the University of South Florida, at Tampa, in 1981, where she was the first woman hired by the history department on a tenure-track line. As she would in every institution that she was a part of, Nancy combined teaching, activism, and scholarship. Hewitt helped to organize a group of professors from the departments of history, theater, and the medical school, where they organized teach-ins, lectures, and showed films on current political issues at home and abroad. She became active in the Coordinating Committee on Women in the Historical Profession/Conference Group on Women's History, the International Federation for Research in Women's History, and the Southern Association for Women's Historians, and served as a founding editor of the journal *Gender and History*. Nancy also directed symposia on Central America and militarism, protests of the Gulf War, and the demand for divestment in South Africa. She helped to write the sexual harassment guidelines for USF, helped to sustain a faculty union, and worked with the Florida Endowment for the Humanities to promote multicultural history programs, which would incorporate race, class, and gender in all of the basic courses.

Hewitt also conducted teaching workshops around Florida for both college and high school teachers, and eventually in other states and in summer institutes. Among her colleagues was a historian named Steven Lawson, her partner for over two decades; and one of those summer institutes—for middle-school teachers, in the late 1980s—was run by a historian and future

Rutgers colleague, Deborah Gray White. Nancy and Steven gave presentations on women's history and civil rights.

By the 1980s, women's history was being transformed by studies of and by African American women, working-class women, and immigrant women. Of course, it was one thing to acknowledge the existence of a diverse group of women on history's horizon, but quite another to absorb the logic of their activism that challenged the unitary primacy of gender oppression and the universalization of women as a category. While a number of historians resisted—or only half-heartedly embraced—an intersectional framework, Nancy's communitarian perspective had long taken into account Black, ethnic, and working-class women and she entered the debate with her essay "Beyond the Search for Sisterhood," published in *Social History* in 1984. In it she critiqued long-held historiographical assumptions about separate spheres, women's culture, identity formation, and gender as the primary source of oppression.

Pulling on "Emma's Thread," Hewitt further synthesized ideas gained from her experience and scholarship in her project researching the lives of Latin—mainly Cuban—and Italian women cigar-workers who settled in Tampa at the turn of the twentieth century. They were the perfect subjects for a narrative that revealed how women activists claimed their various identities. Hewitt understood how these women maintained their multiple identities, while focusing on whichever one was dictated by the situation. This allowed them to be strategic in responding to opportunities and/or oppressive conditions.

For example, during the Spanish-American War, both middle- and working-class women devoted their energies to the independence movement. But as soon as the war ended, a major strike in the cigar factories forced working-class women to differentiate themselves from their wealthier counterparts who owned the factories. Once the strike was settled, the tobacco stemmers, all of whom were women, protested the fact that the male cigar rollers received more benefits. In a very short span of time, they went from organizing around their ethnic identity, to organizing around their class identity, to organizing around their gender identity.

There was an additional complexity to unravel. It soon became apparent that because Tampa was still subject to the rigid Jim Crow laws, women often found their ability to work together constrained by racial divides. For instance, the Spanish-American War at the end of the nineteenth century certainly galvanized Latin women, like the Puerto Rican anarchist and labor organizer Luisa Capetillo, to become politically active, but "it also pulled Black and white women into the conflict, either supporting the troops stationed in Tampa or questioning whether we should be fighting against Spanish tyranny in Cuba when Blacks in the United States were under a kind of white supremacist tyranny."[4]

Clearly, the Tampa study had to expand to include Anglo and African American activists—the latter of whom included three activist women hairdressers. This was another strand of "Emma's Thread" in which Latino and Latina workers wanted to overthrow Spanish rule in Cuba and Puerto Rico and had to contend with the arrival of thousands of white and Afro-Cuban cigar-makers in the 1890s—just as the institution of Jim Crow laws was undermining the gains made after Emancipation. The key elements were the moments of rupture—moments that can serve as catalysts of change rather than stasis or regression—which allowed women to reconfigure rather than reject communal and collective values as the source for their global visions. Hewitt's essay on the Tampa activists, published in *Visible Women*, brought "Tampa into the mainstream of U.S. urban and labor history," according to the *American Historical Review*.[5]

In 2001, the study of Tampa women bloomed into Nancy's full-length masterwork, *Southern Discomfort: Women's Activism in Tampa, Florida, 1880–1920s*. *Gender and History* called it a "highly nuanced and evocative study [that] challenges scholars to rethink and reshape constructions of race, ethnicity, identity, community, and female activism in the South."[6] It won the prestigious Julia Cherry Spruill Prize, awarded by the Southern Association for Women's Historians.

By then Nancy had had a six-year tenure at Duke where she directed the Sawyer Seminar on Women's Leadership and Grassroots Activism. The project included scholars from Africa, Central America, and the Caribbean that fortified the strands of "Emma's Thread" with its creation of a network of scholar-activists practicing communitarian politics. Her mentoring and scholarship at Duke, noted William Chafe, former dean of Arts and Sciences, helped to transform the Duke history department. Following Duke she taught at Rutgers where her teaching, mentoring, and activism guided students and faculty alike through roiling issues of affirmative action, sexual assault on campus, the denigration of the women's basketball team, and of course the 2008 primaries with its heated competition between Hillary Clinton and Barack Obama—a competition that revealed that race and gender were still too often seen as oppositional rather than interrelated.

Nancy's scholarship offers insight into this false dichotomy of race and gender. *No Permanent Waves: Recasting Histories in U.S. Feminism,* an anthology of essays edited by Hewitt, does this in part by challenging the "master" narrative of the beginning of the women's rights movement.

When that narrative frames the movement's origins with the 1848 Seneca Falls convention, where no Black women were present, where women's suffrage became the focus of the movement, and where the dominant struggle became that over the Fifteenth Amendment that allowed Black men to vote but not women, it puts the opposition of race and gender at the heart of the history. In her introduction and chapter entitled "From Seneca Falls to Suffrage? Reimagining a 'Master' Narrative in U.S. Women's History," Hewitt performs the revisionist task brilliantly.

She notes that well before 1848, there had been women's rights activism and biracial organizations where women of color had leadership roles and/or prioritized such issues as the rights of Native American women, the economic demands of working-class and ethnic women, and the plight of Chicanas in the wake of the Mexican-American War, among other issues. As in Tampa and in the political thinking of Goldman and Post, the women's conception of women's rights may have included suffrage but these other issues were seen as at least equally, if not more, important to the activist project.

With this wider intersectional view of the template of the beginnings of women's rights movements, we are less apt to exclude women of color and working-class women—or pit race against gender—in our historical and contemporary imagination. "From Seneca Falls to hip-hop, this striking collection pushes us to rethink the who, what, when, where, and why of U.S. feminist history," said the historian Joanne Meyerowitz about *No Permanent Waves* on the book's back cover. "The wide-ranging essays toss out the overly tidy generational model and replace it with complex, rich, and inclusive accounts of our feminist past."

I ended my talk with words of praise from her former students—a significant number of whom have published their own groundbreaking books—who were both nurtured and inspired by Nancy, a recipient of numerous teaching awards. Both they and her colleagues in this volume attest to a legacy, a vision, a feminist way of being that has enriched us all.

Paula J. Giddings

NOTES

1 Quotations, unless otherwise indicated, are from Nancy A. Hewitt, "The Emma Thread: Communitarian Values, Global Vision," in *Voices of Women Historians: The Personal, the Political, the Professional*, ed. Eileen Boris and Nupur Chaudhuri (Bloomington: Indiana University Press, 1999), 235–247.

2 Sara M. Evans, review of *Women's Activism and Social Change: Rochester, New York, 1822–1872*, by Nancy A. Hewitt, and *The Free Women of Petersburg: Status and Culture in a Southern Town, 1784–1860*, by Suzanne Lebsock, *Contemporary Sociology* 14 (May 1985): 354.

3 Sarah Elbert, review of *Women's Activism and Social Change: Rochester, New York, 1822–1872*, by Nancy A. Hewitt, *American Historical Review* 91 (Feb. 1986): 181.

4 Hewitt, "The Emma Thread," 244–245.

5 Nancy A. Hewitt, "In Pursuit of Power: The Political Economy of Women's Activism in Twentieth Century Tampa," in *Visible Women: New Essays on American Activism*, ed. Nancy A. Hewitt and Suzanne Lebsock (Urbana: University of Illinois Press, 1993), 199–222. Sharon Hartman Strom, review of *Visible Women*, ed. Nancy A. Hewitt and Suzanne Lebsock, *American Historical Review* 100 (Dec. 1995): 1653.

6 Vivien Miller, review of *Southern Discomfort: Women's Activism in Tampa, Florida, 1880–1920s*, by Nancy A. Hewitt, *Gender and History* 15 (Apr. 2003): 171.

ACKNOWLEDGMENTS

The seeds for this volume were planted during a conversation in 2011. Meeting for coffee during the triennial Berkshire Conference on Women, Gender, and Sexualities, Leslie and Annie expressed to Nancy Hewitt our desire to edit a volume in her honor. With her customary graciousness and openness, Nancy recommended Jacki as a third editor and suggested that the volume be less of a commemoration and more of a compilation of new scholarship in women's history. When Nancy's long-time colleague Deborah Gray White began to organize a conference that would gather former students to present research that was inspired or guided by Nancy, we realized those presentations could form the substance for this collection.

Many people provided assistance and support through this process. Deborah Gray White's work was critical; we thank her and her students for coordinating Solidarity and Social Justice, the 2013 conference at Rutgers University where many of these essays were initially presented. Thanks as well to the scholars and students who attended that gathering and shared their interest and their incisive questions. And we owe much appreciation to Steven Lawson. Throughout our process of editing, Steven gave us timely feedback and answered our questions, even the stupid ones, with speed and humor.

We express our gratitude to Rutgers University Press for its enthusiastic embrace of the project. Executive Editor Kim Guinta patiently replied to our many inquiries and prodded and pushed us to make and stick to a schedule—otherwise we still would be revising. Two outside readers supplied thoughtful responses to the initial drafts; their enthusiasm and criticism helped make the volume better.

Working collaboratively as a team of editors and with a cohort of authors—in many cases now friends—tested our communication and organizational skills and forced us to deal with the technical challenges of document sharing, working across operating systems, merging calls on our iPhones, and handling multiple versions of files. We thank the authors for putting up with these challenges and with our sometimes confusing correspondence. It has been a pleasure to work with them and to learn from their fantastic work. We are proud of their contributions and appreciate the opportunity to publish them here.

As we complete this project and as representatives of the authors brought together here, we would like to thank Nancy Hewitt, whom we honor with this volume, for her positive influence on our lives and our work. We also wish to thank all of Nancy's friends, colleagues, collaborators, and family members—far too many to list here—who share her passion for the work of women's history and whose example we hope we emulate.

U.S. WOMEN'S HISTORY

INTRODUCTION

LESLIE BROWN

Nancy Hewitt is one of a cohort of women's historians whose push to move beyond the analytical "search for sisterhood" resulted in a significant paradigm shift in the field's historiography. That shift is reflected in this collection. The following essays concur that race, class, and gender still matter because they inform women's political culture, community, and economic options as well as their activism. But these authors argue other issues of identity matter also: era, location, political perspectives and affiliations, religiosity, sexuality, generation, citizenship status, migration and immigration experiences, marital status, labor outside and inside the home, and claims of motherhood. Each essay in this collection forms a thread that connects back to Nancy Hewitt and forward to other scholars. Sewn together, the chapters in *Untangling the Threads of Sisterhood* convey the state of the field of U.S. women's history in the early twenty-first century. These essays demonstrate why and how U.S. women's history covers the range it does, its propensity to question its own frameworks and analyses, to use fresh approaches to reach new conclusions about familiar and unfamiliar themes, and to follow its threads to new subjects.

In order to understand this process, it is helpful to briefly review the past.[1] Early projects in women's history included celebratory discoveries that identified women of note and commemorated their accomplishments in their communities or in the male-dominated political arena. Simultaneously, scholars hunted for evidence and focused on archival projects; uncovered, compiled, preserved, and shared sources that told stories of women's lives in every region in the United States; and mined libraries for books, articles, manuscripts, and dissertations on women. Published primary source collections made these stories accessible, and sought after.[2] Among their evolving themes, historians recognized women's voluntary associations not only as women's contributions to society, but also as expressions of women's politics and culture, and that communities and families take all sorts of forms.[3] Inserting women into the annals and narrative of U.S. history challenged the broader story, pointed to the ways that patriarchy limited women's personal and political freedom, and revealed a chronicle where select groups of men dominated and restrained the processes of change. The field turned its analyses toward the distinction and differences that separated women from men.

At the same time, feminist and womanist theory and methodologies from other fields expanded the ways that historians read literature, viewed photographs, analyzed art, assessed record books, letters, and diaries, and conducted oral history interviews. By the 1990s, the field of women's history had transformed itself by following threads of differences among women rather than similarities, and turning toward analyses of the distinctions and power differentials that separated women. Those threads led a new generation of women's historians to identity *differences* among women as a theme and a foundational category of analysis for the field.

The publication of Deborah Gray White's book *Ar'n't I a Woman: Female Slaves in the Plantation South* marked a watershed, a directional shift in U.S. history.[4] White's work challenged the narrative of not only African American history and southern history—and by extension U.S. history—but also women's history. The vast distinctions between enslaved women and slave-owning women clarified how sisterhood could neither be inclusive nor expected. Published the same year as White's book, Nancy Hewitt's seminal article, "Beyond the Search for Sisterhood: American Women's History in the 1980s," called for a paradigm shift that would complicate the narrative of women's history by incorporating class and race analyses.[5] Arguing that the field was overly concerned with the experiences of white middle-class northern women, Hewitt joined other women's historians writing on this issue. Interrogating dissimilarities among women by race, class, gender, and other identities, scholars could analyze socially constructed power relations defining women's communities, including the community of women's historians. Elsa Barkley-Brown explained in her pivotal essay "What Has Happened Here: The Politics of Difference in Women's History and Feminist Politics" that the tendency to focus on white women and white women's historians disappeared both Black women's history and Black women historians.[6] Likewise, Evelyn Brooks Higginbotham, in "Beyond the Sound of Silence: Afro-American Women in History," wrote of historians' failure to recognize African

American women's history as a subject on its own.[7] Evelyn Nakano Glenn, Vicki Ruiz, and Hasia Diner engaged historical critiques of white middle-class gender roles by documenting the lives and labors of Asian, Latina, Irish, and Jewish women. Joanne Meyerowitz, Mari Jo Buhle, Alice Kessler Harris, Thomas Dublin, and others focused on women migrants and factory workers, and joining with these, others spun out more threads to follow. The scope of production—monographs, syntheses, community studies, critical biographies, compilations, and textbooks—attests to the synergy, the creative tension among the multiple constituencies of women's history.[8]

Despite fears among some women's historians that pursuing difference over commonality would diminish the importance of patriarchy and oppression, shared by all women, the discourse of difference did not disrupt the project of women's history. Indeed, the matrix of U.S. women's histories recrafted a subject into a credible and challenging field, even as it continued to deepen its own explorations into the construction of gender roles within specific communities and at particular moments in time. As the field has grown, scholars of women's and gender history have answered new calls to look beyond early historical paradigms, to move from a critique of "sisterhood," and, moreover, to nuance race and class differences in order to better examine separate-ness and idiosyncrasy, intersectionality and intrasectionality. Racism, classism, sexism, homophobia, nativism, and other forms of oppression cannot be transected into separate forms of discrimination. Nor can women parse their own race, class, gender, and sexual identities, their region, religiosity, and political affiliation into discrete elements.

Still wary of sisterhood, however, the scholarship of the late 1990s and 2000s revealed different ways that collaboration among women could emerge: around social and political issues expressed, for instance, in antipoverty campaigns, women's health and peace movements, and labor organizing. Tangling and untangling these strands and threads also recast the metaphors once used to describe the frameworks of women's activism. The "waves" metaphor—used to describe how women's movements ebbed and flowed across time, as in first-, second-, or third-wave feminism—gave way to an analysis of women's movements as persistent and continuous "permanent waves." In addition, women's historians returned to familiar themes like suffrage and electoral politics, mothers' campaigns for their and their children's needs, perspectives of (and about) radicals, and more specific mechanisms of oppression and dynamics of power relations.

The essays collected here demonstrate that the feminist project of women's history—or, rather, women's, gender, and sexuality histories—continues to complicate and expand its topics, methodologies, and analyses. Written by junior, senior, and mid-career scholars in history and women's and gender studies, the chapters in this book present community studies, comparative analyses, social movements, and cultural and public history. The authors examine the political demands that emerged from women's perceptions of their identities as wives, mothers, lovers, and citizens, linked to their efforts to fight against gender, race, class, and other constraints. Together the essays take up three broad historiographical issues: examinations of the relationships among groups of women, challenges to accepted historical narratives, and new ways to understand efforts to define and claim women's rights. They attempt to answer perennial questions in the field: What are the prospects for sex-based connections when women of different groups do not face comparable circumstances? What new categories of analysis or avenues of inquiry can women's historians bring to seemingly traditional themes, like motherhood and labor? How can we track the waves of feminism or trajectories of civil rights activism and at the same time capture the tumult within them? The authors bring new answers but even more questions to these and other themes. Thus, even as they challenge established master narratives, these essays singly and collectively further women's history's prospects for engaging new theoretical concepts and alternative lenses to relay a women's history of social and political change.

The first section of the book, "Searching for Sisterhood," seeks out and then complicates commonalities among women. But the works also reconsider the means and meanings of those connections. For example, in "Cleaning Race: Irish Immigrant and Southern Black Domestic Workers in the Northeast United States, 1865–1930," Danielle Phillips discusses women's experiences of migration and labor, comparing immigrant women from Ireland to migrant African American women from the South. Both denigrated groups worked in household labor and confronted damaging stereotypes, while also competing with each other for respectability and employment. The race and gender ideologies swirling in public discourse prevented any alliances among them, however. Rebecca Tuuri reconsiders African American women's activism in the Black freedom movement. In "'By Any Means Necessary': The National Council of Negro Women's Flexible Loyalties in the Black Power Era," Tuuri analyzes the relationship between the moderately positioned National Council of Negro Women (NCNW) and

the radical women of the Student Non-Violent Coordinating Committee (SNCC). Although the two groups differed in their history, membership, and approaches to social change, Tuuri uncovers significant overlap
between them. She argues that in the late 1960s and early 1970s, NCNW
and SNCC women found a common platform from which to continue their
forms of activism. The final essay in this section, Ariella Rotramel's "'This
Is Like Family': Activist-Survivor Histories and Motherwork," analyzes
oral history interviews she conducted with activists from the South Bronx
group Mothers on the Move/Madres en Movimiento (MOM). Drawing on
the concept of "motherwork," Rotramel discusses ways that MOM brings
in women (and men) who seek to support their own growth as survivors
of violence by working to address community concerns. Women's famil-
iarity with violence is deeply personal but Rotramel finds this experience
also connects them to a larger group of activists and concerned community
members who seek to lessen economic, environmental, and educational
inequities.

The second set of essays takes up recent challenges to narratives of wom-
en's history. The field of intersectionality studies provides theoretical under-
pinnings for Danielle McGuire's "The Maid and Mr. Charlie: Rosa Parks
and the Struggle for Black Women's Bodily Integrity," as McGuire considers
the significance of an essay allegedly written by Parks. The essay describes a
sexual assault on Parks, yet because it was found after her death its author-
ship is contested. Critics' efforts to dismiss the essay, McGuire argues, are
intended to silence discussions of Parks's radical political consciousness
and to sustain her image as a moderate civil rights figure. In "Cold War History as Women's History" Jacqueline Castledine also explores the silencing of women's voices, arguing that in the last two decades the trope of the
successful "containment" of postwar U.S. women in their homes has been
widely discredited by historians. Yet Castledine suggests that scholars of
the American left have only recently begun to explore how "deep ideological divides with friends, family, and community" helped to erase radical
women's political activism from cold war historiography. Examining the
activist life of Vermonter Helen MacMartin, Castledine considers whether
women do indeed have a cold war history. The last chapter of this section,
Christina Greene's essay "'I'm Gonna Get You': Black Womanhood and
Jim Crow Justice in the Post–Civil Rights South," explores the legacy of the
Joan Little rape-murder trial and its wide-reaching implications. Tried in
Beaufort County, North Carolina, for the 1974 murder of a jail guard, Little

was vilified and then vindicated for fighting back against a sexual assault by her white jailer. Although the trial ended with an unlikely and celebrated exoneration, Greene writes that one triumph is not a victory against "a long history of discriminatory treatment within the criminal justice system" and cautions against allowing Little's victory to obscure the "roots of our modern carceral state."

The final essays complicate the theme of feminism and movements for women's rights. Jen Manion's chapter, "Gender Expression in Antebellum America: Accessing the Privileges and Freedoms of White Men," de-links mid-nineteenth-century campaigns for dress reform and women's rights from the collection of women who sought to exercise the freedoms of white men by dressing and passing as men. Considering the interplay between the organized women's rights movement and the actions of unknown numbers of gender crossers, including women who donned male clothing and personae in order to escape enslavement, Manion finds that both efforts challenged prescribed gender norms. Indeed, Manion argues, even though they did not work in concert, gender crossers made other women's rights activists appear more reasonable and thereby advanced their cause. Nearly one hundred years later, participants in 1960s and 1970s radical feminist groups sought to craft an activist identity and agenda that continued the opening up of gender roles begun during the antebellum era. Like the women's rights activists that Manion studies, the feminist mothers in Andrea Estepa's "When a 'Sister' Is a Mother: Maternal Thinking and Feminist Action, 1967–1980," challenged gendered expectations of their time. Differentiating between childbearing and child rearing, these activists—feminist mothers—sought to transform parental and familial roles and the forms of gender socialization that supported them. The personal truly became political, as these activists crafted agendas and created childcare arrangements based on the insights drawn from their own families. Feminist mothers, Estepa contends, constituted an important but often invisible subgroup within the larger women's movement.

Kirsten Delegard takes up the subject of activists in Minneapolis, Minnesota, who banded together to make city streets safer for women. As Delegard explains in "Contested Geography: The Campaign against Pornography and the Battle for Urban Space in Minneapolis," a deep attachment to place motivated women to fight to reclaim their neighborhood from a growing commercial pornography district, and to curb the harassment and humiliation that women endured on the streets. Minneapolis activists pressed for changes in zoning, policing, and business practices, but then made an uneasy alliance with feminists who pushed for an all-out ban on pornography. Although that ban was never instituted, Delegard observes that one important legacy of this earlier movement can be seen in continued unease between feminists and gay men in the city. Anne Valk's essay similarly charts the history of how feminist activists have organized Take Back the Night, once an assertive claim for women's right to public space and safety from harassment and sexual violence. TBTN continues as a recognition of the sexual danger confronting women, albeit more recently in the form of closed and quiet assemblies. Looking at the history of this annual event, Valk points out how, nonetheless, history and memory provide a foundation for continuing the project, bringing new generations of participants to the struggle. Like other authors in this section, she considers the impact of this activism on a larger movement for women's rights and on the public perception of that movement.

In addition to these issues, several specific themes and subjects cut across the sections of the book. The essays by Phillips, McGuire, Greene, Tuuri, and Manion focus on aspects of African American women's history. Spanning from Manion's considerations of women's efforts to gain their freedom by posing as men; to Phillips's examination of the ways that popular depictions of African American domestic workers reinforced racial distinctions and established the whiteness of their Irish counterparts; to Tuuri's, Greene's, and McGuire's analysis of forces that shaped Black women's demands for rights within the larger freedom movement—together these articles suggest the necessity of linking race, class, and gender to understand the constraints women faced and the strategies they could employ to improve the economic, legal, and social well-being of their families and communities. The subject of women's changing approaches to combating sexual violence in its many forms also makes up a core theme. Studies by Rotramel, McGuire, Greene, Delegard, and Valk all point to the persistence of violence and the inventive responses women have employed across time and community. At the same time, these essays suggest how cultural expectations and social realities can both increase women's vulnerability and curtail the effectiveness of their political strategies. Tuuri, Castledine, and Estepa add to the analysis of women's political activism. Their investigations highlight the importance of understanding the inner workings of organizations and the diversity of people and ideas that drive social change efforts. They also hint at the critical role that scholars can play in rethinking historiography and contesting the memories of movements that take root over time.

Untangling the Threads of Sisterhood moves forward with the central critique of U.S. women's history, that the sisterhood refrain of presumed commonality stymies the study of women's lives, communities, and activism. Together the essayists in this volume still argue that at its core, women's history scholarship must recognize the distinctiveness of women's experiences with oppression, agency, activism, and feminism, *and* the issues around which groups of women can coalesce, however fleetingly. For these reasons, U.S. women's history joins—and perhaps with African American history leads—recent historical trends toward more complex, if uncomfortable, analyses of the past. What is women's history now, in the early twenty-first century? It is, as always, inspired by questions from the past and the present and creatively dedicated to the project of documenting the lives of women in the United States.

NOTES

1 The texts and articles that should be included in this introduction form a very long list, one far too long for a comprehensive note. Therefore I have listed in the notes below a few select works that exemplify the trends discussed throughout the introduction.

2 For example, Gerda Lerner, *Black Women in White America: A Documentary History* (New York: Random House, 1972); Anne Firor Scott and Andrew M. Scott, *One Half the People: The Fight for Woman Suffrage* (New York: Lippincott, 1975); Jacquelyn Dowd Hall and Anne Firor Scott, "Women in the South," in *Interpreting Southern History: Historiographical Essays in Honor of Sanford W. Higginbotham*, ed. John B. Boles and Evelyn T. Nolen (Baton Rouge: Louisiana State University Press, 1987), 454–509.

3 For example, Carroll Smith-Rosenberg, "The Female World of Love and Ritual: Relations between Women in Nineteenth Century America," *Signs* 1 (Autumn 1975): 1–29; Linda Gordon, *Woman's Body, Woman's Right: A Social History of Birth Control in America* (New York: Grossman/Viking, 1976); Nancy Cott, *The Bonds of Womanhood: Women's Sphere in New England, 1780–1835* (New Haven: Yale University Press, 1977); Kathryn Kish Sklar, *Catharine Beecher: A Study in American Domesticity* (New Haven: Yale University Press, 1973).

4 Deborah Gray White, *Ar'n't I a Woman: Female Slaves in the Plantation South* (New York: W. W. Norton, 1985, 1995).

5 Nancy A. Hewitt, "Beyond the Search for Sisterhood: American Women's History in the 1980s," *Social History* 10 (October 1985): 299–321.

6 Elsa Barkley Brown, "What Has Happened Here: The Politics of Difference in Women's History and Feminist Politics," *Feminist Studies* 18 (Summer 1992): 295–312.

7 Evelyn Brooks Higginbotham, "Beyond the Sound of Silence: Afro-American Women in History," *Gender & History* 1 (March 1989): 50–67.

8 Vicki L. Ruiz, *Cannery Women, Cannery Lives: Mexican Women, Unionization, and the California Food Processing Industry, 1930–1950* (Albuquerque: University of New Mexico Press, 1987); Evelyn Nakano Glenn, *Issei, Nisei, War Bride: Three Generations of Japanese American Women in Domestic Service* (Philadelphia: Temple University Press, 1986); Hasia R. Diner, *Erin's Daughters in America: Irish Immigrant Women in the Nineteenth Century* (Baltimore: Johns Hopkins University Press, 1983); Hasia Diner and Beryl Benderly, *Her Works Praise Her: A History of Jewish Women in America from Colonial Times to the Present* (New York: Basic Books, 2002); Joanne Meyerowitz, *Women Adrift: Independent Wage Earners in Chicago, 1880–1930* (Chicago: University of Chicago Press, 1988); Mari Jo Buhle, *Women and American Socialism, 1870–1920* (Urbana: University of Illinois Press, 1981); Thomas Dublin, *Women at Work: The Transformation of Work and Community in Lowell, Massachusetts, 1826–60* (New York: Columbia University Press, 1979); Alice Kessler Harris, *Out to Work: A History of Wage Earning Women in the United States* (New York: Oxford University Press, 1982).

PART ONE SEARCHING FOR SISTERHOOD

1 • CLEANING RACE

Irish Immigrant and Southern Black Domestic Workers in the Northeast United States, 1865–1930

DANIELLE PHILLIPS

In 1866 the scowling face of Mrs. McCaffraty stared out at readers of *Harper's Weekly* as cartoonist Thomas Nast's "Holy Horror of Mrs. McCaffraty" captured the unsettledness surrounding race and gender following the recent passage of the Civil Rights Act by Congress.[1] In the cartoon, Mrs. McCaffraty's round body and face are contorted with anger and her mob cap and bib apron mark her as employed in domestic service. Her basket overflows with the stuff of working-class women's domestic labor: fish (are we to imagine that it stinks?), vegetables, and bottles. The Black woman next to her epitomizes nineteenth-century ladyhood: slender face and body, lace-trimmed dress, and bonnet with hair neatly held by a snood. Her gentle hands grasp a parasol and purse. Her casual demeanor seems uncaring or unaware of Mrs. McCaffraty's high dudgeon. Although Black, she is the woman of careless leisure. She is Mrs. McCaffraty's "holy horror."[2]

What is striking about the image is that it illustrated a shift in the country's attention—and anxiety—from Irish immigrant and African American men to their sisters, daughters, nieces, and wives. Since Ireland's potato famine, native-born whites had attributed societal ills to degenerate Irish immigrant men and Black men.[3] I argue that after Emancipation, African American and Irish immigrant women's household labors as domestic workers became a medium through which the country gauged and defined racial hierarchies and undesirables. By the late nineteenth century, Mrs.

McCaffraty no longer had to worry about the perception that Black women were more worthy of American citizenship than their Irish counterparts. Although African American and Irish immigrant women were concentrated in the lowest-paid women's work by the late nineteenth century, the newcomers from Ireland would access the privileges of American citizenship before Black women.

Irish women immigrated to the United States in their greatest numbers in the mid-nineteenth century and southern Black women migrated to the North in unprecedented numbers after World War I. While the height of Irish and Black women's movement to the urban North took place in different periods, similar circumstances fueled their migration, and their labor histories in domestic service overlapped. Both entered northeastern cities as racialized beings who had been relegated to tenant farming and household work in their hometowns. They also left the U.S. South and Ireland to escape poverty and violent social and political conflict. Of all the ethnic and racial groups of women who migrated to northern U.S. cities they were most likely to be concentrated in domestic service (except for Caribbean women).[4]

Overall Irish immigration declined in the late nineteenth century, yet a series of crop failures in the late 1870s and 1880s and violent conflicts between British soldiers and Irish nationalists who sought freedom from British rule fueled Irish women's immigration to the United States until the early 1930s, when they chose Great Britain as their primary destination.[5] In 1900, the U.S. Immigration Commission reported that 71 percent of Irish immigrant women in the labor force were classified as "domestic and personal workers" and 54 percent were classified as "servants and waitresses." By 1912 and 1913, nearly 87 percent of the Irish women who had migrated to America worked in some form of private or public domestic service. And as late as 1920, Irish-born women still constituted 43 percent of white, female, foreign-born domestic servants in the United States.[6]

Streams of Irish and Black women from similar, but also very different contexts, flowed into the Northeast, a region fraught with its own political and socioeconomic unrest. Although native-born white northerners had boasted that the North was the pinnacle of American democracy and progress, they remained deeply ambivalent about Irish immigration, women's rights, and Black freedom following the Civil War. They encapsulated these sentiments in portrayals of the Irish and southern newcomers as the source of the "servant problem," or the shortage of reliable, clean, honest, and efficient household servants.[7]

While they cleaned dirt from floors, linens, and dishes, Irish immigrant and African American women also worked at redefining ideologies of race that deemed them "dirty" and thereby undeserving of the promises of American citizenship. As Phyllis Palmer noted, "Dirtiness appears always in a constellation of the suspect qualities that, along with sexuality, immorality, laziness, and ignorance, justify social rankings of race, class, and gender."[8] As can be seen in "The Great Scrub Race" (circa 1870), progress, whiteness, intelligence, and respectable womanhood were mutually constituting categories represented in the labor of women (see figure 1.1).[9]

Only native-born, landowning white men were without markers of racial and gender inferiority. Unquestioned American citizens, they had the right to an education, to own property, to vote, to earn livable wages, and to live in safe and comfortable housing. Irish immigrant and African American domestic workers worked long hours in private homes to access the rights and resources of citizenship. As with work that rearranged household objects, Irish immigrant women reorganized the terms of white female respectability to include themselves. Black women's citizenship-claiming tasks, however, were more daunting. They not only had to clear away entrenched ideologies of womanhood; they also had to eliminate ideologies of race that excluded them from the *human*.

The outcomes and the duration of their work could not have been more different. By the 1930s, Irish immigrant women had exited domestic service and could vote as white women. Today Irish immigrant women are engrained in the American imagination as respectable, God-fearing, hard-working matriarchs who raised their children to become responsible American citizens.[10] Since slavery, ideologies of race relied on the premise that Black women were hypersexual, masculine, immoral, and *permanently* inferior. Hence, the work of eliminating ideologies that categorized Black women as antithetical to American citizenship persisted much longer than it did for Irish immigrant women. Black women also remained concentrated in domestic service until the latter half of the twentieth century.[11] And their project is ongoing. As Melissa Harris-Perry noted in *Sister Citizen*, "Black women are rarely recognized as archetypal citizens."[12]

The questions I explore in this chapter are the following: What do the lives and representations of Irish immigrant and southern Black women tell us about the racial projects of the late nineteenth and early twentieth centuries?[13] What strategies did both groups of women use to redefine race as they cleaned homes and resisted labor exploitation? Because I am interested

FIGURE 1.1 Advertisement for Eureka mops, 1870. Dialogue in the top image: "No use, she's got a Eureka." Dialogue in the bottom image: "I told you so!"(Courtesy of Library of Congress Prints and Photographs Online Catalog.)

in analyzing how domestic workers shaped ideologies of race, I am exploring, as Nancy Hewitt put it, "women who sought to make sense and create
order out of the upheavals of their time."[14]

REARRANGING BOUNDARIES OF
WHITENESS AND RESPECTABILITY

Before Ireland won its independence in 1921, the British had long declared
the Irish a racial "other" to justify England's assertion of political, religious,
and economic dominance over Ireland since the twelfth century. As J. J.
Lee explained, racism occurred in Ireland "where there were no observable
differences" between the Irish and British.[15] Protestant Irish descendants
of early British settlers, the Anglo-Irish established a tenant farming labor
system in the 1800s that seemed to confirm the belief that the Irish were in
fact inferior to the *white* British. Catholic Irish families were confined to living on small tenant farms owned by Anglo-Irish landlords who demanded
exorbitant rents. Irish girls had few options but to quit school at an early age
and learn domestic skills including cooking, knitting, and poultry and dairy
work.[16] Irish women and girls also worked alongside their fathers, brothers,
and husbands harvesting potatoes, vegetables, and eggs and tending to live-
stock for both subsistence and to sell so that they could pay their Anglo-
Irish landlords.

The minimal oversight of agricultural production and the overproduction
of the potato crop to meet the excessive demands of Anglo-Irish landowners
facilitated fungus growth, which in turn compromised the fertility of the soil.
From 1845 to 1847 a strain of bacteria spread across farms, destroying potato
crops that were a source of income and personal consumption for Irish families.[17] Faced with insurmountable poverty, limited options for earning a living, and virtually no political power to change their economic circumstances
under British rule, approximately three million people from Ireland crossed
the Atlantic Ocean to seek domestic service jobs in the United States well into
the early twentieth century. Over 50 percent of the immigrants were women.[18]

Irish women could not have come to the United States at a better time
for domestic service employers. Industrialization expanded employment
options for native-born white women who had been employed as the "help"
in private homes since the early nineteenth century. By the mid-nineteenth
century, native-born white women had exited private household work to

become housewives or work in factories. With housework experience and limited formal education, Irish-born women displaced the smaller population of free Black women in domestic service and became the largest group of servants in the urban Northeast.[19]

Irish immigrant women arrived in the United States as racialized beings entering a racially stigmatized occupation. Although Irish women on both sides of the Atlantic were portrayed as dirty, lazy, and domineering in contrast to their pious white Anglo-Saxon Protestant mistresses, and were concentrated in domestic service in both countries, the circumstances by which Irish women were racialized by the British in Ireland were distinct from the conditions from which the Irish "Bridget" emerged in U.S. racial discourse. The battle between Protestants and Catholics for power in the name of religion and Britain's refusal to release Ireland and its other colonies from its control set apart the Irish from the *white* British race. The racialization of the Irish in the United States, by contrast, had nothing to do with land but had everything to do with political power, jobs, American citizenship, and most importantly, slavery.

The racial shift in domestic service to an Irish-dominated occupation did not diminish the negative stigma associated with it. Despite Irish immigrant women's displacement of free Black women, the newcomers from Ireland entered a labor niche that had been defined as servile, Black, and non-feminine work since slavery. The very term "servant" held significant racial meanings in a country that had long celebrated the republican ideologies of independence and free labor as a certifiable virtue of whiteness and Americanness. According to Leslie Harris, "Whites believed that blacks who had been enslaved and who in freedom held jobs as servants were the most degraded workers and the farthest removed from the ideal republican citizen."[20] As such, *servant* was a term that white domestic workers in northern cities in the early 1800s avoided, preferring to be called "the help" to distinguish themselves from enslaved Black women.

Domestic service was defined as a form of dependent labor that was only suitable for enslaved Black women in the homes of white slaveholders. Irish immigrant women's living arrangements—they obtained food and lodging as well as wages by residing in their employer's home—were different from what enslaved Black women household workers were coerced into doing in the South. Native-born white Protestant employers, however, were suspicious of poor, immigrant, female outsiders who were devoted to a "suspicious" religion and hailed from a country that resisted Anglo-Saxon rule well into the late nineteenth century.[21] Despite their dissatisfaction with Irish servants, employers depended heavily on their labors, which fueled complaints for several decades.[22] Employers accused Irish newcomers of being bossy, impatient, dirty, defiant, incapable of doing household tasks properly and thereby the source of instability in the American home. These incessant complaints were captured in the dark, masculine, and animalistic Irish "Bridget" caricature in print media.

As women who were on the edges of whiteness, Irish immigrant women did not have to completely redefine race. Irish servants inserted themselves into the sphere of white female respectability by linking their concerns to the larger Progressive Era movement to end the labor exploitation of wage-earning white women. Irish immigrant women asserted themselves as simultaneously professional workers and *white* "ladies" who deserved the same treatment as native-born white housewives and white male and female factory workers. Irish serving women created women's branches in the male-dominated Knights of Labor and joined white women's labor organizations to advocate for their own legal protection. They set the clock on the time they would do domestic work in other people's homes and refused to do tasks that were beneath wage-earning white *ladies*. The daughters of Erin also demanded respect and fair working conditions on the job by expressing their candid opinions about white women employers in local newspapers.

An Irish servant who signed her letter "Brave Irish Girl" responded to a letter written by "C.O.P.," a domestic service employer who complained to readers about an Irish servant in her home. According to the employer, the servant stole food from her kitchen and used household toiletries excessively. "Brave Irish Girl" wrote in response to C.O.P.'s letter: "I pity the poor, innocent Irish girls who meet with such as 'C.O.P.' I don't consider her a lady. I guess 'C.O.P.'s' girl must have been starved when she took the bread. I hope she did not eat the soap. 'C.O.P' is more of a servant herself than the lady help that worked for her. I guess 'C.O.P.' is one of those ladies who pays $5 a month and expect everything done first class. . . . I have lived with a lady who always stole my shoe blacking to polish her shoes with. She would not give me a cake of soap in my room. She said she could not afford it."[23]

An Irish servant who signed her letter "Irish Rambler" associated herself with ideas of whiteness and Americanness by drawing an instructive parallel between slavery and the working conditions of Irish immigrant women in domestic service. "Irish Rambler" predicted that if employers continued issuing low wages to Irish servants, "then we will have what Abe Lincoln never thought of—white slavery. It is very near that now."[24] As the letter made clear, "Irish Rambler" based her demand for better working conditions for her fellow Irish women on the fact that they were white and thus deserved the same level of respect as white American workers. Domestic workers collaborated with labor organizers to demand protection in the workplace on the basis that they were white workers. Although Irish American and Irish-born leaders in these organizations rarely spoke about the particular concerns of domestic workers, deciding to focus primarily on the concerns of immigrant women in factories and mills, one of the most outspoken labor leaders, Leonora O'Reilly, did advocate that all wage-earning Irish immigrant women be respected as white workers who deserved better working conditions and higher wages.[25] While delivering a speech about factory workers, O'Reilly argued that labor legislation was also needed to "break up caste and put domestic service on another foundation."[26]

The Catholic Church also charted avenues for Irish immigrant women to achieve white femininity by providing hospital employment to the Irish newcomers, which offered an escape from the racial stigma of domestic service even for Irish women who were not trained nurses. At the insistence of their relatives, some Irish immigrant women sought jobs cleaning floors and linen in hospitals instead of cleaning private homes. Frances Hoffman migrated from Londonderry, Northern Ireland, in 1923 to live with her uncle in New York City. Shortly after arriving in Manhattan, Hoffman told her uncle that she planned to apply for domestic service positions at the employment agency down the street from where he lived. He warned Hoffman, "No, do not go there. That is for colored people. You can work in a hospital." Hoffman followed her uncle's advice and searched for employment at the Brooklyn State Hospital. Three days later, she was hired as a nursing assistant.[27] Her duties were similar to domestic work, but without the racial stigma associated with domestic service. Irish immigrant women who worked as formally trained nurses achieved a degree of racial and social-class mobility. Nursing was a racially segregated occupation considered skilled labor for only white women. As Jane Edna Hunter, founder of the Phyllis Wheatley Association and a nurse trained at the Hampton Institute, was told by a white doctor when she arrived in Cleveland, Ohio, in 1905: "white doctors did not employ nigger nurses."[28]

Many women who had been in domestic service insisted on leaving their jobs to become housewives. These Irish immigrant women adopted the customs of their native-born white women employers, using similar furniture and linens to adorn their homes.[29] Despite Irish immigrant women's advancements, however, they remained concentrated in service jobs, encountered ethnic discrimination in the workplace, returned to domestic service during periods of financial hardship, and remained a generational step behind Jewish women and native-born white women in occupations well into the 1930s.

In contrast to that of Irish immigrant women, the racial identity of Black women was never open to debate. They were undeniably Black, which for native-born whites meant that they were in a permanent state of inferiority to all other races and ethnicities. Attaining freedom required Black women to, as Leslie Brown put it, "redefine black womanhood" and "shed the burdens of labor and reproduction that black women had carried in the past."[30] An additional task, particularly for southern Black women in the North, was to redefine what it meant to be southern, Black, migrant, wage-earning women in the North. As women who were the descendants of enslaved laborers and who entered a region that was culturally distinct from the South, journalists quickly categorized them as outsiders who were akin to immigrants.[31] Reporters also suggested that southern Black women become Americanized before working in northern white homes.[32]

CLEANING RACE: DOMESTIC LABOR AND THE LEGACY OF SLAVERY

After Emancipation, African American women were relegated to the lowest-paid labors of sharecropping and domestic service in the South, with no legal protection. The federal government failed to establish a land redistribution program after the Civil War to allocate property to formerly enslaved Blacks. Whites remained in control of the land and refused to sell their property. Bitter over the economic and political outcomes of the Civil War, they also sought to regain control over Black labor by establishing a sharecropping system. With very little capital, Blacks had few options but to work as tenant farmers for survival, sometimes on the same property where they had been enslaved. While Black women's daily routines consisted of domestic chores, including cooking breakfast for children and male sharecroppers in the household, they also worked alongside men planting, chopping, and harvesting cotton, and digging up potatoes and picking peas on small plots of land. White landowners held Black families in perpetual debt by charging exorbitant prices for tools, seeds, and fertilizer needed to grow crops and they imposed strict rules that required families to pay rent in the form of a fixed amount of cash rather than a portion of the harvest.[33]

Some Black women left the farms to seek higher wages in domestic service in southern towns and cities. Although some domestic workers found "good" employers, the occupation itself remained low-wage work.[34] Not all white employers accepted Emancipation and many refused to recognize domestic workers as wage-earning women. They continued the exploitative labor practices prevalent during slavery. Some employers refused outright to pay domestic workers livable wages, claiming that Black women had gotten lazy since the Civil War. Others paid domestic workers with leftover food or second-hand clothing instead of money. Black women were also accused of becoming dirtier now that they were no longer under the watchful eye of slaveholders. When tuberculosis hit southern towns in the late 1800s, Black women were accused of exposing their employers to the disease such that it became known as "the servants' disease."[35]

In addition to being subjected to a repackaged slave labor system, Blacks had no legal recourse for protection against labor exploitation. They were forced to adhere to the Black Codes, a series of laws passed by southern states in the 1860s that confined them to low-wage work through vagrancy laws. As during slavery, lynchings and sexual and physical abuse remained a constant threat to Black women whether or not they spoke out against their working conditions. The Atlanta city government allowed the Ku Klux Klan to threaten domestic workers who "gave too much lip" or talked back to their employers.[36] The 1896 Supreme Court's *Plessy v. Ferguson* decision further entrenched white supremacy by legalizing racial segregation. Except for the very few southern towns that Blacks established and controlled, Blacks were barred from political and civil service positions, and most institutions, public spaces, and residential neighborhoods remained segregated.[37]

Southern Black women began migrating to northern cities before the Great Migration in the 1910s to escape racial and gender violence and exploitative tenant farming and domestic service. They migrated from rural farms to small towns and then to cities, constantly in search of better wages and living conditions for themselves and their families.[38] Between 1870 and 1910, an average of 6,700 Black southerners migrated north annually to search for better working and living conditions. Over 90 percent of the early migrants worked in domestic service.[39] When Black women left the South during the late nineteenth century, they ventured primarily into cities along the east coast, including Washington, D.C., Philadelphia, Baltimore, and New York City.

The women who took part in this early migration were young, single, separated, or widowed, and they often made the journey alone.[40] Some women traveled north to work in private homes only during the summers while others settled there working in domestic service permanently. They maintained strong ties with their family members in the rural South by sending money and letters about life and work in the urban centers.[41] Family communication with their loved ones helped fuel the Great Migration of southern Blacks to northern cities from roughly the 1910s until the 1970s.[42] As settlement worker and researcher Isabel Eaton discovered in her study of domestic workers in Philadelphia, some employers preferred hiring the southern newcomers over Irish servants. Seventh Ward housewives assumed that southern Black women were "more anxious to please" than Irish servants because slavery instilled in them the importance of having an "agreeable and obliging" demeanor toward whites.[43]

Black women worked at cleaning race by asserting themselves as wage workers through individual acts of resistance, through music, and through collective organizing. Confronted with having to prove themselves *human*, Black women worked across social classes and employed multiple strategies to disrupt dominant racial ideologies that "explained" unequal wages. Black domestic workers toiled to rid domestic service of its ties to slavery by asserting themselves as wage workers deserving of livable wages and safe working conditions. And Black middle-class women, some of them daughters of domestic workers, researched and wrote their mothers, sisters, and aunts working in private homes into the American story of respectable hard, wage-earning work.

Few working Black women left behind letters and testimonials describing their experiences as domestic workers. The voices of Black women in domestic service did not become pronounced and formally organized until they created the Domestic Workers' Union in New York City in 1935. We know, however, from interviews, newspaper articles, song lyrics, and personal stories passed down from generation to generation in Black families that Black women engaged in acts of resistance. Black women developed formal organizing strategies primarily in the South where they far outnumbered immigrants. Washerwomen in Atlanta, Georgia, organized labor strikes against white employers who refused to pay them livable wages and against Chinese immigrants who set up commercial laundries. Washerwomen strikes also occurred in Jackson, Mississippi, in 1866 and Galveston, Texas, in 1877.[44] Some Black women employed resistance methods in the North as they did in the South. They refused to do dangerous tasks and left their jobs when their employers demanded too much of them.[45] Black women also created a blacklist of names to share with family and friends warning them to stay away from employers who refused to pay Black women livable wages, or any at all. And most importantly, the southerners transformed domestic service into a live-out occupation. Although some newcomers lived in their employers' homes, most Black women insisted that they have their own homes so that they could put an end to their workday.[46]

Southern Black middle-class women, some of whom were the daughters of domestic workers or worked in domestic service themselves, entered the national discussions about race, migration, and domestic labor. They delivered speeches, wrote articles, and researched the experiences of Black women in domestic service. Victoria Earle Matthews, a Georgia native born to a white slaveholding father and an enslaved mother, worked as a domestic servant in New York City before becoming a clubwoman and co-founder of the White Rose Industrial Home for Working Class Negro Girls. She established the home to assist other southern migrant Black women with finding safe lodging and domestic service employment. While directing the home she traveled across the United States to drum up support for southern migrant women by dispelling myths that they were immoral women who posed a danger to northern cities. Matthews argued in a famous speech at Hampton University in 1898 that disreputable domestic service employers and the owners of brothels preyed upon innocent and respectable southern migrants. And she asserted Black women's claim to American citizenship by insisting that their exploitation was a national problem. She concluded her speech by demanding that the country do something to help the "long-suffering cruelly-wronged, sadly unprotected daughters of the entire South."[47]

Clubwomen also established distinctions between southern Black women and immigrants to make the case that Black women were in fact American citizens whether or not the country chose to recognize them as such. They also argued that domestic workers in particular deserved adequate compensation and legal protection in the workplace before immigrants were granted such privileges. Women's suffragist and southern migrant Anna Julia Cooper was among the most outspoken nineteenth-century clubwomen on the subject of race, immigration, and domestic service. Cooper witnessed firsthand the exploitation of Black women in white homes as a young enslaved girl in Raleigh, North Carolina. Cooper credited her critical analysis of racial, class, and gender inequalities in the labor sector to conversations that she overheard between elderly women on the plantation who spoke about their work experiences in slaveholders' homes. Cooper was also aware of her mother's experiences as a domestic servant during slavery and after Emancipation.[48] She advocated for legal protections for Black household workers by expressing her disdain for northern whites who were more sympathetic to the labor exploitation of European immigrants. In her classic text, *A Voice from the South by a Black Woman from the South*, Cooper declared:

> How many have ever given a thought to the pinched and down-trodden colored women bending over wash-tubs and ironing-boards . . . ! Will you call it narrowness and selfishness, then, that I find it impossible to catch the fire of sympathy and enthusiasm for most of these [European] labor movements at the North? . . . I feel like saying, I can show you workingmen's wrong and workingmen's toil which, could it speak, would send up a wail that might be heard from the Potomac to the Rio Grande; and should it unite and act, would shake this country from Carolina to California.[49]

Cooper stressed the importance of Black women's household labors seven years later in her *Southern Workman* article entitled "Colored Women as Wage Earners." In the article, Cooper redefined ideologies of domesticity by blurring the line between the public and private spheres and disrupting the Victorian belief that working women defied the norms of femininity. According to Cooper, Black women did not receive wages for the productive work that they did in their own homes and they were severely underpaid for important work that they did for employers. She explained, "The fact remains that a large percentage of the productive labor of the world is done by women . . . ; of 1,137 colored families 650, or 57.17 percent, are supported wholly or in part by female heads. So that in comparison with white, female heads of families and others contributing to family support, there is, by a house to house enumeration, quite a large excess on the part of colored women."[50] Cooper concluded from her research that Black women's labors were grossly undervalued, although their labor required "the capacities in

man, intellectual as well as physical and moral, which have economic significance."[51] Consequently, Cooper argued, Black women were simultaneously
respectable and intelligent wage earners.

Music was another medium through which Black women articulated
their perspectives about their working experiences.[52] In the 1920s, patrons of
blues clubs and juke joints could hear Bessie Smith sing of "bustin' suds" all
day long and doing more work "than forty-'leven Gold Dust Twins."[53] When
Works Progress Administration researcher Vivian Morris interviewed
Rose Reed, a domestic worker in the Bronx during the Depression, Reed
explained that spiritual music gave her the strength to bear the backbreak-
ing work of domestic service and to lead her to better working conditions.
She recalled that after singing "I Got to Get Rid of This Heavy Load" and
"Go Down Moses" while scrubbing floors, she learned later the same day
about the Domestic Workers' Union. After joining the union, Reed's wages
increased and her working conditions improved.[54]

Despite the simultaneous efforts of both Irish immigrant and Black
women to assert their own definitions of race and domestic work, redefining race was much more difficult for Black women. After the Immigration
Act of 1921, racial categories were more rigidly defined and Irish immigrant
women ascended to higher strata of whiteness than previously. In the 1920s,
employment opportunities outside of domestic service opened up for Irish
immigrant women and by the 1930s most had exited domestic service altogether. In cities like New York where the Irish outnumbered other immigrant populations, Irish immigrant women could vote for Irish American
politicians who reserved city contracting and construction jobs for their
husbands, uncles, nephews, and sons. Irish American men held political
office, owned salons and contracting companies, and dominated the police
force, which was instrumental in establishing racial divisions on the ground.
As James R. Barrett argued, newcomers to New York City "could be excused
for thinking that 'Irish' equaled 'American.'"[55]

Black women's racial project continued beyond the Progressive Era.
By the 1930s, Black women dominated domestic service in the North and
South and they continued engaging in multiple forms of resistance by working with women's organizations, Black labor organizations, and educators to
end labor exploitation in domestic service.[56] Formal organizing to address
the particular concerns of domestic workers emerged during the 1930s. In
1934, Dora Lee Jones worked with a small group of Finnish women to create
the Domestic Workers Union of Harlem, which was initially affiliated with

the Building Service Union, Local 149. The National Negro Congress sponsored the Domestic Workers Association in New York City, which worked with Black labor activists including A. Phillip Randolph to fight for legislation to standardize domestic service.

Black women also enlisted for domestic service training programs developed by the Young Women's Christian Association and collaborated with the Women's Trade Union League to upgrade the profession.[57] While domestic workers joined labor organizations, clubwomen like Cooper remained committed to speaking out against the labor exploitation of Black women in domestic service. In a 1930s speech entitled "On Education," Cooper declared that domestic workers were the "cream" of "natural endowment" and represented the "thrift, the mechanical industry, the business intelligence, the professional skill, the well-ordered homes, and the carefully nurtured families that are to be found in every town and hamlet where the colored man is known."[58] Despite these wide-ranging efforts to change the racial terms of domestic service, it was not until after the Civil Rights Act of 1964 that Black women could make the large-scale transition into other occupations.

CONCLUSION

Bringing together the labor and migration histories of southern Black migrant and Irish immigrant women in domestic service challenges the assumption that they did only manual labor. They engaged in both physical and ideological work to redefine blackness and whiteness for wage-earning women. Their histories also complicate understandings of race that rely on the labors and migrations of men. Shifting to a comparative focus on women's domestic labors and migrations opens a new avenue for tracing the messy process of constructing the meanings of whiteness, blackness, and American citizenship after Emancipation. An integrated history of Irish immigrant and southern Black migrant domestic workers challenges the idea that all Irish immigrant struggles with race ended in 1863 when Irish men became members of the white working class. As Catholic immigrant women from a despised country and concentrated in a "Black" occupation, Irish immigrant women worked harder and longer than their male counterparts to ascend to higher strata of whiteness.

A comparative history also challenges perceptions that race sparked either alliances or tensions among immigrant and Black workers. There are no recorded stories of violent conflicts between Irish immigrant and Black women in domestic service. The women's stories, however, reveal the complexity and power of race whereby an imaginary construct could be molded by political interests and anxieties to render distinct groups of women nearly synonymous, although the women's actual paths did not always cross in the homes where they worked. The women, as journal editors, cartoonists, and employers imagined them, illustrated national debates about race, gender, and citizenship. However, these women also created discourses and representations of themselves while engaging in labor actions that molded definitions of race and gender at the turn of the nineteenth century. Thinking about cleaning race through women's migrations and labors expands the theoretical and conceptual terrain on which we can understand the historical and contemporary dilemmas of race.

NOTES

1 After President Abraham Lincoln signed the Emancipation Proclamation in 1863, Democrats and Republicans in Congress engaged in contentious debates over whether Blacks were American citizens. Radical Republicans in the House of Representatives introduced the Civil Rights Act to Congress. Abraham Lincoln's successor, President Andrew Johnson, refused to see Black people as human and tried to restore white supremacy by vetoing the act. The Radical Republican–controlled House of Representatives overrode the veto and the act became law in 1866. See David W. Blight, *Race and Reunion: The Civil War in American Memory* (Cambridge, MA: Harvard University Press, 2001), 45–49.

2 The bracketed caption read: "Mr. McCaffraty Voted against Negro Suffrage"; see "Holy Horror of Mrs. McCaffraty in a Washington City Street Passenger Car," *Harper's Weekly*, Feb. 24, 1866, http://www.harpweek.com/09cartoon/BrowseByDateCartoon.asp?Month=February&Date=24, accessed July 28, 2014. The website comments: "The bracketed remark lets viewers know that she represents the type of disreputable person who opposed black manhood suffrage."

3 Upon arrival, Irish immigrants and free Blacks lived in the same neighborhoods and worked in the same low-wage jobs. Irish immigrant and free Black men worked alongside each other before the Civil War as longshoremen, artisans, apprentices, and dock workers in Boston, New York City, and Philadelphia. See David Roediger, *The Wages of Whiteness: Race and the Making of the American Working Class* (New York: Verso, 1991), 144–149. Cartoon images of Irish immigrant and Black men reinforced their racially inferior, non-American, and non-masculine status in a country in which the model American citizen was defined as a rational, entrepreneurial, land-owning WASP (White

Anglo Saxon Protestant) breadwinning man. See Noel Ignatiev, *How the Irish Became White* (New York: Routledge, 1995), 41.

4 Jewish and Italian women avoided domestic work because they were already married before immigrating to the United States or married soon afterward. They labored either as housewives or workers in factories and stores. See Jennifer Guglielmo and Salvatore Salerno, eds., *Are Italians White: How Race Is Made in America* (New York: Routledge, 2003), 11; Hasia Diner, "A Century of Migration, 1820–1924," in *From Haven to Home: 350 Years of Jewish Life in America* (New York: George Braziller Press, 2004), 75–76.

5 Margaret Lynch-Brennan, *The Irish Bridget: Irish Immigrant Women in Domestic Service in America, 1840–1930* (Syracuse, NY: Syracuse University Press, 2009), xvii.

6 Ibid., 42.

7 David Katzman, *Seven Days a Week: Women and Domestic Service in Industrializing America* (Urbana: University of Illinois Press, 1981), 223–224.

8 Phyllis Palmer, *Domesticity and Dirt: Housewives and Domestic Servants in the United States, 1920–1945* (Philadelphia: Temple University Press, 1989), 140.

9 The woman in yellow is telling the clearly Irish and African American women there is no use competing with the white woman because she has a Eureka mop. Library of Congress Prints and Photographs Online Catalog, circa 1870.

10 Bronwen Walter, *Outsiders Inside: Whiteness, Place, and Irish Women* (New York: Routledge, 2001), 74.

11 Premilla Nadasen, *Household Workers Unite: The Untold Story of African American Women Who Built a Movement* (Boston: Beacon Press, 2015), 7.

12 Melissa Harris-Perry, *Sister Citizen: Shame, Stereotypes, and Black Women in America* (New Haven: Yale University Press, 2011), 20.

13 Like sociologists Michael Omi and Howard Winant, I define race as "an unstable complex of social meanings constantly being transformed [and reasserted—my addition] by political struggle." According to Omi and Winant, racial projects do the ideological work of defining race. A racial project "is simultaneously an interpretation, representation, or explanation of racial dynamics and an effort to reorganize and redistribute resources along particular racial lines." See Michael Omi and Howard Winant, *Racial Formation in the United States: From the 1960s to the 1990s* (New York: Routledge, 1994), 55–56. Like historical sociologist Evelyn Nakano Glenn I argue that racial formation is also a gendered process. See Evelyn Nakano Glenn, *Unequal Freedom: How Race and Gender Shaped American Citizenship and Labor* (Cambridge, MA: Harvard University Press, 2002), 6.

14 Nancy Hewitt, *Southern Discomfort: Women's Activism in Tampa, Florida, 1880s–1920s* (Champaign: University of Illinois Press, 2003), 15. Similar to Nancy Hewitt's analysis of how African American and Afro-Cuban women redefined race through their activism in cigar factories in Tampa, Florida, I examine how Black and Irish immigrant women's activism, household labors, and migrations defined race in the United States during the late nineteenth and early twentieth centuries.

15 J. J. Lee, *Ireland 1912–1985: Politics and Society* (Cambridge: Cambridge University Press, 1989), 3.

16 Diner, "A Century of Migration, 1820–1924," 13.

17 Kerby Miller, *Emigrants and Exiles: Ireland and the Irish Exodus to North America* (New York: Oxford University Press, 1935), 345–346.

18 Lynch-Brennan, *The Irish Bridget,* xix.

19 Leslie Harris, *In the Shadow of Slavery: African Americans in New York City, 1626–1863* (Chicago: University of Chicago Press, 2003), 183.

20 Ibid., 98.

21 Faye Dudden, *Serving Women: Household Service in Nineteenth-Century America* (Hanover, NH: Wesleyan University Press, 1983), 65–66.

22 Hasia Diner, *Erin's Daughters in America: Irish Immigrant Women in the Nineteenth Century* (Baltimore: Johns Hopkins University, 1983), 88.

23 "Hopes 'C.O.P.'s' Girl Did Not Eat the Soap," *Brooklyn Eagle,* Mar. 12, 1897.

24 "'Irish Rambler' Suggests a Servant Girl Trust," *Brooklyn Eagle,* Mar. 11, 1897.

25 Lara Vapnek, *Breadwinners: Working Women and Economic Independence, 1865–1920* (Urbana: University of Illinois Press, 2009), 46–47; 130.

26 Leonora O'Reilly, "A Few Thoughts Suggested on Reading," June 18, 1907, Women's Trade Union League Papers on microfilm, Texas Woman's University Library.

27 Frances Duffy Hoffman, interview by Janet Levine, Feb. 20, 1997, interview EI-853, transcript, Ellis Island's Bob Hope Memorial Library Archive.

28 Deborah Gray White, *Too Heavy a Load: Black Women in Defense of Themselves, 1894–1994* (New York: W. W. Norton, 1999), 30.

29 Maureen Murphy, "Birdie, We Hardly Knew Ye: The Irish Domestics," in *The Irish in America,* ed. Michael Coffey and Terry Golway (New York: Hyperion, 1997), 145.

30 Leslie Brown, *Upbuilding Black Durham: Gender, Class, and Black Community Development in the Jim Crow South* (Chapel Hill: University of North Carolina Press, 2008), 2–3.

31 *San Francisco Daily Evening Bulletin,* July 28, 1879.

32 "Work to Domestic Service," *New York Times,* Oct. 20, 1907.

33 Elizabeth Clark-Lewis, *Living In, Living Out: African American Domestics in Washington D.C., 1910–1940* (Washington, DC: Smithsonian Institution Press, 1996), 9–13.

34 Leslie Brown and Annie Valk, *Living with Jim Crow: African American Women and Memories of the Segregated South* (New York: Palgrave Macmillan, 2010), 81–82.

35 Tera Hunter, *To 'Joy My Freedom: Southern Black Women's Lives and Labors after the Civil War* (Cambridge, MA: Harvard University Press, 1997), 187–190.

36 Testimony of Alfred Richardson, July 1871, in *United States Congress Report: Testimony Taken by the Joint Select Committee to Inquire into the Condition of Affairs in the Late Insurrectionary States, Volume 1: Georgia* (Washington, DC: Government Printing Office, 1872), 12, 18.

37 Glenn, *Unequal Freedom,* 94–97.

38 Brown, *Upbuilding Black Durham,* 90.

39 Jacqueline Jones, *Labor of Love, Labor of Sorrow: Black Women, Work, and the Family from Slavery to the Present* (New York: Vintage Books, 1985), 155–156.

40 Ibid., 111.

41 Clark-Lewis, *Living In, Living Out,* 54.

42 Joe William Trotter, ed., *The Great Migration in Historical Perspective: New Dimensions of Race, Class, and Gender* (Bloomington: Indiana University Press, 1991), 17.

43 Ibid.

44 Hunter, *To 'Joy My Freedom*, 74–97.

45 Bonnie Thornton Dill, *Across the Boundaries of Race and Class: An Exploration of Work and Family among Black Female Domestic Servants* (New York: Garland Publishing, 1993), 92–93.

46 Clark-Lewis, *Living In, Living Out*, 5.

47 Victoria Earle Matthews, "Some of the Dangers Encountered by Southern Girls in Northern Cities," *Hampton Negro Conference Proceedings*, no. II (July 1898): 62.

48 Vivian May, *Anna Julia Cooper, Visionary Black Feminist: A Critical Introduction* (New York: Routledge, 2007), 14.

49 Anna Julia Cooper, *A Voice from the South* (New York: Oxford University Press, 1988), 254–255.

50 Anna Julia Cooper, "Colored Women as Wage Earners," *Southern Workman* 28 (August 1899): 295.

51 Ibid., 296.

52 For a history of Black worker folks songs, see Lawrence Levine, *Black Culture and Black Consciousness* (New York: Oxford University Press, 1997).

53 For the lyrics to Bessie Smith's "Washwoman's Blues," see A. Davis, *Blues Legacies and Black Feminism: Gertrude "Ma" Rainey, Bessie Smith, and Billie Holiday* (New York: Vintage Books, 1999), 98–99.

54 For Lawrence Levine's analysis of the interview, see *Black Culture and Black Consciousness*, 161. To read the full-length interview and Morris's analysis of Reed's story, see Works Progress Administration Domestic Workers' Union, interview by Vivian Morris, February 2, 1939, 2.

55 James R. Barrett, *The Irish Way: Becoming American in the Multi-Ethnic City* (New York: Penguin Press, 2012), 2.

56 Esther V. Cooper, "The Negro Woman Domestics in Relation to Trade Unionism" (Master's thesis, Fisk University, 1940), 2.

57 Eileen Boris and Premilla Nadasen, "Domestic Workers Organize!" *WorkingUSA: The Journal of Labor and Society* 11 (2008): 417–418; Philip S. Foner and Ronald L. Lewis, *The Black Worker during the Era of the American Federation of Labor and the Railroad Brotherhoods* (Philadelphia: Temple University Press, 1979), 256.

58 Charles Lemert and Esme Bhan, eds., *The Voice of Anna Julia Cooper* (New York: Rowman and Littlefield, 1998), 254.

2 ◆ "BY ANY MEANS NECESSARY"

The National Council of Negro Women's Flexible Loyalties in the Black Power Era

REBECCA TUURI

In 1966, when young radical activist Frances Beal left behind her soon-to-be ex-husband in Paris and moved back to the United States with her two young children in tow, she needed to find employment quickly. Through her friends at the Student Nonviolent Coordinating Committee (SNCC), she learned that the National Council of Negro Women (NCNW), the largest Black women's organization in the United States at that time, was looking to hire staff for Project Womanpower, a new initiative targeting Black women from around the country. Project Womanpower supported self-help projects to combat poverty, homelessness, substandard schools, and joblessness.[1] This program may have surprised Beal, as the council had a reputation for moderation, for hosting teas and lobbying congressmen, rather than fighting on the ground for change or working with the poor. Deborah Gray White points out that the council also had been unable to attract young women as members for well over a decade, as they lost potential members to more dynamic, direct-action civil rights projects.[2] However, in 1966, the council achieved tax-exempt status as a nonprofit and began recruiting more militant young women from SNCC to work as staff for the organization.[3] The council hired Beal as legal secretary as well as other SNCC members, including Prathia Hall, Doris Dozier, and Gwendolyn Robinson as staff for Project Womanpower. Unlike earlier council projects in the 1960s, this one was not concerned with working toward interracialism, but instead with developing self-help programs that targeted only Black women, reflecting the shift within the larger Black free-dom struggle from integration to Black separatism.

Enabling the council's push in hiring staff was its new tax-exempt status and a $300,000 grant from the Ford Foundation for Project Womanpower. As Beal recalls, "NCNW hired people who had been in SNCC . . . , so it was like an act, we were young Turks in the group." But Dorothy Height, president of the NCNW, did not disregard the more radical ideas of the newly hired staff members. Instead, as Beal recalls, "she always listened. She always had an open ear."[4] When Project Womanpower ended, Beal stayed on at the council as the editor of its newsletter, *The Black Woman's Voice*, until 1975. During these crucial ten years, Beal wrote the foundational text "Double Jeopardy: To Be Black and Female" and helped found the Third World Women's Alliance.

Radical women's highly principled, outspoken, and often public insis-tence on justice for the oppressed in the 1960s and 1970s has rightfully captured the attention of recent scholars.[5] These women advocated pow-erful and bold positions such as Black separatism and nationalism, and many, like Beal, were committed to overhauling established American political, social, and economic structures in favor of more communal-based systems and using force if necessary. But women such as Beal did not work alone. The story of the council illuminates how in this historical turn toward radicalism in the Black Power era, Black women's organiza-tions and activists could collaborate across cultural and ideological lines, each aiding the other.[6]

As a moderate organization, the NCNW had always been publicly com-mitted to working interracially, nonviolently, and within the established political, social, and economic structures of American democracy and capi-talism. The council was formed in 1935 to unite Black women's sororities, professional organizations, and auxiliaries to act as a clearinghouse to boost the political and professional power of Black women. The council occasion-ally fought for civil rights legislation such as supporting antilynching and anti–poll tax laws, but its primary focus over its first twenty-five years was on lobbying for increased employment and political opportunities for Black women.[7] Although the council tried to recruit lower-income women to its ranks, its most prominent organizations were college-based sororities, and it emphasized networking and professionalization, which were often unat-tainable for poor women.[8] The college-educated background of its con-stituency as well as its emphasis on Black women's entry into mainstream

America contributed to its elitist reputation among Black Americans and moderate reputation among whites.

Beginning in the early 1960s, the council shifted focus under the new leadership of Dorothy Height, who became its president in 1957, to become more directly involved in the civil rights movement and later in the War on Poverty. Meanwhile, the council also gave quiet support to its more radical members, like feminist lawyer Pauli Murray; project participants, like Ruth Batson and Flo Kennedy; and staff, like Beal. All were outspoken in their challenge of racism and sexism.[9] In her study of Black feminist organizations in the late 1960s and 1970s, Kimberly Springer argues that many middle-class Black women did not join Black feminist organizations in this period because they were "already beholden" to moderate groups like the council, which "supported traditional sex roles more in line with their personal aspirations."[10] Although true in terms of the council's public image and actions, this assertion overlooks the inner complexities of its composition. Beal's cohort, just like Murray's, held radical views, which they brought to bear on the council.

The council furthered Black Power through the hiring of staff members, facilitating organizational alliances, and creating council-run programs. Scholars have examined the concept of multiple allegiances when thinking about Black activists' ties to local and national organizations in the civil rights movement. The phrase "flexible loyalties," coined by Françoise Hamlin, illustrates the pragmatic alliances of local activists themselves.[11] The NCNW, as an organization, also utilized flexible loyalties by deploying a public image of respectability with which to fundraise and build political capital.[12] For instance, at the height of the Black freedom efforts of the 1960s and 1970s, council president Height was invited to enter spaces, including President Kennedy's Commission on the Status of Women in 1961, the Council to the White House for International Minority Rights in 1966, and the National Committee for the Protection of Human Subjects (which established the Institutional Research Board, IRB) in 1974, where she was often the only woman or African American.[13] By participating in mainstream political activities, Black women often had to work with men and whites who may not have been sensitive to their particular concerns and struggles, but women in the council saw the opportunity to engage in cross-racial and cross-sex dialogues as an important step in facilitating change. Utilizing flexible loyalties was a smart strategy as it enabled the council to raise money and thrive organizationally while also helping many Black working-class and radical women.

From their positions of power, council members helped to fund the activism of others. Initially, the council helped support others who were fighting on the ground of the civil rights movement. For instance, in 1963 the NCNW sponsored a series of Action Fellowships to help support students whose financial aid had been revoked because of their full-time participation in direct-action campaigns, such as protests and sit-ins. Well-known activists who received such funds in 1963 included Howard-based Nonviolent Action Group members Ed Brown, Courtland Cox, and Stokely Carmichael. These three later became important members within SNCC as well.[14] By November 1964, the NCNW had distributed over $40,000 in scholarship money to students from Massachusetts to California.[15]

While the council supported young activists engaged in direct action projects in the early 1960s, it also began working on the ground of the Movement in 1964 through its sponsorship of the interracial, interfaith civil rights organization Wednesdays in Mississippi (WIMS). WIMS formed in anticipation of Freedom Summer in Mississippi and sent six teams of five to seven Black and white women to Mississippi for three-day trips over seven weeks.[16] Their task was to offer behind-the-scenes support for the voter registration and Freedom School projects in the summer. Two-thirds white and one-third Black, WIMS included middle- and upper-class northern Protestant, Catholic, and Jewish clubwomen from progressive Black and white women's organizations like the Young Women's Christian Association (YWCA), Churchwomen United (CWU), Delta Sigma Theta, and the League of Women Voters (LWV). WIMS tried to build white southern support for and Black solidarity with the Council of Federated Organizations (COFO) and the Mississippi Freedom Democratic Party (MFDP). They visited civil rights projects, but they also met privately with white and Black middle- and upper-class southern women to offer them outside information and support. WIMS hoped that their respectability, which they deliberately displayed by wearing dresses, pearls, and white gloves (despite the oppressive summer heat and humidity), might influence southerners to support these Black-led civil rights efforts around Mississippi more boldly.

Northern WIMS women returned to Mississippi the following summer to work as teachers for Head Start. Their three-day visits over the two summers made limited inroads in fostering white support and long-term aid to the COFO and MFDP projects in Mississippi. But through this project, the council established important ties to Black community members like Annie Devine of Canton and Fannie Lou Hamer of Ruleville, both members of SNCC and the MFDP. Other WIMS women, such as Ruth Batson, created their own civil rights projects in the North, including the Metropolitan Council for Educational Opportunity (METCO), a volunteer organization that transported Black children from urban to suburban schools in Boston. WIMS women also fundraised for the council, and the Black freedom efforts more generally, using their impressive social and political connections. WIMS participants included Jean Benjamin, the wife of Robert S. Benjamin, the chairman of the board of the United Artists Corporation; Laya Wiesner, the wife of Jerome B. Wiesner, dean of science (and later president) of MIT; and Etta Moten Barnett, Broadway star and wife of Claude Barnett, founder of the Associated Negro Press. The head of WIMS was Polly Cowan, heir of the Spiegel mail order catalog business and wife of Louis Cowan, the former president of CBS.[17] Through its sponsorship of WIMS, the NCNW was able to not only offer assistance to Black Mississippians but also build up a network of influential white and Black supporters for the council.

The council used these same elite white and Black women in major fundraising drives. In 1966 Height appointed prominent WIMS woman and Hadassah national board member Gladys Zales and activist entertainer Lena Horne to head the Life Membership campaign. The council hoped to gain 500 life memberships, for a total of $50,000 in dues. Zales and Horne convinced Mary Lindsay, wife of the mayor of New York City, to host a fundraising banquet for the campaign.[18] These money-raising efforts sustained the NCNW's visibility and relevance among white liberals who continued to wield the majority of political, economic, and social power in the 1960s.

But Wednesdays in Mississippi also helped the council create significant relationships with Black activists in Mississippi. The council employed many Mississippi women as staff after it was granted tax-exempt status. Whereas the council had a staff of only three in 1963, by 1975 its programming required sixty regular staff and forty-one more employees for low-income programs like daycare centers in Mississippi; Liberty House, a handicraft-making cooperative; and other projects.[19] One-quarter of these staff women were from Mississippi.[20] Fannie Lou Hamer, best known for her roles in SNCC and the Mississippi Freedom Democratic Party, became a staff member at the NCNW in the late 1960s. Outspoken SNCC activist Unita Blackwell, who was a NCNW staff member from 1967 to 1975, credited Height and the council with building her a house and bringing her "from the world of a grassroots organizer-activist into professional life."[21]

In 1966 the council gained financial support from the Ford Foundation and then sponsored its next major initiative, Project Womanpower, envisioned as an avenue not only to bring aid to a broad base of Black women, but also to further strengthen the council itself.[22] Throughout its two-year existence from 1966 to 1968, Project Womanpower sought to bring Black women from all walks of life together to help them learn how to utilize networking and be "more effective" at identifying sources of governmental and private funding for their volunteer work during the War on Poverty. Beal and the other young women of SNCC were the staff for this new initiative, which they helped shape.

Project Womanpower set out to first identify a core group of 117 women leaders who were already community activists. SNCC activist Charles Sherrod had referred to these types of grassroots leaders as "mamas" who were "in the community, outspoken, understanding, and willing to catch hell, having already caught [their] share," but the council labeled them "Vanguard" women instead.[23] The council's appellation for these activists reveals its deepened respect, thanks largely to its on-the-ground experience in Wednesdays in Mississippi, for the leadership of women of all classes and education levels. By the start of Project Womanpower the council envisioned these women as experts who carried with them the kind of local knowledge that made them indispensable to the program.

The Project Womanpower staff and the Vanguard women then worked together to develop and lead Community Service Institutes ranging from two-day workshops to a series of smaller seminars. They covered over thirty areas of the country, including the rural South, small urban areas such as Plainfield, New Jersey, and large urban areas including Watts, Los Angeles. Between thirty and three hundred Black women attended each of these Institutes. Seminars often focused on the creation of Black self-help projects within the local community, including food production centers, better housing, consumer education programs, and daycare centers. Participants learned about not only the financial resources available for their proposed projects but also Black culture and history. One of the most important and popular parts of the program was the Black heritage kit distributed to all of the participants. The package included information on Black history, especially stories of liberation. As one woman from Mississippi wrote, "The session I liked best was the one on black history, because it told me so much about myself and my people."[24]

Through Project Womanpower, the council provided formal national leadership roles to women who were already leaders in their communities. The NCNW also hoped that through the Community Service Institutes, the council could attract more members. The final report for Project Womanpower suggests that the experience had taught the NCNW much about the needs of the poor in local communities. In its final recommendations in 1968, Project Womanpower stated, first, that "bread and butter pressures" on women were important to sustain their volunteer activities—such as securing money for a car or bus ride to the project location in order to volunteer. Second, the NCNW recognized that "an indigenous local coordinator . . . is vitally important to sustain the ground work, once laid, and to help local groups gain momentum in community service and community action." And finally, the NCNW found that the staff for Project Womanpower needed to stay for a long time in order to offer help to the local coordinator.[25]

Local women such as Fannie Lou Hamer, Unita Blackwell, and those in the Project Womanpower Vanguard educated Height and other middle- and upper-class women of the council about the projects that would best aid impoverished Black communities. Hamer first worked with the council through Wednesdays in Mississippi. She quickly became a part of the poverty initiatives of the council in the late 1960s. In 1968, after witnessing local Black female candidate Thelma Barnes lose an election to a white candidate in 70 percent majority-Black Washington County, Mississippi, Dorothy Height asked Hamer how this was possible. Hamer pointed out that poor people would do anything to have some food, including vote for Barnes's opponent.[26] The council vowed to help this Black community produce its own food, and it purchased fifty sows and five boars for Hamer's cooperative Freedom Farm in Sunflower County, Mississippi. By 1973, the pig bank had produced 3,000 pigs.[27] As one grateful recipient remarked that year, "every time I kill them hogs, I think about the National Council of Negro Women . . . and if Miss Height and your [group had not] come down here, you wouldn't have this meat."[28]

Hamer and other local Mississippi women also worked with the council to develop and staff three daycare centers for low-income women in the Deep South. One of these daycare centers in Okolona, Mississippi, began as a project to house unwed teenage mothers, but was changed after a local congressman, Thomas Abernethy, claimed that the home would harbor prostitutes. Unwilling to publicly fight against his racist and sexist accusation, the NCNW instead created a daycare center on the property.[29] Through this change, the council caved to white resistance but still helped local women in some way by employing them in and also admitting their children to the daycare center.

Another project that revealed the NCNW's increasing concern for the poor was the Turnkey III home-ownership project. This initiative brought together local builders, the housing authority, and Black homebuyers to create a low-cost, high-quality home ownership program from the late 1960s through 1975. Under this program the NCNW worked with the Department of Housing and Urban Development (HUD) to help families that "qualified" for public housing move into their homes without a down payment, but with an agreement to do maintenance on their properties for subsidized payments. Local Black community leaders were the ones who determined who "qualified," not the local housing authority, which often had little understanding of and consideration for the Black community. The NCNW then set up a voluntary Homebuyers Association from the new homeowners and trained them to work with Turnkey III to manage and maintain the homes. After twenty-five years of occupation, residents received deeds of ownership. By the time the project was completed in 1975, the council had helped construct 18,761 homes around the country valued at $407 million.[30]

But the relationship was not one-sided. The council had a tremendous impact on women like Beal, Hamer, and Blackwell. Far from softening her militancy, Beal's ten years of employment with the mainstream council enabled her to shape her radical views. While working at the council she helped co-found the radical Black Women's Liberation Caucus of SNCC, an organization that continued to seek Black liberation, while also combating sexism within SNCC's ranks. The organization broke away from SNCC in 1969 and became the Black Women's Alliance (BWA). Much like the council in the late 1960s, the BWA sought to attract a wide range of Black women, including those from other women's organizations, campus radicals, and welfare mothers. In the following year, founders decided that they should open up their organization to Puerto Rican and other minority women more generally, and the BWA became the Third World Women's Alliance (TWWA). Kimberly Springer points out how difficult it was for the TWWA to raise money. "In the special [case] of the TWWA . . . , it was unlikely that foundations, liberal feminist organizations, or Black community institutions would contribute funds to organizations that adhered to socialist principles and called for a complete revolution of U.S. patriarchal, imperialist, and capitalist modes of oppression." Springer goes on to point out how organizations as radical as the anti-imperialist, anti-racist, anti-sexist TWWA depended on member dues for their survival.[31] As a contributor, Beal—and by extension her allied organizations—relied on the income from Beal's employment at the council.

Unita Blackwell's time with the council was also transformative. She worked as staff from 1967 to 1975, first with Project Womanpower and then with Turnkey III. Not only did this time with the council provide her with income, it also helped her gain entry into national politics. First Lady Pat Nixon worked with Blackwell on the Turnkey III project, and she first met President Richard Nixon during one of the housing meetings at the White House.[32] After her work with Turnkey III, Blackwell went on to become the first Black female mayor in Mississippi in 1976. Once in office, Blackwell used her training from Turnkey III to incorporate the town of Mayersville and establish a water system, sewer system, and paved streets. She was mayor for a total of twenty years, from 1977 to 1993 and then again from 1997 to 2001. She also served on numerous political advisory boards, including President Jimmy Carter's Presidential Advisory Committee on Women; traveled on diplomatic trips to China, India, and many places in Africa, Europe, and Latin America; and received a MacArthur Foundation Genius Award as an "exceptionally gifted individual" in 1992.[33] But she credited Dorothy Height for first teaching her that "if I approached people, even the most highly placed leaders, on their level as an equal, most of them would receive me as an equal."[34]

The council benefited from these connections as well. Thanks to initiatives such as Project Womanpower, Turnkey III, and other poverty projects, many new NCNW chapters, known as sections, were organized. From 1966 to 1968, the NCNW grew, with a 58 percent increase in individual memberships and a 47 percent increase in local sections. Growth in membership was greatest in the Mississippi Delta, where, for instance, membership in the Sunflower County Section doubled from 125 to 250 members.[35] Membership increased so dramatically in these two years that the NCNW created a simplified booklet explaining how to establish a new section so that any women, "regardless of their educational level," could use it. At the national convention in 1967, the NCNW also altered its policy for annual dues. It reduced total annual dues per person from $5 (with $3 going for national dues and $2 staying in the local treasury) to $2 in impoverished areas. The national organization then took only $1 per person and allowed the other $1 to remain locally; moreover, in exceptional cases where women could not even afford that price, they could join for free.[36] Council staff encouraged the beneficiaries of poverty projects, such as those from Turnkey III, to also join the council.[37] In 1969, the council also opened up the possibility of direct membership for women who were members of the affiliated national organization. These women thus avoided having to find a regional council through which to join. It hoped that this would create further avenues to increase membership.[38]

Thanks to these efforts, the council's public image did move slightly to the left during this time. Initially, Height stated that Black Power was a misguided approach and called for its elimination. She proclaimed in December 1966, "It is unfortunate that the phrase 'black power' was ever conceived."[39] But less than three years later, the council's twenty affiliate organizations released a much more radical public statement in the wake of the federal rollback of school desegregation plans and War on Poverty programs: "Now we understand what our black youth have been saying to us. . . . The government by its actions seems to be informing us that it will not protect the rights of the Black community nor the lives of our children." The council went on to state that it would defend the rights of black Americans "by any means necessary."[40] The NCNW's adoption of Malcolm X's own phrase from his 1964 speech announcing the creation of the Organization of Afro-American Unity showed the council's frustration with the current political situation.[41] The council also asked its local sections to strongly promote Black pride through public outreach and education.[42]

In the wake of major changes within the council in the late 1960s, Height and others had come to respect more fully the radical positions articulated by Beal and the other "Young Turks" of SNCC. In a 1975 interview she stated, "I think what many blacks who have had my kind of training and experience with many whites don't realize is that black young people have a whole lot to be angry about."[43] Behind the scenes the "Young Turks" influenced ideas about programming within the council, including several Black self-directed projects to help poor women. Young women radicals encouraged the council to think about the benefits of unifying Black women along class lines. Beal and the other "Young Turks" helped the council develop a new Black nationalist logo (among other projects), including a "prim-looking woman, . . . one woman with an Afro, another with an African dress—to see the kind of different women that existed [in the council]. It said, Unity, Commitment, Self-reliance."[44] Thus the council's public material reflected this new approach.

The council also began to publicly support other radical causes. It supported the Moratorium to End the War in Vietnam on November 15, 1969, and spoke out against the imprisonment of Angela Davis in 1971. Inspired by the controversy surrounding Davis's imprisonment, the council issued national conference resolutions that year on corruption in law enforcement agencies around the country, pointing out the deaths of two Black Panther youth in Chicago and trouble in San Quentin and Attica prisons in "recent months." It stated that American legal institutions had taken an "implacable *adversary* role in relationship to Black Americans."[45] The NCNW Convention then resolved, "As women who are aware of the multiple dimensions of struggle—physical, moral, and intellectual—we do not believe that a strong and wise nation need to [sic] fear its young rebels, but rather to understand their despair." Members then called for the release on bail of Davis for medical and legal reasons, movement of her trial site to San Francisco, and continued support for Davis's defense.[46]

The NCNW also vowed to support rehabilitative programs for incarcerated Black youth, and in 1972 it developed a program named Operation Sisters United, which was funded by the Law Enforcement Assistance Administration of the U.S. Department of Justice. A pilot program was established in Washington, D.C., in 1972 with the intention of moving it to Greenville, Mississippi, St. Thomas in the Virgin Islands, and Dayton, Ohio, by 1975. Operation Sisters United was developed as a rehabilitative program and paired an NCNW member with an at-risk young girl who would otherwise have been sent to juvenile detention. By 1979, over six hundred girls had participated in the program, which used one-on-one relationships with NCNW members as an alternative to institutionalization and offered "sisterly" guidance as well as tutoring and support services to the child's family.[47]

But despite its work with Black Power initiatives, the council's efforts to attract working-class women were not always as successful as it had hoped. The council continued to struggle with recruiting lower-income members. White highlights that an independent evaluation of Operation Sisters United praised the council's outreach, but pointed out that there were too few poor women involved in mentoring. In order to be more successful, the evaluators recommended that the council incorporate a broader range of volunteers—looking beyond the professionally trained to include those with less education, work experience, and socioeconomic status.[48]

Although the council tried to recruit more lower-class women, it did not abandon its former constituency. Instead, it continued to recruit elite white and Black women. In 1969 the NCNW created a Resource and Development Committee for influential members. Far from shunning these women during the militant focus on poverty work in the late 1960s, the council stated, "We recognize a positive role for those supporters of NCNW whose stature on the American scene is so prestigious as to either attract direct contributions or to be able to influence the funding of our various programs as they are developed."[49] The NCNW thus continued to strengthen its alliances with powerful people, rather than alienate them.

The council also continued to make some ideological concessions by adhering to public respectability. White has criticized the council for not speaking on behalf of Black women who had been publicly slandered by the Moynihan Report in 1965.[50] Daniel Geary adds that Dorothy Height initially supported the report, passing out copies to council contacts, and helping push that year's national convention to focus on the Black woman's role in the family and responsibility to her community. However, speakers at that same convention criticized the report and helped alter Height's and the council's opinion of the report. One month after the convention, Moynihan complained that even Dorothy Height had turned on him.[51] The council also never publicly condemned the slanderous attacks of Senator Russell Long, who called the women of the National Welfare Rights Organization (NWRO), an organization of mainly poor, Black women, "brood mares" in 1968. Nor did the council openly advocate the positions of the NWRO, such as its insistence that women receiving welfare should not be forced to endure intrusions into their intimate lives even if they needed aid from the government.[52]

However, NCNW members were privately supportive of welfare rights and found subtle ways to offer support to the movement. For instance, Dorothy Height included Henrietta Rice, a member of the NWRO and vice-chairman of the New York citywide coordinating committee of welfare groups, on a council-sponsored task force panel preliminary to the White House Conference on Food, Nutrition, and Health in 1969.[53] And by 1977, the council had adopted a much more sensitive attitude to women on welfare, pointing out that Black women and families had been maligned in the political debates around welfare. The NCNW encouraged members to push for reforms at the local level, insisting that "workers maintain sensitivity and understanding of the needs of poor people." It urged members to educate Black communities about their right to welfare and to provide job training in public service jobs for women on welfare.[54]

Finally, even as the council began to incorporate some aspects of Black Power, it rejected others. It continued to employ white staff and create projects that partnered with majority-white governmental organizations and private foundations. While Beal claimed that she helped push the council to be more radical, Height at the same time believed that the council had an effect on young activists by helping them to see the potential of working with whites. "When they [Beal and other young more militant women] sat down and worked with white staff, they came to a different view," softening their separatist position, she said in 1975.[55] She also claimed that although Stokely Carmichael had felt "that I was too soft on white people," toward the end of his life he came to appreciate the need to work together with whites as well. Three weeks before his death in 1998, he told Height "I hope we can get together because we need to bring everybody together." He recommended that she try to call together a diverse group of people together to work for change again.[56]

Project Womanpower, the Freedom Farm pig bank, day care centers, and the Turnkey III housing project were just a few of the poverty projects implemented by the council in the late 1960s and 1970s. Because the council mostly maintained a moderate public stance at the height of the Black Power movement, it could channel resources to more radical initiatives and grassroots activists. In this way the council continued to play a role in national politics while garnering money and support from powerful allies in the Office of Economic Opportunity, at the Department of Housing and Urban Development, and at the Ford Foundation for its projects to empower local Black communities around the country. These flexible loyalties during the War on Poverty helped the council thrive as an organization while also supporting groups and individuals deemed too controversial to receive resources.

The story of the NCNW at the height of Black Power shows how some Black activist women used pragmatic relationships to cultivate a wide and deep network of women committed to racial activism. This story also collapses the binary drawn by scholars over the last twenty years between radicalism and liberalism or militancy and moderation in the mid-century Black freedom struggle. Even as the council continued to cultivate its moderate image, internally it shifted its priorities, sustaining its image with establishment entities on the one hand, and on the other supporting the work of radical women and the Black poor.

NOTES

I wish to thank the editors Leslie Brown, Anne M. Valk, and Jacqueline Castledine for their comments and suggestions on this chapter, as well as Nancy Hewitt, Karissa Haugeberg, and Allison Miller who read and commented on parts of this work previously.

1 Frances M. Beal and Loretta J. Ross, "Excerpts from the *Voices of Feminism Oral History Project*: Interview with Frances Beal," *Meridians: feminism, race, transnationalism* 8, no. 2 (2008): 145–149, 151 (hereafter "Excerpts").

2 Deborah Gray White, *Too Heavy a Load: Black Women in Defense of Themselves, 1894–1994* (New York: W. W. Norton, 1999), 183–186.

3 The council achieved tax-exempt status retroactively to December 1, 1965. For more about this status, see Adrian W. DeWind to Polly Cowan, Apr. 28 and May 9, 1966, Series 19, Folder 115, National Council of Negro Women Papers (hereafter NCNW Papers), National Archives for Black Women's History (NABWH), Museum Resource Center (U.S. National Park Service), Hyattsville, MD; and the National Council of Negro Women, "NCNW Progress Report," Fall 1966, p. 1, Series 13, Folder 50, NCNW Papers. For more on hiring SNCC women, see Dorothy Height, Interview by Polly Cowan, May 25, 1975, *Black Women Oral History Project*, 176, Schlesinger Library, Radcliffe Institute, Harvard University, Cambridge, MA (hereafter Height Interview).

4 Beal and Ross, "Excerpts," 151.

5 For some examples of recent and influential literature on radical women, see for example Kimberly Springer, *Living for the Revolution: Black Feminist Organizations, 1968–1980* (Durham, NC: Duke University Press, 2005); Dayo F. Gore, *Radicalism at the Crossroads: African American Women Activists in the Cold War* (New York: New York University Press, 2011); Jeanne Theoharis Gore and Komozi Woodard, eds., *Want to Start a Revolution? Radical Women in the Black Freedom Struggle* (New York: New York University Press, 2009); and Barbara Ransby, *Ella Baker and the Black Freedom Movement: A Radical Democratic Vision* (Chapel Hill: University of North Carolina Press, 2003).

6 While historian Devin Fergus in *Liberalism, Black Power, and the Making of American Politics 1965–1980* (Athens: University of Georgia Press, 2009) applauds the work of foundational Black Power scholars William Van Deburg, Robert Self, Komozi Woodard, and Timothy Tyson for challenging the supposed nihilism, criminality, and geographical origins of Black Power, he criticizes them for "silenc[ing] the dialogue between liberalism and Black Power" and he encourages future scholars to move beyond an "isolationist" view of Black Power (6).

7 White, *Too Heavy a Load*, 150–152.

8 Ibid., 157–160.

9 For more on Pauli Murray, see Glenda Gilmore, *Defying Dixie: The Radical Roots of Civil Rights, 1919–1950* (New York: W. W. Norton, 2008). Florynce Kennedy and Ruth Batson were participants in the NCNW-sponsored project Wednesdays in Mississippi. For more on these two women, see Sherie M. Randolph, *Florynce "Flo" Kennedy: The Life of a Black Feminist Radical* (Chapel Hill: University of North Carolina Press, 2015) and Jeanne Theoharis, "'They Told Us Our Kids Were Stupid': Ruth Batson and the Educational Movement in Boston," in *Groundwork: Local Freedom Movements in America*, ed. Jeanne Theoharis and Komozi Woodard (New York: New York University Press, 2005), 17–44.

10 Springer, *Living for the Revolution*, 85.

11 For instance, Aaron Henry of Clarksdale, Mississippi, utilized whatever national organization was willing to help his community. See Françoise Hamlin, "Collision and Collusion: Local Activism, Local Agency, and Flexible Alliances," in *The Civil Rights Movement in Mississippi*, ed. Ted Ownby (Jackson: University Press of Mississippi, 2013) and *Crossroads at Clarksdale: The Black Freedom Struggle in the Mississippi Delta after World War II* (Chapel Hill: University of North Carolina Press, 2012), 4–5, 53. Likewise, in his study of SNCC, Clayborne Carson pointed out how locals in Lowndes County, Alabama, avoided drawing sharp distinctions between organizations and just referred to all activists as "civil rights workers" or "freedom fighters." Clayborne Carson, *In Struggle: SNCC and the Black Awakening of the 1960s* (Cambridge, MA: Harvard University Press, 1981, 1995), 163–164. For more on black women's pragmatic political alliances, see Julie Gallagher, *Black Women and Politics in New York City* (Champaign: University of Illinois Press, 2012).

12 Both Presidents Johnson and Nixon applauded the council for its efforts in "advancing the American ideal." Quote is from Lyndon B. Johnson to Dorothy Height, Dec. 16, 1966, WHCF, Subject Files "EX ME 3/National Council F–Council R," Box 111, LBJ Presidential Library, Austin, Texas. During the unveiling of the Mary McLeod Bethune statue in 1974, President Richard Nixon offered equally high praise of the council. See "Mary McLeod Bethune—Dedication—Lincoln Park," July 10, 1974, audio recording transcription, 2008, Side 1, 33–34, Series 15, Subseries 5, Folder 86, NCNW Papers.

13 "Dorothy I. Height," Introduction in *The Black Women Oral History Project*, v; and *Encyclopedia of Women in American Politics*, ed. Laura van Assendelft and Jeffrey Schultz (Phoenix, AZ: Oryx Press, 1999), s.v. "Dorothy Irene Height."

14 Stokely Carmichael, *Ready for Revolution: The Life and Struggles of Stokely Carmichael* (New York: Scribner, 2005), 248.

15 National Council of Negro Women, "Convention Handbook, November 11–15th, 1964, 29th Annual Convention," Series 2, Folder 174, NCNW Papers.

16 For more on Wednesdays in Mississippi, see Rebecca Tuuri, "Building Bridges of Understanding: The Activism of Wednesdays in Mississippi" (PhD diss. Rutgers University, 2012); Debbie Z. Harwell, *Wednesdays in Mississippi: Proper Ladies Working for Radical Change, Freedom Summer 1964* (Jackson: University of Mississippi Press, 2014);

and Tiyi Morris, *Womanpower Unlimited and the Black Freedom Struggle in Mississippi* (Athens: University of Georgia Press, 2015).

17 See application forms for each woman in Series 19, Folders 12, 13, and 14, NCNW Papers.

18 "Mary McLeod Bethune Awards Presented," *Cleveland Call and Post*, Dec. 24, 1966.

19 Height Interview, 175.

20 National Council of Negro Women, "Women and Housing: A Report on Sex Discrimination in Five American Cities," U.S. Department of Housing and Urban Development (Washington, DC: U.S. Government Printing Office, June 1975), 149-a.

21 Unita Blackwell, *Barefootin': Life Lessons from the Road to Freedom* (New York: Crown, 2006), 177 and 181.

22 "Capahosic Conference—Capahosic VA, July 8, 1966, Evening Session and July 9 A.M.," Series 15, Subseries 5, Folder 13, Side 1, NCNW Papers, 27–9, internal transcription provided to author by Kenneth Chandler, archivist, NABWH, 2010.

23 Cited in Carson, *In Struggle*, 75, as cited originally from James Forman, *The Making of Black Revolutionaries* (New York: Macmillan, 1972), 276.

24 "Project Womanpower Final Report," Aug. 31, 1968, 125, Series 10, Folder 587, NCNW Papers.

25 Ibid., 131.

26 In her autobiography, Dorothy Height mistakenly refers to this year as 1967, but the election that she refers to was in 1968. See *Open Wide the Freedom Gates: A Memoir* (New York: Public Affairs, 2003), 187–188.

27 "Interviews with Fannie Lou Hamer and others about the Pig Bank," 1973, transcript of audio recording, Series 15, Subseries 6, Folder 1, Side 2, 35, NCNW Papers. On Hamer's cooperative farm, see Chana Kai Lee, *For Freedom's Sake: The Life of Fannie Lou Hamer* (Champaign: University of Illinois Press, 1999), chapter 8; and Kay Wright Mills, *This Little Light of Mine: The Life of Fannie Lou Hamer* (Lexington: University of Kentucky Press, 2007), chapter 14. Mills mentions the council's role in developing the pig bank, but Lee does not. See Mills, *This Little Light of Mine*, 258–259.

28 "Interviews with Fannie Lou Hamer and others about the Pig Bank," 29.

29 Height, *Open Wide the Freedom Gates*, 198.

30 National Council of Negro Women, "Women and Housing," 149-c.

31 Springer, *Living for the Revolution*, 84, 148.

32 Blackwell, *Barefootin'*, 177, 181. Paula Giddings remarks that Blackwell also cherished her initial work with Project Womanpower. See *When and Where I Enter: The Impact of Black Women on Race and Sex in America* (New York: William Morrow, 1984), 287.

33 Blackwell, *Barefootin'*, 207, 210, 214, and 248.

34 Ibid., 181.

35 "Project Womanpower Final Report," 121 and 134.

36 Ibid., 122.

37 Ruth Moffett, "Weekly Report—July 28–Aug. 1, 1969," Series 20, Folder 656, NCNW Papers.

38 White, *Too Heavy a Load*, 208–209.

39 Cathy Aldridge, "Dump 'Black Power' Line, Women Urged," *New York Amsterdam News*, Dec. 24, 1966, 1.

40 "Vow Militant Action," *New York Amsterdam News*, July 26, 1969, 5.

41 Malcolm X, *By Any Means Necessary: Speeches, Interviews, and a Letter by Malcolm X* (New York: Pathfinder Press, 1970), 35–67, accessed Aug. 31, 2015 at http://www .blackpast.org/1964-malcolm-x-s-speech-founding-rally-organization-afro-american -unity#sthash.sbToYQrt.dpuf.

42 White, *Too Heavy a Load*, 206.

43 Height Interview, 179.

44 Beal and Ross, "Excerpts," 150.

45 National Council of Negro Women in National Convention Assembled, "Resolution on the case of Professor Angela Davis," Nov. 6, 1971, 2, Series 2, Folder 226, NCNW Papers. Emphasis in the original.

46 Ibid., 4–5.

47 NCNW, "'Fulfilling the Promise,' 1979 NCNW Annual Report," 4, Series 2, Folder 257, NCNW Papers.

48 White, *Too Heavy a Load*, 254–255.

49 National Council of Negro Women, Inc. "Proposed Constitutional Revisions to be Voted on at the 1969 National Convention [final draft]," Revisions to Page 6, Article VII, 3, Series 2, Folder 218, NCNW Papers.

50 White, *Too Heavy a Load*, 201.

51 Daniel Geary, *Beyond Civil Rights: The Moynihan Report and Its Legacy* (Philadelphia: University of Pennsylvania Press, 2015), 142–143.

52 White, *Too Heavy a Load*, 234–235.

53 "Press Conference of Nat. Council of Negro Women," Nov. 26, 1969, audio recording transcription, 2010, Side 1, 2., Series 15, Subseries 5, Folder 85, NCNW Papers.

54 National Council of Negro Women, "Plan of Action: A Plan to Identify and Intensify Productive, Constructive Actions toward Greater Progress for the Black Woman during the Decade for Women 1975–1985," Report at 38th National Convention, Nov. 6–13, 1977, 14, Series 2, Folder 251, NCNW Papers.

55 Height Interview, 178.

56 Dorothy Height, *Living With Purpose: An Activist's Guide to Listening, Learning and Leading* (Washington, DC: Dorothy I. Height Education Foundation, 2010), 59.

3 • "THIS IS LIKE FAMILY"

Activist-Survivor Histories and Motherwork

ARIELLA ROTRAMEL

I did very much feel separated from everything and everybody for most of my life. . . . I still struggle with . . . not putting up barriers, not communicating with people without being present, not saying things that I need or want. . . . That's one of the reasons why I love Mothers on the Move too, was because where things deeply concern me . . . just being here . . . [encourages you] to step out, to say what you think, to say what you feel, to discuss it, to talk to other people that are going through the same things.

—Jocelyn

As a survivor of poverty, child abuse, and domestic violence, Jocelyn learned to create distance from others in an attempt to protect herself.[1] Activism offered her a means of developing supportive relationships based on a shared commitment to social justice. Such connections were particularly critical for her as a young single mother encountering the staggering inequities in housing, schooling, and street safety that characterized New York City's South Bronx, the poorest congressional district in the United States. In the early 2000s, Jocelyn opened her apartment door to a housing organizer doing neighborhood canvassing. As Jocelyn recalled, the organizer "door knocked to ask people in the neighborhood what they thought about community and any issues that they had saw coming up. . . . I talked to her for two or three hours, and that's how I got involved. . . . [T]o me [it] was the beginning of my informal family in New York . . . the people that share my ideals for justice and that there could be some type of equality, we could create this." She had been deeply moved by the stories of social justice she saw in films growing up, but was largely isolated in her own life. In Mothers on the Move/Madres en Movimiento (MOM), she found a community of people that also cared and supported her own growth as a survivor.

MOM was founded in 1992 when parents mobilized in response to educational inequalities between schools in the South Bronx and those in other parts of the same district.[2] The students in an adult education program at Bronx Educational Services taught by former community organizer Barbara Gross were shocked by the math and reading scores in their children's schools. With the support of founding directors Gross and Mili Bonilla, a community organizer, the parents decided to make changes in their children's education and formed the Parent Organizing and Education Project; in 1994, this became MOM. The group's name change served to center its interest in engaging mothers in an area where an estimated one-third of all households were headed by single women.[3] At the same time, from its inception, MOM included men as parents and grew to include grandparents, non-parents, and youth. From the start, MOM was inclusive of the men who participated in the adult education program and were as outraged by education inequalities as their women peers. Those roots and the interest of some men in the work of MOM created a sustained legacy of a mixed-gender, women-centered organization.

Over its first five years, MOM focused on solving educational inequalities. Dire statistics from the annual New York Times rankings of public schools showed Hunts Point students were struggling in comparison to other students within the same Community School District 8.[4] MOM members responded by demanding changes in the school administration, an equitable distribution of funding, and an end to school board election fraud.[5] Successful in achieving these reforms, in 1996 MOM expanded its mission beyond educational activism to include "tenant rights, environmental justice, and safe streets," based on the demands of South Bronx residents. Former MOM organizer Lisa Ortega described their approach: "Our issues come from the needs of the people. . . . If someone complains about the need for a stoplight at the corner, MOM goes out and investigates if this is indeed a community concern."[6]

MOM became a small community organization with a storefront office, a maximum of six paid staff at a time, a core of approximately twenty active members, and a much wider community of MOM affiliates and allies. MOM activists used a motherwork frame to embolden South Bronx residents as they claimed that their community deserved quality schools, safe streets, relief from environmental burdens, and economic opportunity. According to sociologist Patricia Hill Collins, motherwork is public action that extends beyond families and "recognizes that individual survival, empowerment, and identity require group survival, empowerment, and identity."[7] Temma Kaplan calls this concept "female consciousness." Looking at women's activism in a global historical context, Kaplan argues that female consciousness comes from "cultural experiences of helping families and communities survive."[8] In the case of the MOM activists, it is apparent that while mothers are centered in the organization's work, non-mother women, men, and young adults also are drawn toward motherwork to express their commitment to their community's future. This chapter examines activists' experiences of community and interpersonal violence within the context of MOM, an organization where the practice of motherwork is paramount.

MOM's Gloria attended a government employment program and her experience demonstrates that the motherwork ethos extends beyond parents. She observes, "I don't have kids. . . . So imagine a person going through these programs having kids . . . that you got to deal with childcare and the doctors. . . . You have all these other barriers on top of it. . . . I know it's more frustrating to other people."[9] Gloria's statement reveals her belief that all South Bronx residents have a right to access services and receive the support they need, particularly when caring for children. MOM's Cassie narrated how her own life experience taught her that a motherwork approach to family is indeed necessary. She recalls her childhood in the 1980s as a period of increasing drug addiction and incarceration: "My grandmother raised me and my sister . . . most parents wasn't there . . . most of the children was raised by grandparents or other relatives."[10] Through her work with MOM, Cassie connected with a broader community of support and addressed the gaps in many family networks that result from incarceration. Other MOM members, such as Manny, overtly embraced their identities as MOMs despite not identifying as women or mothers. Manny saw the organization as having room for people with a range of familial identifications, and stated, "What got me involved was the fact that the people are sincere and committed to what they're doing." Manny's experience of navigating gender contradictions as a young man likely informed his ability to embrace MOM's mission. As Manny recalled, his mother taught her sons to be self-sufficient in "housecleaning, cooking, sewing . . . [but] we stayed away from the windows so nobody on the street could see us doing this work, because the rumor was that men don't do this kind of stuff."[11] Taken together, these three MOM activists showed a history of addressing challenges faced by caretakers and children in the South Bronx. Importantly, they all recognized the need for a community of support that reached beyond the confines of the nuclear family ideology that was frequently distant from the realities of residents.

The MOM activists whose oral history interviews are at the core of this chapter shared a foundational identity as South Bronx residents concerned for the well-being of their community, and particularly the community's children. Their histories provide an opportunity to reflect on the intimate connections between an embrace of motherwork and activists' own experiences with violence. Having survived violence, activists dedicate themselves to efforts to contest multiple forms of violence that impact their communities. Recognizing these connections is critical, as "studies of historical trauma must be balanced by analyses of how political and economic dynamics interact with community wellbeing."[12] In a world saturated with violence, such activist-survivors' histories offer an important opportunity for examining the dynamic relationship between experiences of violence, social justice efforts, and membership within community organizations.[13] In recounting life histories, activists such as Jocelyn named their trauma as an important part of their own experience as activists. In addition, they recognized the ways that micro and macro forms of violence are braided together and negatively impact their local and global communities. This political consciousness shaped both their social justice work and their reflections on their own lives.[14]

FEMINIST HISTORIOGRAPHY AND MIXED METHODS

As a gender and women's studies scholar, my approach to feminist historiography emphasizes interdisciplinarity as a necessary means of understanding that contemporary social movements and actors have a history. This chapter centers on five oral histories that I collected from core activists in MOM during a broader research project examining community organizations as sources of knowledge production about major social issues. I conducted ethnographic and archival research in MOM's office between 2008 and 2011. I also compared information generated through interviews, observations, and archival research to mainstream media and governmental representations of the same issues, communities, and activists. Through the oral history interviews and ethnography I was in direct dialogue with research participants and learned first-hand about their work and experiences. The interview subjects included in this chapter were chosen based on their centrality to the work of MOM during that period. These activists ranged in age from their twenties to their sixties and are a mix of Puerto Rican and Black residents of the South Bronx. As volunteers or paid organizers, each person had demonstrated a strong involvement in MOM's work to address environmental justice and housing rights in the area. They were thus knowledgeable about both the issues in the South Bronx and MOM's agenda. Our interactions at MOM's office and in the community during outreach, protests, and celebrations helped me establish a significant level of rapport with each interview subject. They became familiar with me in terms of my own life and circumstances, rather than simply knowing me as a researcher. Over time, I correspondingly became acquainted with their personalities and interests, enabling me to understand their work with MOM as part of their larger life stories. Thus, rather than embracing a positivism-informed approach to interviewing research subjects, I understood this mixed-methods approach and the resulting larger sense of my subjects beyond our interviews through feminist theoretical insights.

In the 1980s, feminist scholars such as Sandra Harding and Donna Haraway established the need to trouble the lines between the knower and known, which in turn has led to calls for a politically informed feminist research praxis by key figures such as Chandra Mohanty.[15] These critical interventions value the use of oral history interviews within a broader ethnographic project as a means to more fully contextualizing and engaging with interview subjects.

The interviews I conducted focused on learning about individuals' life histories and experience as activists working with MOM. It is important to note that the socio-political context within which narrators are living both makes possible and limits the content of their oral histories. A narrator's decision to participate is structured by identifying or participating in particular communities as well as a desire to provide "what the narrator thinks the researcher wants to hear."[16] Within this dynamic, I was struck that many interviewees decided to talk about the role of violence in their lives when asked to discuss their activism. This revelation was initially surprising to me in revealing individuals' openness about a highly stigmatized subject. I learned that their openness demonstrated a recognition of the important role played by violence in their lives and an unwillingness to divorce this aspect of their histories from their paths into social justice work.

The openness in the interviews I conducted reflects the focus on politicization and personal empowerment at the heart of MOM's work. As Leigh Gilmore suggests in her study of fictionalized autobiographical trauma narratives, "The knowing self in contrast to the sovereign or representative self does not ask who am I, but how can the relations in which I live, dream, and act be reinvented through me?"[17] In the case of MOM interviewees, they reflected upon questions of violence through their effort to make positive social change. For MOM activists the ability to claim a knowing self is often contested due to the mix of oppression they encounter in the form of racism, xenophobia, classism, and sexism. Moreover, paths toward understanding the role of violence in their lives are too frequently blocked by common expectations in mainstream culture and within social movements. Women of color in particular are often asked to engage only parts of their identity and communal history, rather than to acknowledge the complex ways they interact with the multiple identity-based movements that matter in their lives. Recognizing intragroup differences rather than pushing "the identity of women of color to a location that resists telling" enables a complex approach to identity-based organizing.[18] MOM's motherwork history provided the flexible basis for this approach to community work by incorporating members with many differences but a shared aim of achieving an improved future for the South Bronx's children and broader community.

The ability of MOM to connect issues such as education, environmental racism, and housing rights reflects the overlapping of maternalist, racial, and economic justice movements over time. As Deborah Gray White argues, "The definition of 'mother's' responsibilities was wide ranging" at the turn of the twentieth century; and across the century, participants in Black women's clubs, the National Welfare Rights Organization in the 1960s–1970s, and emerging environmental and reproductive justice movements have drawn upon the power of motherhood to build organizations and work across identity lines.[19]

In the 1970s and 1980s, low-income communities in New York City faced numerous crises. Arson fires frequently engulfed residential buildings when building owners sought to collect insurance and move out of the area. Inequitable schools, inadequate affordable housing, high rates of poverty, environmental abuses, and insufficient public services demonstrated public and private disinvestment in the area.[20] MOM has a history of adopting a holistic approach to its activism that reflects the interest of community members in the South Bronx to respond to such challenges. In 2011, a study found that "more than two-thirds of public housing tenants responding to a survey conducted by Mothers on the Move and the Urban Justice Center earlier this year said they want jobs that would help improve housing conditions and air quality."[21] MOM's work thus has sought to elevate the voices of community members and further residents' awareness of the roots of these overlapping issues. The opportunity to participate in activism that recognizes intragroup diversity made MOM a place where survivors of violence developed resilience and became advocates for their communities. In this woman of color–led organization, survivors of violence pursued their own healing, built collective resilience, and challenged institutionalized forms of violence.

REFLECTIONS ON COMMUNAL AND FAMILIAL TRAUMA

The recent past of MOM suggests that to fully understand the roots of social justice activism scholars must connect histories of violence at the micro level to macro forms of structural violence. This effort starts by listening to the way that activists understand how surviving violence provides a catalyst for their journey into political activism. In order to contextualize the individual stories included in this article, it is critical to recognize the disturbing ordinariness of the violence experienced. It is not their victimization that is exceptional—sexual and domestic violence continue to be a critical social issue across communities. Rather, activists' ability to name their experience and use it to improve our world makes their stories important to explore using a historical lens. Finally, it is important to note that while this chapter focuses on the experiences of activists of color, violence is prevalent across communities and its significance to survivors participating in social justice movements merits further study.[22]

MOM activists' life histories reflect the dynamic relationship between the trauma that their community has experienced generally and the specific issues that played out in their families. One initial theme that emerged in interviews was the impact of the damaging destabilization of the South Bronx in the 1970s. Gloria's family migrated to the South Bronx in the early 1970s when she was six years old. She remembered the neighborhood as initially safe and that "you was able to leave your doors open, your windows open. You could sleep in your fire escape. You could go up and down your building and go to your neighbor's house because they had the door open."[23] By the late 1970s, however, her family had moved three times because fires were set in buildings where they were tenants. Similarly, MOM's Janna remembered that as a child "I started refusing to wear pajamas because one day there was a fire and we went outside in our pajamas . . . there were like a lot of fires around that time."[24] Eventually, Janna's family followed her aunt to Queens for a few years to escape the danger. The real fear that caused Janna to wear street clothes to bed speaks to the ways that the fires destabilized the lives of residents during this period. The experience of MOM activists with an increasingly unstable South Bronx in the 1970s and the 1980s framed their shared sense of being from a marginalized community that could not obtain accountability from the state. They retained this sense of the insecurity of their families as they became adults.

Some MOM activists shared the combined struggles of neglect, substance abuse, and violence that were a defining component of their lives. Prior to coming to the South Bronx, Jocelyn experienced child abuse and domestic violence in her key relationship as an adult. As she noted, it was her choice to leave the abusive relationship: "that [was the first time] my family's even had to think about what abuse looks like in a family or how to deal with that in a way that you're still respected, because I was very real about I'm not going to let somebody beat up on me."[25] After growing up in poverty and facing complex forms of abuse from her mother and men, Jocelyn slowly recognized what she had experienced and refused to be abused by her husband. She eventually gained her family's support to get a divorce, seek custody of her son, and pursue her lifelong dream of migrating to New York City from the Midwest. After moving to the South Bronx she encountered a MOM organizer canvassing about educational issues. Jocelyn recalled, "I talked to her for two or three hours, and that's how I got involved with the parent organizing piece here, you know involved with schools, fliering at schools, trying to talk to other parents about it."[26] Through her interest in her son's education Jocelyn viewed MOM as an organization through which she could express her concerns and begin to act.

MOM's Manny recalled his struggles as a child and young man living with an alcoholic father. He recalled his father's continual abuse: "It was a beating every other day . . . he would also take it out on Mom. . . . More than one time I wanted to leave him and just take Mom, just say 'Let's get out of here. Come on. Let's get out of here.' And she wouldn't do it."[27] In vivid detail, Manny retold a conflict he had with his father after a particularly severe assault on his mother. Importantly, his brother intervened in his attempt to attack his father and as Manny surmised, "I probably wouldn't be here talking to you at this point . . . because otherwise I'd either be dead or in jail, one or the other. . . . But she never left him and wouldn't."[28] Manny's recognition that his defense of his mother would have ruined his future reveals his understanding of the lack of resources that were available to his family. While fully able to describe the anger and disgust that his father's behavior elicited from him, Manny also discussed how after his father quit drinking he learned about the sense of inadequacy that drove his father's behaviors. He learned that "although he didn't admit it to us, he felt like he couldn't stand next to us . . . like he wasn't on the same level. And to me, that's not true."[29] Manny's ability to analyze the contradictions of his parents' relationship demonstrated his capacity to both criticize and empathize with human struggles. This ability served him well when he became an active member of Mothers on the Move.

While Jocelyn and Manny struggled with their relationships with their parents, Cassie's childhood was filled largely with absence. She recalled, "My mother was never around, she was on drugs. We couldn't have no more dealings with my mother, like, you would wake up in the morning and see the time on the microwave and then one morning it's gone and you're like, 'Where's the microwave?'"[30] As her parents' lives became dominated by addiction, Cassie and her younger sister were sent to live with her disabled grandmother in a public housing complex in the South Bronx. The responsibilities she felt were intense. Cassie shared that "I sort of raised my sister from birth, changed the Pampers, fed her, and I also had to tend to my grandmother . . . I had to become an adult. At the age of eight, I was always doing it all."[31] The outsized obligations that Cassie took on at this young age, coupled with her longing for her parents to be an active part of her life, left her feeling isolated. She concluded, "My childhood, I feel, was taken from me. . . . I really experienced a lot of things by myself. I didn't have nobody, so I'm kinda traumatized still. Like I said, I just really thought about just surviving."[32] Cassie's experiences led her to be particularly appreciative of the opportunities available at MOM, both personally and professionally. Moreover, the issues she and other MOM activists encountered growing up provided them with the background necessary to connect deeply with South Bronx residents whose struggle with similar issues leads them to seek support from MOM.

FINDING COMMUNITY AND MAKING CHANGE

Since the 1990s, MOM has proved to be a group where people could find deeper forms of connection through community-based social justice work to address the impact of violence in their communities. While they continue to face challenges as survivors of violence, they seek out community as they struggle for positive change. As Gloria observed about first coming to MOM, "when I came in here I didn't know nothing about social justice. . . . So little by little I learned about door knocking and fliering, one-on-ones with the community, inviting people to come to meetings to talk about the issue at hand, whether it be the environment or the buildings, the housing, education."[33] Beyond learning about the idea of social justice and how to do community organizing, she noted, "I didn't know there was a term, 'movement.' Now I see movement is people getting together for different issues."[34] She emphasized that MOM's approach is focused on empowering residents: "I'm not going to do the work for you. I'm going to empower you so you could do the work. . . . So they give you that power, because if I know I fought for the elevator to get fixed and they came and they fixed it, well, I'm going to be happy. 'Oh, they came because I fought for them to fix it. I fought for them to put the supermarket with healthy food in the community.'"[35] The ability to gain basic improvements in housing and access to fresh produce are of particular value to residents who lived through the neglect and withdrawal of resources from their community during the 1970s and 1980s. Having become a participant in the work of MOM, Gloria concluded, "So this movement, these people getting together and fighting for all these issues I'm grateful that I am a part of, because now I could say that I'm part of this movement."[36] Gloria's education in social justice organizing and sense of belonging to a movement that was capable of making positive change in her community is echoed in the histories of other MOM members who found connection and strength through working with the group.

Manny first encountered MOM activists during a door knocking campaign to lower air pollution in the area. When he attended his first meeting, he recalled, "It was eye-opening . . . they were talking about their first victory was the one to get rid of the superintendent."[37] MOM's ability to secure change in the leadership of their schools assured Manny that the group was capable of taking on the issues he cared about as well. He shared, "I was helped quite a bit in learning how to organize and how to think through these problems, in terms of identifying exactly what the problem is, and identifying those people that can help you solve the problems."[38] Manny had obtained a high level of formal education, but learning organizing skills at MOM empowered him in a new way. He became involved in their work as they sought to make concrete changes in the community including fighting for improvements in air quality and rejecting proposals to open more prisons in the area.

Manny was particularly committed to MOM's work around environmental justice, and became knowledgeable about the intricacies of waste processing. He spoke out against the New York Organic Fertilizer Company's unregulated operations in the South Bronx. This issue presented an opportunity to push against one source of the toxic air created by industrialization in the area. As Gloria noted, "That small core [of MOM activists that included Manny], they kept on with the fight . . . they kept on going with the rallies, with the meetings, and they kept on fighting until they got done. Sometimes it's not the quantity. It's the quality of the work that you were doing."[39] Even after he moved to Queens and the fertilizer company was shut down after a public uproar and lawsuit, Manny stayed connected to MOM and hoped to maintain a lifelong relationship with the organization. He put it plainly, "because this is like family, these people are committed, they're sincere, they love the community, and I think they want to make it stronger and grow."[40] For Manny, MOM provided a unique context where he could grow as a person, fully express his care for the South Bronx and build relationships with people equally invested the neighborhood's future.

Jocelyn was quick to point out that while she had initially been drawn to MOM through parent organizing, the many responsibilities of her life caused her to not become fully engaged in the group's work. But her need to respond to problems she and her son experienced as tenants brought her fully into the group. She recollected,

> I really actually became a member . . . during our housing campaign. So, our building was definitely going through its share. . . . [MOM members and building residents] was trying to form a tenant association because we had a lot of repair issues. Our landlord really was like one of those landlords that if they could not be involved they would. We had a lot of prostitution, drug selling in our building. . . . We did surveys, actions, you know, the whole MOMs everything that I could be involved in.[41]

The complicated challenges of forming a tenant association and securing follow-through on building issues necessitated the mix of tactics that Jocelyn used with other MOM activists. Her investment in having a safe building for her son to grow up in motivated her to become more fully engaged in this work. Finally, MOM's director, Wanda Salaman, encouraged her to take on a leadership role. Jocelyn recalled, "We were having the annual meeting, she was like, 'Yeah, so I need you to give the update on housing,' and I'm like, 'Well, I haven't been that involved in housing. I don't know what to say, you know.' She said, 'Oh, we'll work with you on that.'"[42] Salaman's words and commitment to supporting Jocelyn provided her with a level of encouragement that she had largely missed in her life. As she reflected, MOM connected her to "the people that share my ideals for justice and that there could be some type of equality, we could create this. . . . And I just felt infused by the very different people."[43] Over time, she gained a sense of her own value and belonging within the diverse community tied to MOM. Through her work as an activist and performer, she found that "I bring out the older people who want to take care of me, you know, and the men want to hold me up, you know what I mean."[44] Her personal growth and ability to develop healthy and supportive relationships with community members provided a foundation for continuing to recognize and address the scars left from the past abuse she had experienced.

For Cassie, MOM has overtly provided the support that she missed as a child. After her reconciliation with her own mother, she framed the important role of the organization in maternal terms. She stated, "[MOM is] like a surrogate mother, it kinda feels to me. Because I didn't have that. So when I'm here, they give me the love, and the 'Hey, how you doing!' I just love being around them."[45] Having a dynamic and supportive community whenever she was at MOM's office provided her with the positive engagement that she had wished for as a child. Cassie argued, "So that's another thing that I feel like we need more organizations like that in communities that suffer from parents not being there and doing drugs, and people who've been raped and things that happen to them, at least they have somewhere to go to feel safe and feel like someone cares about them."[46] She pointed to the continuing issues related to interpersonal violence, addiction, and incarceration that have been part of her life and the important role groups like MOM can play by creating a network of care and support.

Similarly to Jocelyn and Gloria, Cassie also learned of her own value through MOM. When it was time for her to shift from MOM to another site as a government program worker, she was offered a part-time position and told "we really want you here, we see something in you."[47] This acknowledgment was critical for her as she recalled that "[MOM] gave me the opportunity to look inside myself to see something I never thought I'd want to do or would be able to do. . . . I always feel like I'm not good enough . . . I just have to work at McDonalds or work at these underpaid jobs just to survive and that's I really felt [like those jobs were the ones] I was good enough to do."[48] Cassie had grown up frustrated by a lack of opportunity, but also without a support network to help her complete high school and find work opportunities that reflected her talents.

The tone she took when describing her work with tenants reflected her shift in understanding of what is possible for South Bronx residents. She stated, "We really want to create leadership in these tenants and create unity first and foremost because without the unity, without that trust between the tenants, knowing that we're all in this together, it really doesn't go nowhere."[49] Her ability to believe in and pursue the connections necessary to grow tenant organizing efforts underscored her new sense of the possibility of community and building ties among residents. Finally, MOM provided her with experiences to connect with activists beyond the South Bronx. She reflected: "I do want to help change the world, or try to change at least my community in some way, not only to benefit me but to benefit everybody else who lives within it. It was a real good experience to see that [attitude among other activists]. It is life out of the South Bronx, it is life and people trying to make life better all over."[50] Like Gloria, Cassie found through MOM's embrace that participation in a contemporary social justice movement offered not only a form of empowerment but connection and hope for the possibility of positive social change.

CONCLUSION

Since the early 1990s, Mothers on the Move has been fighting to address myriad challenges and forms of violence faced by residents of the South Bronx. MOM has built a diverse coalition by bringing together activists who simultaneously recognized the need for social justice while appreciating the life-sustaining potential of community and value of embracing motherwork. Organizing under the banner of MOM, these activists demonstrated the continued valuing of mothering, even as their ranks were more heterogeneous and underscore the complexity of this frame.[51]

The stories that make up this chapter gain even sharper relief five years after the last set of interviews, as issues of state and interpersonal violence became a larger part of mainstream discussions in the wake of Black Lives Matter protests, sexual violence on and off college campuses and in the military, and the increasing recognition of violence as a public health issue.[52] MOM activists' choice to share their experience with violence as part of their oral history interviews demonstrates the significance they give to its role in shaping their activist paths. Feminist methodology offers an opportunity to both honor such decisions and draw upon them to develop a complex and empathetic understanding of how histories of violence and social justice struggles are interwoven. The activists profiled in this chapter demonstrate the continued salience of the Afro-Caribbean New Yorker feminist Audre Lorde's claim that "I am not only a casualty, I am also a warrior."[53] After surviving the violence enacted upon their community and within their families, each of these activists refused to live in isolation and instead chose to work together to gain resources and respect for themselves and their community. Their refusal to erase the role of violence in their lives confirmed their awareness that such commonplace occurrences cannot be ignored, given how deeply they informed their understanding of the ongoing struggles within their communities and beyond.

NOTES

1 Interview with Mothers on the Move activist, 2008. Pseudonyms are used for all interview subjects and easily identifying characteristics have been removed.
2 Mothers on the Move, "Who We Are," MOM, accessed Apr. 22, 2007, http://www .mothersonthemove.org/about.html; Kavitha Mediratta and Jessica Karp, "Parent Power and Urban School Reform: The Story of Mothers on the Move," New York University Institute for Education and Social Policy, 2003.
3 Alan Feuer, "Single Mothers, Far From Alone; In the Bronx, More Than 30 Percent of Households Are Led by Women," New York Times, Jan. 8, 2004.
4 Mediratta and Karp, "Parent Power and Urban School Reform," 3.
5 Mothers on the Move, "Timeline," MOM, accessed Apr. 22, 2007, http://www .mothersonthemove.org/timeline.html.
6 Mothers on the Move, "Who We Are."

7 Patricia Hill Collins, "Shifting the Center: Race, Class, and Feminist Theorizing About Motherhood," in *Mothering: Ideology, Experience, and Agency,* ed. Evelyn Nakano Glenn, Grace Chang, and Linda Rennie Forcey (New York: Routledge, 1994), 47.

8 Temma Kaplan, "Female Consciousness and Collective Action: The Case of Barcelona, 1910–1918," *Signs* 7, no. 3 (Spring 1982): 545–566.

9 Interview with Mothers on the Move activist, 2010.

10 Interview with Mothers on the Move activist, 2008.

11 Interview with Mothers on the Move activist, 2010.

12 Laurence J. Kirmayer, Joseph P. Gone, and Joshua Moses, "Rethinking Historical Trauma," *Transcultural Psychiatry* 51, no. 3 (2014): 312.

13 Other examples include Danielle L. McGuire's "The Maid and Mr. Charlie: Rosa Parks and the Struggle for Black Women's Bodily Integrity" in this collection as well as Paula J. Gidding, *Ida: A Sword among Lions* (New York: HarperCollins, 2008); and Jacqueline Castledine, *Cold War Progressives: Women's Interracial Organizing for Peace and Freedom* (Urbana: University of Illinois Press, 2012), 113.

14 Hill Collins, "Shifting the Center," 45–66.

15 Sandra Harding, "The Instability of the Analytical Categories of Feminist Theory," *Signs* 11, no. 4 (1986): 645–664; Donna Haraway, "Situated Knowledges: The Science Question in Feminism and the Privilege of Partial Perspective," *Feminist Studies* 14, no. 3 (1998): 575–599; and Chandra Mohanty, *Feminism without Borders* (Durham, NC: Duke University Press, 2003), 231.

16 Nan Alamilla Boyd, "Who Is the Subject? Queer Theory Meets Oral History," *Journal of the History of Sexuality* 17, no. 2 (2008): 189.

17 Leigh Gilmore, *The Limits of Autobiography: Trauma and Testimony* (Ithaca, NY: Cornell University Press, 2001), 148.

18 Kimberlé Crenshaw, "Mapping the Margins: Intersectionality, Identity Politics, and Violence against Women of Color," *Stanford Law Review* 43, no. 6 (1991): 1242.

19 Deborah Gray White, *Too Heavy a Load: Black Women in Defense of Themselves, 1894–1994* (New York: W. W. Norton, 1999); Alexis Jetter, Annelise Orleck, and Diana Taylor, eds., *The Politics of Motherhood: Activist Voices from Left to Right* (Hanover, NH: University Press of New England, 1997); Jael Silliman et al., *Undivided Rights: Women of Color Organize for Reproductive Justice* (Cambridge, MA: South End Press, 2004); Julie Sze, *Noxious New York: The Racial Politics of Urban Health and Environmental Justice* (Cambridge, MA: MIT Press, 2007); Mary S. Pardo, *Mexican American Women Activists: Identity and Resistance in Two Los Angeles Communities* (Philadelphia: Temple University Press, 1998).

20 Evelyn Diaz Gonzalez, *The Bronx* (New York: Columbia University Press, 2004); Jill Jonnes, *South Bronx Rising: The Rise, Fall, and Resurrection of an American City* (Bronx, NY: Fordham University Press, 2002).

21 Mothers on the Move, "City Owes Mott Haven Tenants Jobs, Advocates Contend," *On the Move/En Movimiento* (blog), http://mothersonthemove.blogspot.com/2011/05/city-owes-mott-haven-tenants-jobs.html.

22 Callie Rennison and Mike Planty, "Nonlethal Intimate Partner Violence: Examining Race, Gender, and Income Patterns," *Violence and Victims* 18, no. 4 (August 2003): 433–443.
23 Interview with Mothers on the Move activist, 2010.
24 Interview with Mothers on the Move activist, 2008.
25 Ibid.
26 Ibid.
27 Interview with Mothers on the Move activist, 2010.
28 Ibid.
29 Ibid.
30 Interview with Mothers on the Move activist, 2008.
31 Ibid.
32 Ibid.
33 Interview with Mothers on the Move activist, 2010.
34 Ibid.
35 Ibid.
36 Ibid.
37 Ibid.
38 Ibid.
39 Ibid.
40 Ibid.
41 Interview with Mothers on the Move activist, 2008.
42 Ibid.
43 Ibid.
44 Ibid.
45 Ibid.
46 Ibid.
47 Ibid.
48 Ibid.
49 Ibid.
50 Ibid.
51 Molly Ladd-Taylor, "Toward Defining Maternalism in U.S. History," *Journal of Women's History* 5, no. 2 (1993): 110–113; Susan Logsdon-Conradsen, "From Maternalism to Activist Mothering," *Journal of the Motherhood Initiative for Research and Community Involvement* 2, no. 1 (2011): 9–36.
52 Linda L. Dahlberg and James A. Mercy, "History of Violence as a Public Health Issue," *AMA Virtual Mentor* 11, no. 2 (Feb. 2009): 167–172.
53 Audre Lorde, *Sister Outsider* (Freedom, CA: Crossing Press, 1984), 42.

PART TWO CHALLENGING ESTABLISHED NARRATIVES

4 • THE MAID AND MR. CHARLIE

Rosa Parks and the Struggle for Black Women's Bodily Integrity

DANIELLE L. McGUIRE

Six years after her death in 2005, Rosa Parks made national news when an essay she penned in the 1950s was released to the public by Guernsey's auction house. The six-page handwritten document, part of a trove of private documents and household goods offered for sale to settle a legal dispute, detailed Parks's steely resistance to a white man she called "Mr. Charlie," who assailed her in 1931 while she was working as a domestic in Montgomery, Alabama. "He offered me a drink of whiskey," Parks wrote, "which I promptly and vehemently refused. He moved nearer to me and put his hand on my waist. I was very frightened by now." "I was ready to die," she wrote, "but give my consent, never. Never. Never."[1] Guernsey's hoped this essay about a "near-rape" would garner media attention and lure potential buyers to the $8 million collection.

Almost immediately, however, some of the self-appointed guardians of Rosa Parks's legacy argued that the essay was fictitious and meant to be private. "It never should have been part of the memorabilia collection," Steven Cohen, a lawyer for the Raymond and Rosa Parks Institute in Detroit, told the Associated Press.[2] By dismissing the essay as private and/or imagined, Cohen virtually silenced any discussion about how the iconic civil rights activist (and other working-class Black women like her) may have been subject to and even testified about sexual violence and what that meant for the development of her political, racial, and gender consciousness, her movement activism, and how we remember her today.

While we have no way of knowing how much of the essay is true or why and for whom Rosa Parks wrote it, given that many of the details in the essay match her history and biography and can be substantiated in historical and autobiographical accounts, we can assume that it was not simply a figment of her imagination even if there may be some discrepancies between the actual events that evening in 1931 and her memory of them. And since she was not a professional writer, nor given to lengthy literary exercises, the actual writing of the story, the offering up of her testimony, is important in and of itself. It would have taken an unusual expenditure of time and effort to document the assault by "Mr. Charlie" and it might have endangered her if it fell into the wrong hands. Clearly Parks thought the story was meaningful; so much so, in fact, that she wrote it down and saved it in her personal files for decades.[3] And it seems she worried about language or how the story might sound to others since you can see her careful edits on the original document—adding more substantive verbs here and more descriptive adjectives there.[4]

In the finding aid to her papers at the Library of Congress, which is where this essay ended up after Howard G. Buffett, the son of billionaire Warren Buffett, purchased the collection in 2014, archivists note that many of Parks's writings "may have been written as notes for interviews or speeches, or she may have considered writing her memoirs in either article or book form."[5] Whatever the case may be, Parks did not include the story about "Mr. Charlie" in any of her memoirs, published essays, or interviews, or talk about it with media figures.

Parks's public reticence about this incident, along with her use of the pseudonym "Mr. Charlie" may help validate Cohen's assertion that the essay was meant to be private or that it was fictional. But her silence may have served other, more personal and private purposes. For example, by referring to her white assailant as "Mr. Charlie," a condescending, if not derogatory term for a white man, she may have been protecting herself and her family from retribution.[6] Naming names could have consequences—especially in the segregated South of the 1950s, when accusations of interracial rape or assault justified heinous racial violence.

She may also have kept the story private to maintain her respectability. Was her silence part of what Darlene Clark Hine called the "culture of dissemblance" among Black women who created, as she put it, the "appearance of openness and disclosure but actually shielded the truth of their inner lives and selves from their oppressors?"[7] Did Rosa Parks's husband want her to share the story? Did he urge her to keep quiet about it? Did her mother caution her or share advice that she had gotten from her grandmother and great-grandmother about the lack of justice for Black women who were victims of white men's lust? Would telling impugn her respectable reputation as a married woman and upstanding citizen? It may have been even harder to share the details in her essay after she became known as the iconic "mother of the civil rights movement," when her identity as a saintly seamstress with tired feet helped justify the bold action against segregation.

While Parks may have used dissemblance to protect her reputation or her family's safety, the act of writing about her assault positions her in a tradition of testimony and resistance among Black women, like Harriet Jacobs and Ida B. Wells, who spoke out about racialized sexual violence in the nineteenth century and early twentieth century. By choosing to write about "Mr. Charlie" instead of her specific assailant, she universalizes this experience for a like-minded audience who shared similar burdens and vulnerabilities. Indeed, working-class Black women like her were susceptible to the racial and sexual proclivities of white men *and* were often unprotected by Black men. Rosa Parks's essay—true testimony, allegory, or some combination of both—places her squarely within this history. That some rushed to invalidate Parks's essay or suggest it should remain hidden when it was rediscovered in 2011 speaks to ongoing issues of power and control over Black women's bodies, their history, and the way we remember the powerful women who helped lead the modern civil rights movement.

ROSA PARKS'S ESSAY

It was the spring of 1931 and Rosa McCauley (later Parks) was unmarried and eighteen years old. She had recently dropped out of the laboratory school at Alabama State College because, as she put it in this essay, "poverty kept me from paying tuition to continue."[8] In order to supplement her mother's income, she took a job as a "maid of all work" for a white family. The position paid a paltry $4 a week for around-the-clock childcare and housekeeping services. She might earn an extra "50 cents or a cast off article of the white lady's clothing" for staying late into the night. On one of these nights, after finishing her daily tasks, putting the baby to bed, and washing the dishes, she was eager to relax. "How tired I was," she wrote, "after a long day of cleaning, cooking, baby tending, I really anticipated getting some rest and relaxation." She was about to go to the den and read the newspaper or "listen to the radio or phonograph records" when a knock came at the back door. The groundskeeper, a Black man whom she called "Sam," told her he had left his coat behind and asked if she would go to find it. When she returned, she wrote, Sam was gone. In his place was a tall, heavyset white man.[9]

She called him "Mr. Charlie." He stood in the kitchen and poured himself a glass of whiskey. She suggested he take his drink into the living room to wait for the white homeowners. He declined and instead offered her a drink. "Jones won't miss it," he said. Parks refused. "I told him I didn't drink whiskey and didn't want him there to visit me." Then, she wrote, "he moved nearer to me and put his hand on my waist." She was terrified: "I jumped away as quickly as an unbridled filly," she said. "I was very frightened by now . . . or just plain scared to death." He asked her to "be sweet to him," she said, and promised her money.[10]

At that moment, she wrote, she realized that Sam had set her up. "Sam's mission here was not a forgotten coat," she said. "I felt trapped and helpless. I was hurt and sickened through with anger." She thought of Sam as a trusted friend, but now she saw him as "a procurer." "I felt filthy and stripped naked of any shred of decency," she wrote. "In a flash, I was no longer a decent, self-respecting teenage girl, but a flesh pot, a strumpet to be bargained for and parceled out as a commodity from the Negro to the white man." As Mr. Charlie grew intoxicated and more "lustful for my body," she feared for her life: "My puny 5-foot-2; 120 pound frame," she recalled, was no match "against this tall heavy set man . . . six feet tall . . . possibly 200 pounds." More than his size, perhaps, was the power embodied by his race and gender. "So many frantic thoughts raced through my mind. His strength, my weakness physically. The white man's dominance . . . [and our] subjection throughout the history of chattel slavery to the semi-freedom of this moment," she wrote. She knew all too well that white men could attack Black women with impunity.[11]

To be sure, the history of such interracial encounters weighed heavily on her mind. "I thought of my poor great-grandmother," she wrote, who was "bred, born, and reared to serve no other purpose than that which resulted in the bastard issue; to be trampled, mistreated, and abused by both Negro slaves and [her] white master." Her great-grandmother was a rare beauty and a skilled seamstress who died young. She left behind three children, the eldest of whom was Rosa Parks's grandfather, Sylvester Edwards. Parks lived with Edwards as a child and understood that his milky-white complexion and straight brown hair testified to this tangled interracial history.[12] As she traced this personal archive of Black women's lack of sexual sovereignty in the essay, Parks was also reminded of the ways in which whites' sexual and racial double standards affected African American men accused of interracial excursions. Indeed, not many miles away, she wrote, "the state of Alabama was doing everything possible to electrocute nine young Negro boys, the Scottsboro boys, for the alleged rape of two white women hoboes."[13]

Standing in the shadows of a ruthless past and in the throes of a present threat, Parks began to pray: "The Lord is my strength, of whom shall I be afraid? The Lord is my light, my salvation, whom shall I fear?" Suddenly, she wrote, "all my fear had been replaced by a hard-as-tempered-steel determination to stand . . . against this formidable foe for as long as I drew the breath of life." "I knew that no matter what happened, I would never yield to this white man's bestiality. I was ready and willing to die," she said, "but give my consent, never. Never, never."[14]

A sense of righteousness and strength filled her as she unleashed a verbal tirade against Mr. Charlie. "I taunted him about the supposed white supremacy, the white man's law drawing the color line of segregation," she wrote. "I would stay within the law—on my side of the line." She refused to be intimate, she said, highlighting her morality and respectability, "with a man that the law did not permit me to be married to and respected by." She continued to rail against him and the history of white supremacy. "Without the least bit of quaking or quivering of my voice," she wrote, "I talked and talked about everything I knew about the white man's inhumane treatment of the Negro. How I hated all white men [and would] never stoop so low as to have anything to do with him."[15]

She shared a similar sentiment in both her autobiography and later interviews. For example, she said she was unimpressed when she first met Raymond Parks in the spring of 1931, around the same time the incident with Mr. Charlie occurred. "I thought he was too white," she admitted; "I had an aversion to white men." Indeed, she only seemed interested in light-skinned Black men if they adopted a kind of radical freedom politics. It was not until she realized that Raymond Parks was a charter member of the Montgomery chapter of the NAACP, carried a pistol in his pocket, and was part of Alabama's underground network of Black radicals that she finally consented to a date.[16] If Rosa Parks was drawn to "Race Men," it may have had something to do with her deep respect and love for her shotgun-toting Garveyite grandfather, Sylvester Edwards, who taught her that a "proud African American can simply not accept bad treatment from anybody."[17] This may be why she also vehemently condemned Sam as a "procurer" in this essay. Sam did not "own me," Parks wrote. He could not "offer me for sale." With simmering rage and what she called a "cold and cruel, controlled anger," she recounted how she "hated Sam as much as I did [Mr. Charlie] and I would not wipe my foot or spit on either of them."[18]

Despite her disdain for weak Black men like Sam, Parks saved most of her vitriol for Mr. Charlie. Throughout the entire episode, Parks described being chased around the living room and just barely dodging his groping hands by jumping behind furniture and in front of tables. "He need not think," she wrote, "that because he was a low-down, dirty dog of a white man and I was a poor, defenseless helpless colored girl that he could run over me."[19]

Finally, she decided to stop trying to escape. Perhaps she realized there was nowhere she could safely turn—alone in a white family's home, it was unlikely that she would find assistance among the neighbors. If she ran out of the house, where would she go? And what would happen to her job—a necessity in the midst of the Great Depression—if she left the baby alone? What consequences would she and her family suffer? It is hard to know what drove her decision to stop resisting, but her surrender seemed to work. "I was so tired and spent physically and emotionally," she wrote, that she just sat down and picked up the newspaper. She told him "if he wanted to kill and rape a dead body, he was welcome." But "while I lived, I would stand alone in my belief, no matter who, no matter how many Negro men's permission he could get, it would do no good." "I don't care if you line them up, pile them or stack them against me . . . [my] answer is still NO!"

"At long last," she wrote at the end of her essay, "Mr. Charlie got the idea that I meant no, very definitely no. He said he would not bother me further." He sat down next to her on an ottoman and she got up and moved to another chair. "I didn't want to see him," she said. "It made me sick to look at him." She opened her newspaper wide and held it, as she put it, "where I couldn't see him." And she started to read.[20]

BLACK WOMEN, SEXUAL VIOLENCE, AND "MR. CHARLIE"

Rosa Parks's experience fits into a long and brutal history. For decades, African American women spoke publicly and privately about the everyday sexual harassment and sexualized racial terror that they and their loved ones faced during and after slavery. In 1892, the respected Washington, D.C., author, educator, and clubwoman Anna Julia Cooper argued that the "Colored Girls of the South" lived in the "midst of pitfalls and snares, waylaid by the lower classes of white men."[21] The next year, in a speech at the World's Columbian Exposition in Chicago, she condemned the assault of Black women and girls by white men and testified to the "painful, patient and silent toil of mothers to gain a fee simple title to the bodies of their daughters."[22] The great educator and reformer Fannie Barrier Williams echoed Cooper's comments. She told the same audience of Black and white clubwomen in Chicago about the "shameful fact that I am constantly in receipt of letters from the still unprotected women of the South" who asked for assistance placing their daughters in jobs "to save them from going into the homes of the South as servants, as there is nothing to save them from dishonor and degradation."[23] In a 1912 editorial for *The Independent*, a weekly magazine founded by abolitionists, a "Negro Nurse" argued that "a colored woman's virtue in [the South] has no protection."[24]

Like Rosa Parks's essay about "Mr. Charlie," the "Negro Nurse" described the dangers and risks associated with working as a domestic in white homes— from the low wages and long hours ("from sunrise to sunrise") to psychological, physical, and sexual abuse. She was fired from one job, the nurse said, "because I refused to let the madam's husband kiss me." Her husband was arrested and fined when he confronted the white man who attacked her. The message from the judge was clear, she said: "This court will never take the word of a nigger against the word of a white man." This was not an isolated incident. "Many and many a time since," the nurse wrote, "I have heard similar stories repeated again and again by my friends. I believe nearly all white men take, and expect to have, undue liberties with their colored female servants— not only the fathers, but in many cases the sons also."[25]

In 1925, the clubwoman Maggie Lena Walker spoke specifically about the dangers facing wage-earning Black women. "Poverty is a trap for *women* and especially for our women," she said. "When I walk along the avenues of our city and I see our own girls employed in the households of the whites, my heart aches with pain. . . . When I see the good, pure honest colored girl who is compelled to be a domestic in a white man's family—while I applaud the girl for her willingness to do honest work in order to be self supporting, and to help the mother and father who have toiled for her, yet I tremble lest she should slip and fall a victim to some white man's lust."[26]

Understanding this history and learning how to survive, navigate, negotiate, and endure the threat of sexual harassment and sexualized racial terror was part of the socialization process of coming of age as a Black woman
and, as a result, part of the long struggle for freedom. Rosa Parks's narrative reveals her vulnerability to this kind of terror as much as it underlines
her resistance, suggesting perhaps that other women who faced similar
situations could resist as well. Parks opens her narrative by recalling how
helpless she felt once she realized the danger she was in. She asks, "Lord,
What can I do?" And then details not only how she verbally and physically
resisted Mr. Charlie's advances, but also how she used her knowledge of the
past to counter sexual stereotypes of Black women and dominant narratives
of white supremacy. She makes it clear, for example, that she was no "strumpet" and cites the state's antimiscegenation laws as part of the cause for Mr.
Charlie's assumption of her sexual availability. She asserts her respectability
and her morality—she is no law-breaker or pushover—which establish her
as a woman deserving of respect, protection, and bodily integrity. In that
sense, Rosa Parks's essay is as much a personal testimony as it is a model of
bold, yet respectable resistance to white men, much like the model Harriet
Jacobs provides in *Incidents in the Life of a Slave Girl*, that could be utilized in
the larger campaign for civil and human rights.[27]

Since Guernsey's auction house dated the essay in the mid-1950s, it could
have been developed as a talk for one of the many fundraising efforts Parks
made on behalf of the Montgomery Improvement Association and the bus
boycott. In addition to the daily support she devoted to the boycott, Parks
also raised significant funds for the movement in 1956 by delivering speeches
throughout the country—at Anderson College in Indiana and Highlander
Folk School in Tennessee; at an NAACP event in Pittsburgh and the militant UAW Local 600 in Detroit; to the National Council of Negro Women
in D.C. and a massive civil rights rally in Madison Square Garden in New
York City; and up and down the Pacific Coast including the 47th annual
NAACP convention in San Francisco.[28] Little is known about what she said
at these events and conferences, but given the gender and racial restrictions
of the time, it is unlikely Parks would have delivered a speech about her
own experience with interracial assault. Other African American women,
like Mamie Till Bradley, who traveled around the country on behalf of the
NAACP in the wake of her son Emmett Till's brutal murder, were careful to
toe these racial and gender lines as well.[29]

What is more likely, however, is that Parks had small speaking engagements in and around Montgomery, Alabama. She was, after all, the secretary of the local NAACP, she directed their youth council, worked for the Brotherhood of Sleeping Car Porters and, in 1948 she was the secretary for the Statewide Conference of the Alabama NAACP, among other things. In other words, she was well acquainted with activists and organizations across the state. It is in these intimate spaces "behind the veil" where her testimony about "Mr. Charlie" could have had the most impact.[30] For example, if the point of the essay was to encourage others to think about "What Can I Do," then it seems possible that Parks's bold stand against Mr. Charlie would be a useful talk for the working-class Black women and girls who found themselves in similar situations. Parks's testimony about how she resisted Mr. Charlie could help others locate their own inner strength and conjure up the courage not only to stand up to their own Mr. Charlie, but to believe in themselves and their ability to shape the world around them. This is speculation, of course. But given the history of the Montgomery bus boycott as a women's movement for dignity and Parks's history as a radical activist, it may not be pure fantasy.

Although popular portrayals of Parks reduce her protest against racial segregation to a singular, silent act, she devoted her life to what Hasan Jeffries calls "freedom rights."[31] Parks was a seasoned organizer long before the 1955–56 Montgomery bus boycott began. Racial pride and resistance to white supremacy was something she learned at her grandfather's knee. She grew up in a household that celebrated Black history and believed in armed self-defense. She and her husband labored together in the Scottsboro struggle and hosted voter registration workshops in their little shotgun house in Montgomery in the 1930s and 1940s. For more than a decade, her work with the local and state NAACP, the Brotherhood of Sleeping Car Porters, and other militant groups placed her at the center of Alabama's civil rights movement long before she was told to go to the back of a bus.[32]

Most importantly, in the ten years before the bus boycott began, Rosa Parks investigated and organized campaigns to help defend Black women assaulted or raped by white men.[33] For example, when she heard that a group of white men kidnapped and raped Recy Taylor, an African American mother and sharecropper in Abbeville, Alabama, in the fall of 1944, she rushed to investigate. After meeting with Taylor and taking notes on her testimony, Parks and Montgomery's most militant activists—labor leaders, women's groups, and community organizers—formed the "Committee for Equal Justice for Mrs. Recy Taylor," and helped launch what the *Chicago Defender* called "the strongest campaign for equal justice to be seen in a decade."[34]

As secretary for the Montgomery NAACP since 1943, Parks had notes on nearly every case of racial and sexual brutality in Alabama in the 1940s and 1950s. She knew that what happened to Recy Taylor was not unusual in the segregated South. "There was a lot of white violence against blacks," she recalled. "Things happened that most people never heard about."[35] Indeed, from slavery through the better part of the twentieth century, white men abducted and assaulted Black women with alarming regularity and often with impunity. They lured Black women and girls away from home with promises of steady work and better wages; attacked them on the job and assailed them while traveling to or from home, work, or school; and sexually humiliated and assaulted them on buses and streetcars and other public spaces. Montgomery seemed to have more than its fair share of what Roy Wilkins, the executive director of the NAACP, called "sex cases."[36] And Rosa Parks was often at the center of any organizing activity to defend Black womanhood and bring their assailants to justice.

In 1946 she worked with E. D. Nixon—a prominent activist in Montgomery whose lifelong work with the Brotherhood of Sleeping Car Porters and the NAACP connected him to national leaders like A. Philip Randolph—and others on the campaign to expose the white police officers who abducted and raped the sixteen-year-old daughter of a Black woman who challenged a police officer on a bus.[37] Three years later, in the spring of 1949, African American activists and community leaders mobilized to defend Gertrude Perkins, a twenty-five-year-old Black woman who was kidnapped and raped by two white Montgomery police officers. The "Citizens Committee for Gertrude Perkins" launched a public protest to demand an investigation and a trial.[38] Their efforts forced a grand jury hearing and brought the city's disparate Black ministers together for the first time.[39] In 1951, Sam Green, a white grocer in Montgomery, raped a Black teenager named Flossie Hardman who worked as his babysitter. After an all-white jury returned a not-guilty verdict, community activists launched a boycott of Green's grocery store, which served a mostly Black clientele. After only a few weeks, the organizers delivered their own guilty verdict by driving Green's store into the red.[40] The successful boycott was incredibly important and highlighted its potential power as an instrument of justice.[41]

Many whites in Montgomery chose to ignore these protests, notably the city's bus operators, who brutalized Black passengers daily. In Montgomery, buses were not only segregated, they were often sites of racial violence. Besides the daily indignities of Jim Crow, like paying your fare in the front of the bus and entering in the back, or the ever-changing color line, which could shift dramatically from one stop to the next, African Americans who stepped out of their "place" were arrested, beaten, and sometimes even killed. Since working-class Black women, many of whom were domestics, made up nearly 70 percent of the Montgomery City Lines ridership, they often bore the brunt of these racialized and sexualized attacks.[42]

Black women complained that bus drivers hurled nasty, sexualized insults at them, touched them inappropriately, and physically abused them. One woman remembered bus drivers sexually harassing her as she waited on the corner. "The bus was up high," she recalled, "and the street was down low. They'd drive up and expose themselves while I was just standing there. It scared me to death."[43] Another remembered that bus drivers treated Black women "just as rough as can be, like we are some kind of animal."[44]

This abuse fueled resentment and anger among African Americans, especially those domestics and day laborers who spent hours on their feet cooking, washing, and ironing for white people. "You spend your whole lifetime in your occupation," Rosa Parks said later, "making life clever, easy, and convenient for white people. But when you have to get transportation home, you are denied an equal accommodation." Mistreatment on the buses, she argued, emphasized the fact that "our existence was for the white man's comfort and well being; we had to accept being deprived of just being human."[45] Harassment and abuse by Mr. Charlie, whether on the buses, on the streets, or in white homes, was an all-too-familiar part of being a Black woman or girl in Montgomery, Alabama, and throughout the country.

Rosa Parks's experience with racial violence and sexual harassment may have served as a catalyst for her own antirape work and provided added meaning to the activist work she did on behalf of others who suffered similar abuse. The fact that she wrote about her own battle with Mr. Charlie during the 1950s, when white bus drivers, policemen, and employers felt free to attack Black women without fear of punishment, speaks to the ways in which the boycott centralized the issue of protecting Black women's bodily integrity and dignity. After all, if we listen to the testimonies of Black women who risked their lives to walk instead of ride the bus, the boycott was never just about segregated seating, it was also about the right to move through the world without being touched inappropriately, sexually or racially harassed, or physically assaulted.

Those are the issues Parks speaks to in her essay, especially when she points out that the segregation laws enabled the disrespect and ill-treatment of Black women. ("I would not be intimate with a man that the law did not allow me to be married to and respected by."[46]) And those are the issues Rosa Parks addresses throughout her nearly seventy years as an activist. In a sense, Rosa Parks had been working on the issue of sexual harassment and racialized sexual violence and talking about it with her fellow activists at least since 1944 when she got involved in the Recy Taylor case. Perhaps now she was ready to reveal how deeply she felt about it—and why.

We do not know if Rosa Parks shared her story with audiences or wrote it just for herself, but what we do know is that she did not include it in her memoirs or any of the hundreds of interviews she gave to the press over the course of her lifetime. We should not assume that this means that she dissembled about, fictionalized, or kept the story about "Mr. Charlie" a total secret. Instead, the silence about it may reflect her own understanding and consciousness of her various audiences especially once she became a public figure. She seemed to know who could actually *hear* what she was saying and who would have resisted the lessons she offered. Jeanne Theoharis's biography of Parks notes that she rarely offered detailed or intimate information about her personal life to reporters and interviewers. Parks mainly responded to questions—which were almost always about her 1955 arrest and the bus boycott—with the most direct and least detailed answer.[47] It is important to note that few, if any, reporters or historians asked Parks directly about issues of sexuality and sexual violence.

However, while she may not have talked specifically about her own racial and sexual vulnerabilities and victimhood with journalists and biographers—a character trait she maintained throughout her life—she did not shy away from speaking about racial and sexual violence, even when it was very personal. In the autobiography she wrote with Jim Haskins—as in the essay about "Mr. Charlie"—for example, she notes that her enslaved great-grandmother was a survivor of interracial rape and that her grandfather, Sylvester Edwards, was the product of this coerced relationship. He taught his daughters and his granddaughter to be especially wary of white men.[48] This was a lesson that was repeated over the course of her life as she bore witness to (and organized against) attacks on Black women and girls by white men—from the Recy Taylor case in 1944 to the "Free Joan

Little" movement thirty years later.[49] She also worked to defend Black men accused of rape by white women, understanding clearly that, as Tim Tyson put it, the "much traveled sexual back road between the races was clearly marked 'one-way.'"[50] Why did she include these stories of racial and sexual violence in her memoirs, but not her own? Did her editors and co-authors play any role in shaping these narratives? What did they have to gain or lose by including Parks's testimony about Mr. Charlie?

When Guernsey's trotted out a small, salacious section of the essay in 2011 and called it a "near rape" they were not trying to understand, educate, or enlighten the public about Rosa Parks's life and history, her personal agency, or what it might tell us about Black women's long struggle for freedom in the United States. They were trying to *sell* the collection. In that sense, they focused mainly on the *act* (the "near rape") rather than her resistance to it; on her semi-victimhood (it was a "near" rape, after all) rather than her passionate disavowal of both white men and white supremacy and her important defense of Black women's respectability. Perhaps the guardians of Parks's image—those who too often profit from her iconic status as the sweet, silent, "mother of the civil rights movement"—rushed to delegitimize the essay because they feared it would mar her public image; would raise questions about her purity as a symbol for racial integration and reconciliation; and would limit *their* ability to profit off the popular martyr-like image of Parks as the woman who "sat down, so we could all stand up."[51]

We may never know if Rosa Parks meant the essay as autobiographical or allegorical, as a story to be kept locked away or told in front of a crowd. In a handwritten document in her archival collection, she mused about what to declare and what to keep hidden: "Is it worthwhile to reveal the intimacies of the past life?" she wrote. "Will the people be sympathetic or disillusioned when the facts of my life are told? Would they be interested or indifferent? Will the results be harmful or good?"[52] The answers are uncertain, but a first-person account of sexualized racial violence from a young working-class Black woman is very rare and that alone marks it as important. That it was also written by one of the most important historical figures of the twentieth century, a woman whose life we are just beginning to understand, makes it not only important, but necessary. Black women's and girls' stories are often not visible in historical archives, but fragments of this history can sometimes be found in court documents, in clubwomen's speeches and letters, in the pages of African American newspapers, and in the oral tradition where grandmothers told their daughters, aunts told their nieces, and friends warned each other about the dangers that awaited them in white spaces.

Despite these glimpses into the past, we still have an incomplete record of the kind of daily terrors and indignities Black women and girls faced in the Jim Crow South and how they resisted (if they could) and recovered from (if and when they did) the trauma of racial and sexual brutality. Their invisibility in the archive and our discomfort and unwillingness to engage with the powerful fragments we have speak to Black women's historic powerlessness and disfranchisement as citizens and human beings in the United States, and their continued subjugation today. However, it is from those fragments and testimonies that we can craft a new history of empowerment and active citizenship, of Black women's agency and leadership in the struggle for freedom and human dignity. At the very least, we can better understand the history we think we know.

NOTES

1 Rosa Parks, handwritten essay c. 1950s or early 1960s, Scanned Document II-A-1; "Sample Documents from the Rosa Parks Archive," Guernsey's Auctioneers, copy in author's possession. Hereafter cited as "Rosa Parks Essay."

2 Ula Ilnytzky, "Rosa Parks Essay Appears to Discuss Rape Attempt," *Seattle Times*, July 29, 2011.

3 Parks donated many of her papers to the Walter P. Reuther Library at Wayne State University in 1971, but this essay was not part of that collection. See Jeanne Theoharis, *The Rebellious Life of Mrs. Rosa Parks* (New York: Beacon Press, 2013).

4 See, for example, Douglass Brinkley, *Rosa Parks* (New York: Penguin Press, 2000); Theoharis, *The Rebellious Life of Mrs. Rosa Parks*; Danielle L. McGuire, *At the Dark End of the Street—Black Women, Rape, and Resistance: A New History of the Civil Rights Movement from Rosa Parks to the Rise of Black Power* (New York: Knopf, 2010); Rosa Parks and Jim Haskins, *Rosa Parks: My Story* (New York: Dial Press, 1992).

5 Margaret McAleer, Kimberly Owens, Tammi Taylor, Tracey Barton, and Sherralyn McCoy, Rosa Parks Papers, "A Finding Aid In the Collection of the Library of Congress," 7, Library of Congress Online Catalogue, accessed Feb. 19, 2016, http://lccn.loc .gov/mm2014085943.

6 For more on the term "Mr. Charlie," see, for example, Lawrence Levine, *Black Culture, Black Consciousness* (New York: Oxford University Press, 2007); see also Maciej Widawski, *African American Slang: A Linguistic Description* (Cambridge: Cambridge University Press, 2015), 224.

7 Darlene Clark Hine, "Rape and the Inner Lives of Black Women in the Middle West," *Signs* 14, no. 4 (Summer 1989): 912.

8 Rosa Parks Essay. See Theoharis, *The Rebellious Life of Mrs. Rosa Parks*, 10.

9 Rosa Parks Essay.

10 Ibid.

11 Ibid.

12 Parks with Haskins, *Rosa Parks*, 15.

13 Rosa Parks Essay.

14 Ibid.

15 Ibid.

16 Parks with Haskins, *Rosa Parks*, 55–60.

17 Brinkley, *Rosa Parks*, 23, 27; Parks with Haskins, *Rosa Parks*, 31.

18 Rosa Parks Essay.

19 Ibid.

20 Ibid.

21 Anna Julia Cooper, *A Voice from the South* (Xenia, OH: Aldine Printing House, 1892), 24–25.

22 Paula Giddings, *When and Where I Enter: The Impact of Black Women on Race and Sex in America* (New York: William Morrow, 1984), 31.

23 Ibid., 84–85; Estelle Freedman, *Redefining Rape: Sexual Violence in the Era of Suffrage and Segregation* (Cambridge, MA: Harvard University Press, 2013), 119.

24 A Negro Nurse, "More Slavery at the South," *The Independent*, Jan. 25, 1912, 196–200. UNC-CH digitization project, *Documenting the American South*, accessed Oct. 15, 2013, http://docsouth.unc.edu/fpn/negnurse/negnurse.html.

25 Ibid.

26 Elsa Barkley Brown, "What Has Happened Here," *Feminist Studies* (1992): 311n25.

27 Harriet Jacobs, *Incidents in the Life of a Slave Girl* (New York: Dover Thrift Editions, 2001).

28 Theoharis, *The Rebellious Life of Mrs. Rosa Parks*, 105, 122, 126–130.

29 Ruth Fieldstein, "I Wanted the Whole World to See: Race, Gender, and Constructions of Motherhood in the Death of Emmett Till," in *Not June Cleaver: Women and Gender in Postwar America 1945–1960*, ed. Joanne Meyerowitz (Philadelphia: Temple University Press, 1994), 263–303.

30 For more on "the veil" see W.E.B. Du Bois, *Souls of Black Folks* (New York: Dover Thrift Editions, 1994).

31 See Hasan Jeffries, *Bloody Lowndes: Civil Rights and Black Power in Alabama's Black Belt* (New York: New York University Press, 2009), 4.

32 McGuire, *At the Dark End of the Street*, 78.

33 Ibid.

34 Fred Atwater, "$600 to Rape Wife? Alabama Whites Make Offer to Recy Taylor Mate!" *Chicago Defender*, Jan. 27, 1945; McGuire, *At the Dark End of the Street*, 13.

35 Parks with Haskins, *Rosa Parks*, 94.

36 Timothy B. Tyson, *Radio Free Dixie: Robert F. Williams and the Roots of Black Power* (Chapel Hill: University of North Carolina Press, 1995), 109.

37 E. G. Jackson, "Attack Case Drags On; No Arrests Made," *Alabama Tribune*, Apr. 22, 1949.

38 "Rape Cry against Dixie Cops Falls on Deaf Ears," *Baltimore Afro-American*, Apr. 9, 1949, 1.

39 See McGuire, *At the Dark End of the Street*, 52–54.

40 Case 2, folder IV, box 30 and 14, Martin Luther King Jr. Papers, Howard Gotleib Archival Research Center, Boston University, Boston, MA; J. Mills Thornton, *Dividing Lines: Municipal Politics and the Struggle for Civil Rights in Montgomery, Birmingham, and Selma* (Tuscaloosa: University of Alabama Press, 2002), 30. See also *Montgomery Advertiser*, Feb. 15, 22, Mar. 1, May 24, June 7, 1951.

41 McGuire, At the Dark End of the Street, 58.

42 See, for example, Lamont H. Yeakey, "The Montgomery, Alabama Bus Boycott 1955–56" (PhD diss., Columbia University, 1979); "Incidents and Complaints—Transportation Department, Race Question . . . Birmingham Electric Company's Transportation System," Cooper Green Papers, Department of Archives, Birmingham Public Library, Birmingham, AL; Thomas Gilliam, "The Montgomery Bus Boycott of 1955–56," in *The Walking City: The Montgomery Bus Boycott*, ed. David Garrow (PLACE?: Carlson Pub., 1989), 198.

43 William H. Chafe, Raymond Gavins, and Robert Korstadt, eds., *Remembering Jim Crow: African Americans Tell About Life in the Segregated South* (New York: The New Press, 2001), 9.

44 Stewart Burns, *Daybreak of Freedom: The Montgomery Bus Boycott* (Chapel Hill: University of North Carolina Press, 1997), 70.

45 Earl and Miriam Selby, *Odyssey: Journey Through Black America* (New York: Putnam, 1970), 54.

46 Rosa Parks Essay.

47 Theoharis, *The Rebellious Life of Mrs. Rosa Parks*, xiii–xiv.

48 Parks and Haskins, *Rosa Parks*, 15.

49 Rosa Parks helped lead the "Free Joan Little" chapter in Detroit, Michigan, in 1975. See McGuire, *At the Dark End of the Street*, 215.

50 Timothy B. Tyson, *Radio Free Dixie: Robert F. Williams and the Roots of Black Power* (Chapel Hill: University of North Carolina Press, 1999), 94.

51 This was a common refrain at Parks's funeral in Detroit in 2005. See, for example, E. R. Shipp, "Rosa Parks, 92, Founding Symbol of Civil Rights Movement, Dies," *New York Times*, Oct. 25, 2005, http://www.nytimes.com/2005/10/25/us/25parks.html?_r=0.

52 Emmarie Huetteman, "Who Rosa Parks Was, Not Just What She Meant," *New York Times*, Feb. 5, 2015, http://nyti.ms/1zSWIBK.

5 ♦ COLD WAR HISTORY AS WOMEN'S HISTORY

JACQUELINE CASTLEDINE

In late autumn 2011 I traveled to Moscow with a delegation of U.S. historians on an eight-day cultural exchange tour, where the highlight of my trip was presenting a paper at a Moscow State University (MSU) meeting with Russian historians. Increased access to government documents after the fall of Communism in the early 1990s had sparked a Russian "archival revolution." There was palpable excitement among scholars about the potential disclosures these Soviet records held, and the ways they may help revise paradigms central to not only Russian but also post–World War II global history. I looked forward to discussing how an unprocessed manuscript collection of a little-known U.S. grassroots organizer had prompted my own historical reassessment.

Our meeting started with a number of MSU faculty presentations and I sat intrigued as we discussed current trends in Russian historiography. It was difficult not to share in their enthusiasm, and as I listened to my Russian colleagues I believed that my research had much in common with theirs. In the last two decades, historians of the American left have also challenged well-established paradigms by documenting a history of radical women. Indeed, Erik McDuffie, Dayo Gore, and I are among those who have questioned the widely held assumption that harsh political repression in the McCarthy era caused radical women to leave public life until civil rights and women's movements in the late 1950s and 1960s provided new outlets for their activism.[1] Our research reveals the power of a paradigm that obscured women's work in global cold war movements and suggests new possibilities for understanding radical history. This recent scholarship laid the groundwork for my Moscow presentation, which examined how women's cold war politics affected U.S. family relations—especially women's relations—in ways that significantly expand our assessments of the political impacts of these conflicts.

Yet when I began my talk I sensed that some in the room were surprised by its focus on the historical implications of radical U.S. women's activism. A few audience members shifted restlessly in their seats as I described my discovery of Vermont activist Helen MacMartin, who in 1948 was a state organizer for the short-lived Progressive Party (PP) movement led by Henry Wallace. For over a decade Wallace had represented the left wing of the Democratic Party and before becoming a third-party presidential candidate for the PP, he served as a member of Franklin Roosevelt's cabinet and as his second vice president.[2] Roosevelt, however, replaced Wallace with Harry S. Truman in his fourth and final run for president, making Truman FDR's successor.[3]

In his 2000 study of the 1948 U.S. presidential election, Zachary Karabell provides a sympathetic depiction of MacMartin, describing the Burlington grandmother's best attempts to organize a large crowd for a Wallace appearance in her city. Although the mayor refused to rent city property to the Progressive Party because of its leftist agenda and MacMartin had difficulty finding a minister to give the invocation, she persevered. Karabell wrote, "The visit was a brief moment for Wallace . . . but for MacMartin it was the high point of the campaign"; despite claims she made to the contrary, Karabell also concluded that MacMartin was understandably disappointed by the rally's outcome.[4] She appeared an earnest but inexperienced and ineffectual organizer, making her a fitting symbol of the long and often unsuccessful battle waged by women throughout the nineteenth and twentieth centuries to influence U.S. politics. Karabell's characterization of MacMartin's work reinforced a narrative familiar to women's historians, though one that had been widely challenged outside the cold war period.[5]

In 1948's crowded and ideologically diverse field of presidential candidates, MacMartin was drawn to Henry Wallace by his status as the "peace candidate" who would focus the nation's resources not on military spending but on promoting postwar domestic programs. Others included Republican New York governor Thomas Dewey, "Dixiecrat" South Carolina senator Strom Thurmond, and incumbent Harry Truman. The Wallace campaign's promotion of a foreign policy that would engage the Soviet Union diplomatically to avert a cold war proved unpopular, however, and was overwhelmingly rejected by a voting public entering an era soon defined by the term "McCarthyism."

Harsh redbaiting by anticommunists on both the political left and right had been effective in discrediting the Wallace movement, whose leadership did indeed include Communist Party members. As a result, Wallace earned less than 3 percent of the national vote and Progressives across the nation running for statewide offices faced a similar fate. In conservative Vermont, Wallace fared even worse, receiving just over 1 percent of the vote. An election postmortem by the national PP committee claimed that despite the resounding defeat of its candidates, "We will carry on the fight . . . the Progressive Party has a large and important place in America"—a belief that Helen MacMartin shared.[6] Nonetheless, in the collective public memory, Wallace and his 1948 campaign for president are largely forgotten.

Given the election outcome, Karabell's argument that in 1948 Helen MacMartin personified the futility of the PP movement is convincing. Her civic participation before the Wallace campaign had centered on work as a Parent Teacher Association volunteer in the schools her children attended and membership in the American Association of University Women. Like other Progressives she believed Wallace's stature as a former vice president meant that even if he did not reach the Oval Office in this election, a respectable showing would create opportunity for a strong run in 1952. Considering their ambitious goals, when the final vote was tallied Progressives felt the sting of a significant loss in this election and concerns for the future.

It is easy to understand why MacMartin's first experience with political organizing appeared to represent the near total repression of leftist women's activism in the immediate postwar years. One can envision a physically and emotionally depleted MacMartin following her experience in the 1948 campaign. Karabell writes of the next years of her life, "People stopped giving money, stopped listening to Helen, and stopped answering her letters," as she grew increasingly isolated at the margins of a rightward-shifting political landscape. I was not surprised, therefore, to read that the activist died shortly afterward in 1951.[7]

As I read of MacMartin's travails I was struck by what a compelling story they tell. Later, in *Cold War Progressives* I wrote that from a distance, "The recounting of MacMartin's latter years supports a well-established narrative of the cold war era that depicts American leftists 'contained' by increasingly anticommunist U.S. foreign policies, at the same time that domestic containment of women valorized their role in the home. Indeed, this story appears to dramatically illustrate the postwar silencing of political women as they retreated from public view."[8] Yet as I wrote this I had already discovered closer examination of MacMartin's experience suggested something quite different. A trip to view the Progressive Party Papers at the University of Iowa revealed to me that MacMartin's activism extended well past the decline of the Progressive Party in the early 1950s. The year of her death was actually 1987.

Phone calls to institutions in MacMartin's home town of Burlington disclosed that the University of Vermont (UVM) had a dusty, unprocessed collection of her papers. Fittingly, these were stored on an uppermost shelf in its library annex, half a mile from the university's Special Collections holdings, reflecting MacMartin's ongoing position on the margins of mainstream political culture. Working from a number of large, timeworn cardboard boxes, I found an amalgam of political ephemera, newspaper clippings, and personal correspondence between MacMartin and family members. Topics covered in the cards and letters addressed to Helen suggested that her leftist politics had dramatically complicated personal relations during this time in her life. They also revealed that following a period of melancholy quite possibly brought on by the Wallace loss, MacMartin enjoyed nearly forty years of leftist activism, as a member of such organizations as the Committee to Abolish the House Un-American Activities Committee and the early feminist group, Older Women's Liberation (OWL).

Most interesting to me about this discovery was the window that the MacMartin papers opened into the private world beyond her public life. I learned the names of her two now deceased children, and spoke with several grandchildren. During one interview, a MacMartin granddaughter copied a number of pages from a diary her mother Louise—wife of Helen's son MacGregor—had kept in the 1950s. This document had not been archived in MacMartin's UVM collection, and in it Louise wrote poignantly about the stress that her mother-in-law's activism placed on the family during the early years of the cold war. Although lengthy, I read in Moscow several dramatic entries expressing Louise's concerns about this activism:

[Helen] has been interested in Russia for many years, and did a considerable amount of reading about it between the first and second world wars. Her background and sense of duty combined to make her quit her job . . . to become the Vermont Chairman of the Wallace for President Committee.

We respect her as a person, and love her as a mother, but we cannot subscribe to many of her beliefs. From a personal loyalty angle it was difficult to refuse to sign a petition for Wallace, but we did so refuse.

Louise also wrote about the family's attempt to curtail Helen's activism: "[Helen] told [son] Mac that she realized that it might hurt him, but that she *must* continue with her political work, and that she *would* regardless of whom it might hurt." Finally, Louise concluded: "Perhaps this is something like the tension which arose among families which were divided by the Civil War."[9]

The stillness in the room as I read Louise's words written nearly sixty years earlier suggested that the emotion of these diary entries was not lost on my Moscow audience.

At the end of my talk a number of women in the audience quickly raised their hands and attempted to ask me questions, while others in the room seemed impatient. Soon a faculty member approached the podium where I stood and explained that the effects of the cold war on family life were not often studied in Russia because they raise two important questions. Who would buy such books? And where would this history be taught? He then pointed out to me and those in the audience that there was a schedule to keep to, signaling it was time to move on. As our U.S. delegation leader, Elaine Tyler May, stood and suggested we spend more time answering audience questions about gender and cold war history, I began to wonder if it was not the marketability of this history that was in question but whether or not the narrative of MacMartin's activism, and its effect on her family, was historically significant. More specifically, I wondered if there was doubt that women had a place in cold war historiography.

We did briefly continue our discussion, until a MSU professor proposed that not only Russian but also U.S. historians could do a better job of documenting women's lives in the postwar period. Having found something on which we all agreed, the audience turned its attention to our final presenter. Even as we moved on, however, I was left with questions about what the family papers of Helen MacMartin had revealed to my audience and why its response surprised me. Later I considered how some at our meeting had defined the archives as government repositories and the historical records they contained, a view that contrasts sharply with the practice of women's history. Because historically far fewer women's records have been collected in relation to those of men, women's historians often hold a more expansive definition of the archive. Although family diaries like the one kept by Helen MacMartin's daughter-in-law may be viewed by a diplomatic, military, or cold war historian as less "objective" than a document issued by a government authority, a women's historian is likely to believe the reverse is true, and that the concept of the archive is "in flux, constantly being redefined."[10]

Years after first encountering MacMartin's papers, in collections in Iowa City and then in Burlington, I now considered whether the idea of the archive had shaped differing perceptions about the historical meanings of MacMartin's radical activist life and, perhaps more broadly, about whether there is, or should be, a cold war history of women.

COLD WAR ACTIVISM, POSTWAR WOMEN

The work of Joanne Meyerowitz, Kate Weigand, Daniel Horowitz, and Helen Laville published in the 1990s and early 2000s established a historical subfield exploring activist lives of postwar women.[11] With the exception of Laville, this research focuses primarily on the broadly defined postwar years and not specifically on the cold war waged during these years, when the United States and the Soviet Union engaged in a political and military rivalry to develop "spheres of influence" across the globe. There now appeared to me an important distinction separating postwar and cold war history in the mind of those who do not see a significant relationship between the *grassroots* activism of postwar U.S. women radicals and the *global* cold war. Progressive women like Helen MacMartin understood this differently. Drawing significant links among anticolonial movements in postwar Asia and Africa, global peace, and U.S. prosperity, they believed attention to each was required to create a peaceful and just world.

Following the Wallace loss MacMartin had taken the low-paying position of Vermont Progressive Party secretary, working to keep the Progressive movement alive in her home state. The job proved difficult, as conservative tradition in Vermont politics was longstanding and reflected not only in voting patterns but also by the editorial boards of the state's major newspapers.[12] In the summer of 1950 at a public forum at the University of Vermont MacMartin and four other panelists considered how Americans could "Reduce the Threat of Communism within the United States." When the PP secretary asserted that "native Fascists" and not Communists were the larger threat to Americans, she set off a round of stinging accusations led by Vermont newspaper editorialists. MacMartin's intrepid public performances, however, masked her uncertainty about the future of the PP. In the spring of 1950 she wrote to her state director, "Sometimes I wonder how long I will continue beating my head against a stone wall," yet she seemed resigned to the fact that "I get so encouraged by small responses . . . that I figure I shall go on trying."[13]

MacMartin's efforts included a 1950 campaign for U.S. Congress intended to keep the issue of peace on the Vermont ballot. Press coverage of her congressional campaigning as a cold war peace candidate illustrates the emotionally charged and gendered political discourse of the times. The *Burlington Daily News* characterized the Progressive Party candidate's views as "rants" and "wild bleatings," and suggested she may be a woman worthy of pity.[14] As it turns out, the *Daily News* had little to worry about. With the state party down to forty-nine dues-paying members, PP canvassers were only able to gather four hundred of the over twelve hundred petition signatures required to put her on the ballot. Clearly upset, MacMartin complained to national secretary C. B. Baldwin, "No one got started soon enough or has worked hard enough to accomplish this very easy goal . . . So PEACE Will Not Be On The Ballot In Vermont In November!"[15] Less upset was the *Burlington Free Press*, which announced the PP's failure to qualify under the headline "Mrs. MacMartin Won't Run for Congress After All."[16]

MacMartin fought other battles at the time as well. Most significantly, she found herself unable to regain her job as an employment counselor for the state of Vermont, a position to which she hoped to return following the 1948 election. In 1926 MacMartin had fled Brooklyn, New York, leaving an unhappy marriage to a college sweetheart, and settled in Vermont with her two young children. Perhaps attuned to the politics of respectability, both before and after her divorce a decade later, in Vermont she would claim to be a widow and single mother. Yet even a degree from William Smith College during these depression years would not open doors as she sought employment and MacMartin found herself working a number of odd jobs that included caring for the children of a man in Rutland while also running his two farms and overseeing rental properties. With a federal scholarship from the New Deal's Emergency Relief Administration, in 1934 she began a training program at the Simmons School of Social Work in Boston and two years later, after graduation, joined the United States Employment Services (USES) as an employment counselor doing case work in rural Vermont. When she was unable to return to USES after the 1948 election, MacMartin was convinced that she was being blacklisted due to her leftist politics. Removing from her resumé all mention of her work with the Progressive

Party did not remedy the situation; she was offered only positions caring for children and the elderly—which she took to make ends meet.[17]

MacMartin's post-election financial and emotional slide greatly concerned family members, so much so that in the winter of 1951 sister Bess Buck asked Helen to join her in Washington, D.C., as live-in help. Bess hoped this would be a temporary measure that would allow her sister to look for other work and gain a more stable financial footing. Yet Bess also wrote that the offer was "null and void" if Helen did not give up Progressive Party politics, explaining that her husband, historian Solon Justus Buck, could not have his job as an archivist and assistant librarian of Congress jeopardized by Helen's picketing the White House. Urging her to be "less idealistic," Bess, perhaps with tongue in cheek, suggested this was Helen's "chance to be of service to mankind." Not the type of service she had envisioned, Helen refused the offer.[18]

Correspondence from the late 1940s and the 1950s reveals that Bess and Louise MacMartin were not the only family members concerned about the possible consequences of Helen's politics. While they supported liberal causes, Helen's daughter Margo and Margo's husband Nick found MacMartin's activism irresponsible, and at times resented that their financial support allowed Helen to dedicate her life to radicalism.[19] In one letter Margo wrote, "I . . . understand what you say about having ten or fifteen years more to live and wanting to realize it to the fullest"; however, "I think for that very reason that you ought now to try to be very realistic and practical and should protect yourself from your over tendency to all or nothingness."[20] Such comments reflect not only Margo's genuine concern for her mother's well-being, but also the growing anxiety Helen's family felt about being implicated in her politics.

Louise's diary entries also vividly detail how tensions came to the fore in 1950 when Helen gave Mac and Louise a subscription to the Progressive Party weekly *The Guardian*. The couple cancelled the subscription because they feared the subscribers' list for the publication might be used to identify "dangerous persons," and because, as Mac observed, they hoped "to avert any self-appointed patriot from accusing us of being Communists."[21] Two years later, as the persecution of suspected American subversives intensified throughout the country, Mac and Louise considered how they might "go on record as not being politically associated with Mother," even approaching Vermont senator George Aiken about their concerns.

Yet Aiken provided little solace. Louise wrote that he "was of the opinion that we were unduly alarmed about Mother Mac and her politics and the effect that it could have on us," and he suggested that the family attempt to change Helen's political views by engaging her in debate. The family found little comfort in this suggestion and in Aiken's puzzling confession that he knew a man who was turned down for employment in the Justice Department because twenty-two years earlier his brother-in-law "held a [Communist] party card." Instead of calming MacMartin family fears, the senator's story helped to illustrate the degree to which the politics of family members could in fact influence the employment of government workers, prompting Louise to ask, "Where does that leave us?" and conclude, "Right in the middle of nowhere."[22]

Louise's sense of urgency was justified by her family's numerous ties to government employment. Besides the federal job held by Bess Buck's husband, Margo's husband worked as an engineer on federally funded research projects at Princeton University. Louise's father and her husband were also Vermont state employees. Government security clearance was vital to their continued employment and to the financial security of these families. Clearly exasperated by her sister's political commitments, Bess complained to Louise that Helen "makes the darn thing a religion—just as an early Xtian [Christian] might refuse to abandon Xtrianity [Christianity] tho' it meant he and all his pagan family would be tossed to the lions."[23] Fears of being "tossed to the lions" would continue to significantly shape relations among MacMartin family women.

A disagreement between Louise and her mother-in-law over the significance of the controversial Stockholm Peace Petition demonstrates the depth of feeling associated with their increasing political divide. In March 1950 the leftist World Peace Committee met in Stockholm, Sweden, and issued a document calling for the "outlawing of atomic weapons" with international control of enforcement.[24] A mass signature campaign ensued, with more than one million Americans signing on. Yet most Americans saw the petition as a condemnation of U.S. foreign policy by a Communist-inspired peace movement unwilling to criticize Soviet aggression. Louise's refusal to sign the petition in 1951 resulted in a scene, with Helen accusing her daughter-in-law of approving of "the indiscriminate use of the atomic bomb." "Later," Louise wrote, "Mother Mac and I both apologized to each other; but since then any discussion of politics has been nonexistent between us."[25] Avoiding political differences would do little to lessen family tensions.

On visits to Vermont, Margo, who lived in Princeton, conferred with family members about how to handle the problem of Helen's politics. Following one visit Louise wrote, "Margo has tried with some success to discuss the total situation and the effect that it could have on all of us with Mother Mac." Her conclusion that Helen "certainly realizes what could happen, but I don't believe that she will cease, or be less active" reveals how well Louise understood her mother-in-law.[26] Like others in the family, Louise was angered and frustrated by Helen's insensitivity to the possible impact of her actions on their lives. At the same time, she abhorred redbaiting and well understood Helen's concerns about the implications of McCarthyism for American institutions. By 1954 Louise confessed that her earlier fears about the danger of Soviet Communism had given way to her belief that "Today . . . our fear of the Soviet Union and Communism is our greatest danger."[27] Commenting on Helen's increasing alienation from her family, she was equally reflective, writing, "I feel that we ought to see her more often and really act as though she were one of the family."[28] Dissociating from Helen's politics while still maintaining family ties remained a painful dilemma.

Adding to Louise's troubles were concerns about Helen's physical and emotional well-being, as it became increasingly apparent to her family that Helen suffered from bouts of depression that worsened with age. Unsettled by the impending execution of accused spies Julius and Ethel Rosenberg, in 1953 she wrote, "I can't seem to get anything done . . . I do a little and then get so overwhelmed I just drop it."[29] A 1963 letter from Bess indicates that Helen had confided in her sister about her struggle with depression.[30] In her later years her condition required medication and on at least one occasion hospitalization.[31] The relationship, if any, between her depression and her feelings of isolation is difficult to prove. Correspondence between MacMartin women relatives attests to the concerns they had about the potentially harmful effect that political alienation had on Helen.[32] Despite family concerns, MacMartin remained active in a national network of radical women who helped keep the peace movement alive in the 1950s and provide a bridge to the antiwar and antinuclear movements of the 1960s and 1970s. Their work proves the point of historians Dee Garrison and Harriet Alonso, who argue that the political repression of leftists in the McCarthy era may have weakened radical pacifism, but it did not kill it.[33]

In the spring of 1965 MacMartin experienced what was probably the pinnacle of her activism when she traveled to London as a representative of Women Strike for Peace (WSP), a group founded in late 1961 in response to President John F. Kennedy's decision to end a moratorium with Russia on nuclear testing. When MacMartin joined fellow activists in London to protest a ministers' meeting of the North American Treaty Organization, it was her first overseas trip. A London *Daily Worker* article profiled the seventy-four-year-old activist, explaining that her expenses had been paid with funds raised by Vermont peace workers. Those who worked to bring her to London described MacMartin as "a woman who has worked for peace, civil rights, civil liberties . . . for longer than many of us have been alive."[34] Following her return from Europe MacMartin threw herself into the battle to abolish the House Un-American Activities Committee, which had launched an investigation of the potentially subversive activism of WSP.

A decade later, near the end of her life, MacMartin wrote in her own diary about changes she saw in U.S. politics and culture. Now physically limited because of her age, she engaged the world largely through television viewing. Diary entries suggest that MacMartin was a fan of news programs and talk shows, and in 1973 she reviewed a Gloria Steinem appearance on the *Phil Donahue Show*. Revealing feminist leanings, MacMartin wrote, "'Women serve while men lead,' the old cliché—womens [*sic*] movement really here to stay—all changes involve some risk but they do happen." For these reasons, the Steinem appearance earned a "very good" diary rating.[35]

CONSTRUCTING COLD WAR WOMEN'S HISTORY

When Helen MacMartin died in a Vermont rest home in 1987, despite their past battles the *Burlington Free Press* portrayed the ninety-six-year-old as a respectable Yankee matron.[36] MacMartin's obituary noted that in 1948 she left her job with the state of Vermont "to devote her time to her life-long concern with peace, racial relations, and social justice, which she did until she was more than 75 years old."[37] Neither the Progressive Party nor Women Strike for Peace was included on the lengthy list of organizations to which MacMartin belonged. The list did include the Daughters of the American Revolution, a group she left in the 1940s to protest its conservative politics.[38] MacMartin's radicalism was erased from this historical record.

It is easy to understand the MacMartin family's apprehension about how to publicly characterize in Helen's obituary her years of activism. She, too, was concerned about the way history would remember postwar leftists. During a decades-long correspondence with journalist and Progressive Party member Curtis MacDougall, MacMartin questioned how he planned to address the issue of "naming names" as he worked on a book project chronicling the Progressive movement. "How do you handle names of people who may wish they had never been connected? That bothers me a little," she wrote in 1955. MacDougall attempted to ease her fears, answering, "I use as few names, especially of those who operated at local levels, as possible," and went on to explain, "I know what I've done will be considered a contribution to American historical knowledge someday."[39] When MacMartin posed the same question to her good friend and fellow Progressive Irma Otto, she received a similar reply. "No I have no qualms about any names, Helen," Otto wrote, "this is history and important history—even if we lost."[40]

Although she never attempted to distance herself from the Progressive Party, even years after its demise MacMartin was well aware of the possible repercussions of being associated with the party, and especially the consequences of exposing former activists.

MacMartin's concern about "outing" leftists highlights complex forces at work in the writing of cold war women's history. As Landon Storrs and Daniel Horowitz have convincingly demonstrated in the cases of Mary Dublin Keyserling and Betty Friedan, redbaiting—or fear of it—led some leftist women to reconstruct their political histories. Storrs writes that Keyserling, a Commerce Department official, "sanitized" her leftist past in order to protect her career during government investigations in 1948 and 1952. Likewise, according to Horowitz, Friedan omitted left-wing labor union involvement in the 1940s and 1950s from her personal and professional history to avoid accusations of Communist influence in her feminist activism.[41] The story of Helen MacMartin also suggests a complicated process of deradicalization whereby grassroots leftists, their families, the press, and historians each took part in historical reconstruction. MacMartin's reluctance to implicate those involved with her in the Progressive Party, her family's anxiety about possible repercussions due to her politics, the Burlington press's hostility to her peace politics, and historians' assumptions about the successful containment of postwar women, like those evident in Zachary Karabell's political analysis, came together to obscure the radicalism of MacMartin's later years.

Helen MacMartin has left to historians rich and often dramatic documentation of her cold war activism, including the ripple-like fashion in which it affected both her personal and public lives. In the years since I first discovered her University of Vermont collection, it has been processed, removing, I'm certain, the birdseed and handkerchiefs once scattered in the bottom of its numerous corrugated boxes. I have also discovered that the Vermont State Historical Society holds a smaller collection of MacMartin's Progressive Party papers. Correspondence found in these collections, and the University of Iowa's Progressive Party holdings, suggest MacMartin's experiences were not unique and that women she worked with in her leftist organizing following World War II had similar tensions and disruptions in their own lives. These were often reflected in financial and personal strains caused by deep ideological divides with friends, family, and community. Their radical activism represents a significant chapter of women's cold war history in a book that is still being written with wide-ranging archival sources.

NOTES

1 See Erik McDuffie, *Sojourning for Freedom: Black Women, American Communism, and the Making of Black Left Feminism* (Durham, NC: Duke University Press, 2011); Dayo F. Gore, *Radicalism at the Crossroads: African American Women Activists in the Cold War* (New York: New York University Press, 2010); and Jacqueline L. Castledine, *Cold War Progressives: Women's Interracial Organizing for Peace and Freedom* (Urbana: University of Illinois Press, 2012) (hereafter *CWP*).

2 The name Progressive Party was used by an earlier Vermont organization and the Vermont party established in 1948 was officially named the Independent Progressive Party. As they did, I use the Progressive Party or PP to identify the 1948 Vermont party.

3 Wallace was given the Commerce secretary position in return for stepping down as vice president. He served from March 1945, the month before Franklin Roosevelt's death, through September 1946. After public disagreements about President Truman's foreign policy, Truman asked for Wallace's resignation.

4 Zachary Karabell, *The Last Campaign: How Harry Truman Won the 1948 Election* (New York: Alfred A. Knopf, 2000), 238. In a letter to Curtis MacDougall MacMartin claimed to be pleased that with barely a month for planning she had pulled off the Wallace event. See MacMartin to MacDougall, no date, Progressive Party Papers, University of Iowa Special Collections, Iowa City, box 58, folder 255. Hereafter PP Papers.

5 Karabell, *The Last Campaign*, 287.

6 "The Elections of 1948 and the Job of the Progressive Party," American Labor Party Papers 1948–1949, Series I, F-NA, box 2, Rutgers University Special Collections and Archives, Rutgers University, New Brunswick, New Jersey.

7 Karabell, *The Last Campaign*, 238.

8 Castledine, *CWP*, 68.

9 Diary of Louise MacMartin, Aug. 5, 1952 entry, emphasis in the original. Diary in author's possession. See also *CWP*, 76–77 and 82–83.

10 Alexis Ramsey, "[Ad]dressing the Past: A Critical Methodology for Archival Research in Rhetoric and Composition" (PhD diss., Purdue University, 2008), 2–3.

11 See Joanne Meyerowitz, ed., *Not June Cleaver: Women and Gender in Postwar America, 1945–1960* (Philadelphia: Temple University Press, 1994); Kate Weigand, *Red Feminism: American Communism and the Making of Women's Liberation* (Baltimore: Johns Hopkins University Press, 2001); Daniel Horowitz, *Betty Friedan and the Making of "The Feminine Mystique"* (Amherst: University of Massachusetts Press, 1998); and Helen Laville, *Cold War Women: The International Activities of American Women's Organisations* (Manchester, UK: Manchester University Press, 2002). Also see Gerda Lerner, *Fire Weed: A Political Autobiography* (Philadelphia: Temple University Press, 2002).

12 For a comprehensive discussion of the effects of the cold war on Vermont politics see David R. Holmes's *Stalking the Academic Communist: Intellectual Freedom and the Firing of Alex Novikoff* (Hanover, NH: University Press of New England, 1989), 116–125.

13 Helen MacMartin to Lucien Hanks, Apr. 27, 1950, PP Papers, box 38, folder 80.

14 "Mrs. McMartin [sic] for Congress?," *Burlington (VT) Daily News*, Aug. 6, 1950, PP Papers.

15 Helen MacMartin to Beanie Baldwin, Sept. 14, 1950, PP Papers, box 38, folder 80.

16 "Mrs. MacMartin Won't Run for Congress After All," *Burlington Free Press*, Sept. 23, 1950, clipping in Helen MacMartin Papers, Special Collections, University of Vermont Library University of Vermont Library. Hereafter MacMartin Papers.

17 "Education and Work History of Helen MacMartin," no date, MacMartin Papers.

18 Bess Buck to MacMartin, Feb. 15, 1951, MacMartin Papers.

19 Author interview with (grandson) John Turitzin, Jan. 2, 2004.

20 Margo Turitzin to Helen MacMartin Feb. 14, 1951, MacMartin Papers.

21 June 15, 1950, diary of Louise MacMartin. Copy in possession of author.

22 Aug. 8, 1952 diary of Louise MacMartin.

23 Letter from Bess Buck to James and Louise MacMartin, Sept. 9, [no year], copy in author's possession.

24 For a list of the demands of the petition see Mar. 15, 1950, "Stockholm Appeal issued—By—The Committee of the World Congress of Defenders of Peace To—All men and women of good will," PP Papers, box 8, folder 33.

25 Aug. 5, 1952 diary of Louise MacMartin.

26 Ibid.

27 Feb. 7, 1954 diary of Louise MacMartin.

28 Aug. 4, 1952 diary of Louise MacMartin.

29 Feb.2, 1952 Helen MacMartin to Louise, copy in author's possession.

30 Nov. 9, 1963 Bess to Helen, MacMartin Papers.

31 MacMartin's eldest grandchild, Stephen Turitzin, believes his grandmother may have been diagnosed with a bipolar disorder and remembers her being on lithium later in her life. He believes that her depression worsened with age as dementia took over, especially in the last ten years of her life. Mar. 20, 2004 telephone interview with author.

32 An Aug. 8, 1952 entry in Louise's diary and Aug. 21, [no year] letter from Margo to Louise reveal the level of Margo's concern that her mother faced ostracism in Burlington because of her politics; copies of both in author's possession.

33 See Garrison's "'Our Skirts Gave Them Courage': The Civil Defense Protest Movement in New York City, 1955–1961" and Alonso's "Mayhem and Moderation: Women Peace Activists during the McCarthy Era," both in *Not June Cleaver*. Also see Alonso, *Peace as a Women's Issue: A History of the U.S. Movement for World Peace and Women's Rights* (Syracuse, NY: Syracuse University Press, 1993).

34 No date, flyer, MacMartin Papers.

35 MacMartin diary, MacMartin Collection.

36 MacMartin's chief nemesis, the *Burlington Daily News*, ceased publication in 1961, and thus left no record of MacMartin's death.

37 Obituary of Helen H. MacMartin, *Burlington Free Press*, Nov. 5, 1987, n.p., clipping in MacMartin Papers.

38 "National Progressive Party Convention Headquarters Press Release" 1952, Mac-Martin Papers.

39 MacDougall wrote MacMartin that he "also started out trying to protect several at the national level and am still doing so in a number of cases." Yet his comment concerning Wallace leaves unclear whether MacDougall believed Henry Wallace wanted to keep his own name or the names of others who had worked at the "national level" out of the book. June 25, 1955, MacMartin Papers.

40 Irma Otto to Helen MacMartin, Feb. 5, 1966, MacMartin Papers.

41 See Landon Storrs, "Red Scare Politics and the Suppression of Popular Front Feminism: The Loyalty Investigation of Mary Dublin Keyserling," *Journal of American History* 90, no. 2 (2003) and Horowitz, *Betty Friedan and the Making of "The Feminine Mystique."*

6 • "I'M GONNA GET YOU"

Black Womanhood and Jim Crow Justice in the Post–Civil Rights South

CHRISTINA GREENE

In the wee hours of an August morning in 1974, prison officials found the jailer, Clarence Alligood, slumped on a bunk in the women's section of the Beaufort County jail in eastern North Carolina. His lifeless body bore eleven stab wounds, including one that pierced his heart. Naked from the waist down, one hand held his trousers, the other loosely gripped an ice pick. A trail of dried semen trickled down his left thigh. On the floor was a negligee; a bra hung on the cell door. The prisoner, Joan Little, was nowhere in sight. She was five feet, three inches tall, twenty years old, poor, Black, and in trouble. He was white, sixty-two years old and at 200 pounds, nearly twice her size. On these facts, both sides would agree.[1]

Those who believed Joan Little was guilty saw a "hardened criminal . . . with the instincts of a black widow spider," a Jezebel who had lured the unsuspecting Alligood into her cell with promises of sex.[2] In the moment of his climax, the wanton young woman ruthlessly stabbed the poor, defenseless man and fled from the jail. On the other side, her supporters saw a victim of racism and sexism, a vulnerable Black woman who had valiantly defended herself against one of the age-old and unforgivable crimes of white supremacy. But this was not simply a southern tale. The Joan Little case quickly became a national and international cause célèbre, attracting feminists of all kinds, Black Power and traditional civil rights activists, working-class Black church ladies, and prisoners' rights advocates.

Joan Little remained on the lam for only a few days. After officials invoked a Reconstruction-era fugitive law that allowed anyone to shoot and kill her on sight, she turned herself in to authorities in Raleigh, the state capital.[3] A Beaufort County grand jury wasted no time indicting her for first-degree murder. If convicted, Joan would face a mandatory death penalty in North Carolina's gas chamber.[4] However, a well-oiled defense fund and a broad-based Free Joan Little campaign led a biracial, majority-female jury to acquit her in 1975 after deliberating for just over an hour. But none of this had come easily, and without the funds and the activist support, Little might well have been sentenced to death.[5]

Four decades later, her case continues to attract scholarly attention and fuel activist inspiration, most recently in Danielle McGuire's path-breaking study of African American women's testimony and organizing against sexual abuse and rape.[6] And yet, the Joan Little rape-murder trial is both a triumphalist narrative of hope and promise as well as a cautionary tale about the contradictions surrounding campaigns for social justice and about how we tell this story. On the one hand, the case underlined a woman's right to defend herself against sexual assault, including the use of lethal force. It also focused national attention on racial disparities in capital punishment sentencing. On the other hand, Joan Little's acquittal silenced critics of the criminal justice system by showing that even a poor Black woman—and a convicted felon at that—could emerge a winner in a southern courtroom.[7] The story thus can serve both liberatory as well as more normative, even conservative, aims.

Despite the notoriety of the Joan Little story, no one has fully investigated why she was imprisoned in the first place. By redirecting our attention toward the circumstances that landed Little in the Beaufort County jail, this essay joins an emerging field in U.S. and African American women's history that explores the roots of our modern carceral state. Heather Thompson has observed that until recently, scholarship on mass incarceration was dominated almost entirely by sociologists, criminologists, and legal scholars rather than historians. She persuasively argues that attention to mass incarceration is essential for a fuller understanding of post–World War II U.S. history more generally. And yet, as Kali Gross and Cheryl Clark note, discussions of crime and punishment focus almost entirely on Black and brown men while paying scant attention to Black women. This is all the more surprising considering that African American women have a long history of discriminatory treatment within the criminal justice system and have become the fastest-growing prison population.[8]

Most assessments of the Joan Little case have proceeded on the assumption that Little was simply a common street criminal. She was arrested several times in the early 1970s and in 1974 she was convicted of three felony counts of breaking and entry, larceny, and possession of stolen merchandise. Following her acquittal in the murder trial, Little faced a seven- to ten-year sentence on the felony theft convictions at the North Carolina Correctional Center for Women (known as Women's Prison) in Raleigh. She escaped in 1977, but was picked up in New York City two months later. After losing a six-month extradition fight, Little was sent back to North Carolina and received an additional six months' to two years' prison time for the escape. She was paroled in 1979, left the state, and disappeared from public view. Among her detractors, all this reinforced Joan's image as a lawless young woman, and historians have done little to challenge or complicate this view. Only passing notice has been given to her 1974 felony theft conviction, or to Little's earlier experiences in the criminal justice system *prior* to the highly publicized murder-rape case. After all, she confessed to the theft and therefore her guilt seemingly requires no further investigation.[9]

Certainly there is good reason for the focus on the sexual assault and murder case by the media, by activists, and by scholars. Indeed, the massive Free Joan Little campaign helped to secure a change of venue and to reduce the first-degree murder indictment when halfway through the trial the judge cited the prosecution's lack of evidence and dropped the charge to second-degree murder.[10] Her case fueled the debate about a woman's right to defend herself against sexual attack. But it also increased awareness of racial bias throughout the criminal justice system nationally and in North Carolina's capital punishment cases in particular. The state had more inmates on death row than any other state; and 68 percent of those sentenced to death were African American. Most importantly, the Free Joan Little campaign was instrumental in her acquittal.[11]

However, Joan Little's earliest encounters with the criminal justice system are as worthy of consideration as the more widely heralded rape-murder trial and the Free Joan Little campaign. Our tendency toward triumphalist narratives with Rosa Parks–like heroines has pointed our attention to the more celebratory aspects of the Joan Little saga at the expense of an equally compelling and far more representative story about widespread abuses in the policing, sentencing, and imprisonment of Black women. This largely unexamined aspect of the Joan Little story is important for a number of reasons. First, it moves the experiences of Black women from the margins to the center of historical inquiry.[12] Second, this essay joins an emerging body of scholarship that locates the roots of our contemporary carceral state in harsh penal policies of the American South *prior* to the War on Drugs.[13] As recent historical work has revealed, the ideological basis for mass incarceration was created decades earlier in a pervasive criminalization of Blackness, but in ways that were highly gendered.[14] By the 1960s and 1970s, urban uprisings and Black Power militancy simply recast the age-old "condemnation of Blackness" in the racially coded "tough on crime" rhetoric and policies of both liberal Democrats and conservative Republicans. Third, this interpretation moves beyond a simplistic assessment of Joan Little's guilt or innocence. As growing numbers of scholars and activists have insisted, our treatment of the guilty, not only the innocent, is the more accurate measure of a society that espouses equal treatment under the law.[15] Finally, greater scrutiny of Joan Little's initial experiences with law enforcement challenges the trope of the "strong Black woman." Too often this heroine-survivor, an image that Little's supporters thrust upon her, has become the signifier of Black women's worth, marginalizing those who were unable to make "a way out of no way" and neglecting the structural forces that shaped individual choices and behavior.[16]

Space does not permit a full discussion of each of the above points. However, a closer examination of Joan Little's more extensive experience within the criminal justice system reveals a pattern of racially discriminatory practices that was typical of the kind of "justice" low-income African Americans were likely to find in North Carolina and across the country, despite the victories of the 1960s civil rights movement. Moreover, Little's encounters with law enforcement *prior* to and *apart from* both Richard Nixon's "law and order" policies and Ronald Reagan's "War on Drugs," suggest that her treatment may well have been fueled by unprecedented federal financing of local crime control, begun in the mid-1960s and reaching $7 billion by 1979.

Little was born and raised in Beaufort County in eastern North Carolina. Largely rural, poor, and with a long history of entrenched racism that belied the state's more progressive image, the area has often been compared to the Deep South. Her hometown Washington, "Little Washington" as the locals call it, is the county seat and in 1970 its population of 12,350 was 38 percent Black. The town sits at the base of the Pamlico River and Pamlico Sound, shielded from the Atlantic Ocean by a thin strip of islands known as the Outer Banks.[17] Lumbering, commercial fishing, and ship building once thrived in the county; but silt filled the river bottom, closing the docks in Washington and flattening the area's economic base until light manufacturing jobs came to the county in the mid-1960s. A white journalist and attorney from "Little

Washington" had a more disparaging description of the town: "a county seat with a past but no future. . . . Washington stagnated, its period of expansion and vitality at an end, its racially segregated neighborhoods standing side by side, separate and unequal, two towns within one." Jim Crow laws and customs had relegated most African Americans to "a jumbled collection of hutches and shanties" and although the civil rights movement brought some improvements, including the election of an African American city councilman, the town retained many of its old ways.[18]

In the 1960s, the region saw a huge Ku Klux Klan (KKK) revival, attracting thousands of new members and even larger crowds to mass rallies. "Little Washington" had its own Klavern; and nightriders terrorized Black activists in the northern part of the county, often in response to NAACP school desegregation efforts.[19] Sheriff Otis ("Red") Davis may have boasted that he received the vast majority of the Black vote. However, local Blacks filed voting rights lawsuits into the 1990s; and Beaufort County remained under the preclearance section of the 1965 Voting Rights Act until the legislation was gutted by the U.S. Supreme Court in 2013.[20] Davis also complained that African Americans received preferential treatment in the criminal justice system at the expense of whites. Jerry Paul, Joan's white lawyer, saw things a bit differently from the sheriff. Paul was born and raised in "Little Washington" and had built a reputation defending African Americans and civil rights activists. "I know these people [i.e., local whites]. I know what they are," he said. "They're racists in Eastern North Carolina and they know they're racists, but in 1975 it may not be a good thing to admit you're a racist."[21]

Joan Little had neither Rosa Parks's aura of respectability nor her activist credentials.[22] Even before her felony convictions, Little was viewed by some in her hometown as an unruly young woman. Her mother, Jessie Williams, worked at night and problems with her stepfather pushed Joan to sneak out, running with "brothers that . . . live in the hood. . . . They protect you," she explained.[23] Unable to control her teenage daughter's behavior, Williams convinced a Beaufort County judge in 1968 to send Joan to the Dobbs Training School for delinquent girls, in Kinston, North Carolina. The state ranked first in the nation in the number of youth per capita sentenced to juvenile training schools, the euphemism for youth jails. A 1969 report by Duke University's Center on Law and Poverty and another in 1971 by the North Carolina Bar Association noted that race determined placement in these institutions, despite official policy prohibitions. Both studies also found deplorable conditions, calling the state's training schools a "total failure," and recommended closing them in favor of community-based services for troubled youth.[24] Joan soon ran away from the Dobbs Train-ing School and headed north. She stayed with relatives in Newark and in Philadelphia where she attended school. In 1970, health problems related to a thyroid condition led her back to North Carolina within weeks of finish-ing high school. By the time she was eighteen, Little was on her own and had rented a small house in "Little Washington." Hanging out in poolrooms, she drifted in and out of a series of low-wage, dead-end jobs. She soon took up with Julius Rogers, a man nearly twice her age who owned a small club in the Black section of town. Rogers taught her sheet-rocking and they did odd jobs throughout the Piedmont and eastern North Carolina.[25]

Between 1973 and 1974, Joan was picked up several times for shoplifting. All but one of these charges was dismissed. On one occasion, the arresting officer admitted he had never actually seen her with any stolen merchandise. Later, a local policeman testified that Black residents complained that Joan and Julius ran a theft ring, sending thieves to commit robberies, and then selling the stolen property. The officer also claimed that Joan had allowed her brother's fourteen-year-old girlfriend, Melinda Moore, to take the rap for one of the petty theft charges. "That's just about the reputation that she has," the policeman asserted. However, in a recent conversation, Joan dis-puted all these assertions.[26] In one instance, a friend of hers was arrested and gave the police Joan's name, but the charges were dropped. Joan pleaded guilty to one of the petty shoplifting charges, acknowledging later that she had stolen earrings from a Woolworth's store, and she received a six-month suspended sentence.[27]

Evidence suggests that Little may well have been a target of police harass-ment spurred as much by her presumed reputation as a "bad" girl as by any actual criminal activity on her part. In a 2013 interview, Joan remarked that Sheriff Davis had threatened her after one of her false arrests: "I'm gonna get you," he allegedly warned her.[28] A study of juvenile training schools indi-cated that such placements frequently stigmatized and handicapped adju-dicated young people leading to "heightened police surveillance," and thus lending credence to Joan's claim.[29]

Little's local reputation as a "wild" girl included rumors about her sexual behavior as well. "Ladies of the night" supposedly sold their wares at Julius Rogers's club; and police also suspected that Joan and Julius ran a prostitu-tion ring outside Camp Lejeune, a nearby marine base. But Joan was never arrested on any of these charges. "I was just a teenager out there doing stupid things. I didn't know anything," she recalled. She admitted that some of the people she hung with were involved in prostitution. "It was about making money," she said. "I didn't, they did." During the murder trial, Joan was also accused of being a lesbian.[30] Thus Joan's alleged sexual behavior cast her as immoral and sexually deviant.

Historically, African American women who did not adhere to strict rules of propriety in both the North and the South frequently were accused of prostitution. But even "respectable" Black women were vulnerable. As Cheryl Hicks has shown, simply appearing in public spaces unescorted by a man could land a Black woman in jail for solicitation in the first decades of the twentieth century. Shoplifting also has historically been both gendered and racialized, viewed as "an ancient, if not honorable, art," particularly for white middle-class women. Medicalized as "kleptomaniacs," such women often escaped imprisonment and retained at least some measure of respectability. As certain immigrant groups attained social and cultural "whiteness," working-class and immigrant women were sometimes viewed as "fallen women" and thus also deemed worthy and capable of rehabilitation.[31] However, no such options were available for African American women. Marked by their race as "born thieves," Black women criminals were portrayed in the press as "colored amazons." The image cast aspersions on offenders and non-offenders alike. According to Kali Gross, while the vast majority of Black women (and men) did not break the law, "the image of the Colored Amazon cast long shadows." The caricature portrayed African American women not only as criminals but as defeminized sexual aggressors too, a reconfiguring of the age-old Jezebel image.[32]

In the small-town South, many of these ideas found fertile ground well into the 1970s. As a local car dealer in Little's hometown remarked about Black women, "Hell to them, fucking is like saying good morning, or having a Pepsi Cola." A textile executive echoed similar sentiments: "I tell you one thing," he said, "she didn't lose her honor in that cell, she'd lost that years ago at Camp Lejeune." His comment reflected Little's rumored link to prostitution and the prosecution's contention that she had lured the jailer into her cell with promises of sex. Yet Karen Bethea-Shields, a young Black lawyer who was defense co-counsel in Joan's murder trial, painted a different picture. Joan "was probably more conservative as a young person," she said. The attorney saw great potential in Joan's largely undeveloped gifts: "I was just impressed with her writing ability. . . . Because she was so talented . . . if she had a teacher . . . that pushed her, where would she have ended up? . . . I always wondered about that," she added wistfully.[33]

Little was deeply disturbed by many of the public portrayals of her: "That ain't me," she insisted at the time. While she admitted she was hardly "a saint," neither was she "the worst sinner in the world." Writing from Women's Prison at age twenty-two, she vowed not to "go back to the old way of life." But the "way of life" she described was more bleak than criminal and reflected an aimless despair that was distressing coming from such a young person: "I looked at myself as being almost a tramp on the street, someone that had no future or meaning in life. If I were to pass away I . . . felt like I was just another corpse making room for somebody else that was coming into the world that could do something meaningful."[34]

Today, Little still maintains that people who really knew her did not hold unfavorable views of her. However, even some of her supporters harbored rather harsh judgments about her character (though none thought she was guilty of murder). Winston-Salem Black Panther Party leader, Larry Little (no relation), who later headed the national Joan Little Defense Committee, echoed Joan's own self-assessment: she's "not a saint," he acknowledged. Golden Frinks, the colorful African American field secretary for North Carolina's Southern Christian Leadership Conference (SCLC), claimed that Little had "the reputation of a wayward girl . . . and was a bad girl in that community." The civil rights leader raised money for Little's defense during the murder trial, but was prevented from speaking on her behalf at her mother's church, presumably because the pastor didn't want crime discussed from the pulpit. "She wasn't church," Frinks said. "[B]ecause of her past life which the local people did not exactly feel was up to the general moral standard of the community, they had ostracized her." Years later, several African American women in "Little Washington" recalled that local Blacks were reluctant to help Joan because of her "reputation." But Frinks also believed that Joan's older friends and "society" had led her astray. "You can't blame Joan for being Joan, but we can blame society for creatin' a Joan Little," he said. When Frinks initiated a lawsuit against Little's attorneys over allocation of the defense funds, Joan dissociated herself from him, calling him Golden "Freaks." He later dropped the suit, but insisted that he would continue to support Joan "morally."[35]

Joan's defense attorneys also were concerned about her reputation. "She's no angel," one said. Jerry Paul, Joan's white attorney, pointed to Little's "negative side" and claimed she was neither an "honest" nor a "kind" person.

Like Frinks, Paul blamed her "environment" for creating her presumed "personality flaws." Joan "couldn't stay out of jail, because her talents never were encouraged," he said.[36] However, Christine Strudwick, a Black Durham activist who helped organize Concerned Women for Justice for Joan Little, refused to judge Joan. Similarly, African American women at a local college vigorously defended Little during the murder trial against Black male students who felt that Joan "kind of got what she deserved." Other Black men derided Little as "a nappy headed, evil, loud mouth Sapphire."[37] Whatever the truth about Little's local reputation, these comments suggest that negative perceptions of Black womanhood were pervasive and were harbored more often by men than by Black women. More importantly, such views both obscured and justified discriminatory penal practices against African American women who were deemed "disreputable."

Joan's more serious legal troubles began when she and her brother, Jerome Little, were arrested in January 1974. They were charged with three felony counts for breaking into Black-owned trailer homes and stealing property valued at $1,300. Both pleaded not guilty.[38] The trial was fraught with problems and inconsistencies, including Jerome's sudden about-face confession of receiving stolen goods and his testimony against Joan. After the jury reached its verdict, but before sentencing, Joan then confessed, possibly hoping to reduce her prison time. "If you don't have money you're gonna stay in jail," Joan explained later. "Most people get tired of being in there and they're gonna take a plea bargain." Some thought her confession was a desperate attempt to protect her boyfriend, Julius Rogers.[39] However, Rogers was never charged. Jerome was found guilty of a misdemeanor and placed on probation, while Joan received two consecutive seven- to ten-year prison terms. Hoping to appeal her conviction but with no money for a lawyer, Joan languished in the Beaufort County for nearly three months before her encounter with Alligood took her on a more perilous journey through the criminal justice system.[40]

When Jerry Paul and his team of attorneys took on Joan's murder-rape case in 1974–75, they also appealed her earlier felony convictions, citing fourteen errors in the 1974 theft trial. They argued that evidence was improperly admitted and that "a serious question of effective representation by counsel" marred the court proceedings. According to Bethea-Shields, Joan's lawyer in the felony theft trial knew almost nothing about the case before appearing in court to represent her, and he had spoken to Jerome first. "That concerned me more than anything," Bethea-Shields remarked.

Nor was the jury informed about the reasons for Jerome's surprise testimony and sudden change of plea. Instead, the court allowed Jerome to testify against Joan while giving her lawyer little opportunity to cross-examine him.[41] Many believed that Jerome had reached a plea bargain with the prosecution, although his lawyer denied making any kind of deal. And finally, there was no direct physical evidence linking Joan to the theft.[42] Even the prosecution later admitted the evidence against Joan was weak. According to prosecutor Sam Grimes, the state had a strong case against Jerome, who was arrested with the stolen items, but that "Joan was the one we were really after, and we never would have convicted her without him [i.e., Jerome's testimony]." The prosecution's real target may have been Joan's boyfriend, Julius Rogers, who had had his own brushes with the law. Jerome had named him as mastermind, a view shared by both the prosecution and Joan's mother. Thus, prosecutors may have hoped that Joan might lead them to Rogers. However, no one thought that Joan was merely a dupe. She was "too alert, not dumb-witted by any means," Grimes said.[43]

Despite her attorneys' efforts, the North Carolina Court of Appeals struck down Joan's appeal of the felony theft convictions. In December 1975, four months after her acquittal in the murder trial, the state Supreme Court, with no explanation, denied her motion for a new trial. Louis Randolph, a Black city councilman in Washington, North Carolina, who helped raise money for Little's defense in the murder case, had his own explanation. Randolph believed that Jerry Paul's mockery of the criminal justice system had hurt her chances of an appeal and squelched any chance of a reduced sentence when she was returned to prison on the original felony convictions. During the murder trial, Paul had demanded that the judge recuse himself, claiming that Little could not receive a fair trial. After Joan's acquittal, he boasted to the press that the verdict had been "bought" with a $325,000 defense fund, that the trial process was a "charade," and that the prosecution was inept, even hinting that she may have been guilty of the murder. Paul's antics earned him a contempt citation and nearly cost him his law license.[44]

But even assuming Joan was guilty of the theft—and she acknowledged in a recent interview that it had been her idea, although she insists she broke into one trailer, not three, and stole only food and clothing—her treatment raises important questions about race and the criminal justice system in North Carolina and the nation in the 1970s, particularly around sentencing.[45] For example, Judge Robert Martin failed to grant Joan "committed youth offender" (CYO) status. Youthful felons under the age of twenty-one, excluding those convicted of first-degree murder or rape, were eligible for CYO status. This meant they could be granted parole at any time during their sentence, usually for "good behavior" or "gain time" (i.e., work). Just under 50 percent of youth offenders received CYO status in North Carolina. However, the judge ruled that Joan must serve at least two years before becoming eligible for parole. According to Jerry Paul, youth were especially vulnerable in eastern North Carolina. "You've got more young people in jail than anywhere else, and I had defended many of them," he said. One prosecutor in the area had put more people on death row than the combined death row population in twenty-four of the thirty-four states that had capital punishment statutes.[46]

Judge Martin suspended Joan's second seven- to ten-year sentence, which was consecutive not concurrent, in lieu of a five-year probation. But she was forbidden to have any contact with Rogers, unless they were married; and she was barred from the "vicinity" of his club. If Joan violated these terms, the court would impose the second seven- to ten-year consecutive prison term. Efforts to control Black women's sexual behavior had a long history, but in 1974 the court's prohibition against Joan's association with Rogers, *unless they were married,* seemed especially onerous. Indeed, the potential fourteen- to twenty-year sentence for a nonviolent property offense was excessive for a nineteen-year-old with no prior prison time or felony convictions. As attorney Bethea-Shields concurred nearly forty years later, "The sentence was extremely stiff for a first offender."[47]

A closer look at Judge Martin's judicial record as well as his political leanings may shed some light on Joan Little's sentence. Martin had recently gained notoriety in two high-profile, racially tinged cases in North Carolina. The first involved the acquittal by an all-white jury of three white men (one of whom was a known KKK associate, and perhaps member) for the 1970 murder of a twenty-three-year-old Black veteran in front of scores of witnesses in Oxford, North Carolina. Two years later, Judge Martin presided over the notorious Wilmington Ten case, in which nine African American civil rights activists and one white female were falsely convicted on felony charges of arson and conspiracy to assault emergency personnel. Seven of those convicted were under age twenty-one, but Judge Martin sentenced all the defendants, including civil rights leader Ben Chavis, to various terms of fifteen to thirty-four years. A broad-based campaign emerged in support of the defendants and, as with Little's murder trial, well-known activists such as Angela Davis helped bring national and international attention to the case. In 1976, Amnesty International took up the Wilmington Ten cause, citing human rights violations. Four years later, a federal appeals court overturned the convictions, ruling that the judge and prosecution had allowed perjured testimony, limited defense cross-examination of key prosecution witnesses, and withheld crucial evidence from the defense. Four decades later, in 2012, the defendants finally were "pardoned with innocence," by outgoing North Carolina governor Bev Perdue, meaning no crime had been committed. Judge Martin also had campaigned in 1960 for gubernatorial candidate I. Beverly Lake, a hard-core segregationist. As attorney general, Lake proposed that the state fund private schools in order to skirt the U.S. Supreme Court's *Brown v. Board of Education* decision. But Martin insisted that he harbored no animosity toward African Americans. During the Oxford murder trial, he told one reporter, "I was raised in a mainly black county. I ate with them and played with them. We had an instinctive love for the Negro race. Why, my secretary is black," he pointed out. "That should show you how I feel about them."[48]

Judge Martin's behavior was not unusual, but that was precisely the point. North Carolina had vastly differing sentencing practices within the state, and plea bargaining was a particular problem. With no formal sentencing guidelines and with judges actively participating in the plea-bargain process, differential sentencing was widespread across the state. One legal scholar in the mid-1970s found that white middle-class defendants received much more "lenient treatment." Defendants who pled guilty had reduced charges and shorter sentences. Not only "character and past record," but race and class, were key factors shaping "indeterminant" sentences (i.e., the broad discretion granted to judges and parole boards to determine prison sentencing). In 1979, the North Carolina legislature enacted the Fair Sentencing Act, which eliminated indeterminant sentences and prevented judges from setting both minimum and maximum prison terms. However, it was delayed until 1981 and even then judges retained wide latitude in sentencing.[49]

The North Carolina General Assembly Commission on Correctional Programs acknowledged that such disparities in sentencing were a major cause of prison unrest. In 1975, the Women's Prison in Raleigh—where Little was incarcerated during and after her rape-murder trial—was the site of a sit-down strike by about one-third of the approximately 450 women inmates. Even Little's hometown newspaper conceded that "[c]onditions at Central Women's Prison have been ripe for an explosion for a long time."[50]

Little herself was out on bail at the time of the strike, but she later spoke in support of the women prisoners at public rallies organized for her upcoming murder trial. The peaceful prison protest quickly erupted into violence; guards beat the women and herded them into the gymnasium, segregating the participants and sending the leaders to a men's prison. Considering the court testimony by Little and other women inmates about prison sexual abuse, the retaliatory transfer of the women protesters to a men's prison clearly threatened their safety. As Bethea-Shields noted, the sexual abuse of incarcerated women in North Carolina was widespread.[51]

Along with despicable prison conditions and discriminatory sentencing practices, North Carolina had the second-highest rates of confinement in the early 1970s for both felony *and* misdemeanor convictions. Felons had the third-longest average sentences and even misdemeanor sentences were twice the national average. By 1980, the state had the highest incarceration rate in the country.[52] Although African Americans were 22 percent of North Carolina's population, racial disparities among prisoners, especially women, were striking. In 1972, only 3 percent of the state's prison population was female, but Black women made up two-thirds of those held at Women's Prison. (African American men were 55 percent of Central Prison's all-male population.[53]) The over-representation of Black women continued as the inmate population expanded in North Carolina and across the nation.[54] While it is widely assumed that a rising crime wave was responsible for the prison population explosion nationally, scholars have found little correlation between increasing crime rates and imprisonment during this period.[55]

However, another, more insidious factor fueled arrest, sentencing, and incarceration practices in North Carolina and throughout the country. Well before Richard Nixon's "law and order" campaign and Ronald Reagan's War on Drugs, financial incentives established in the mid-1960s played an important role in driving the growing prison population. The 1965 Law Enforcement Assistance Act (LEAA) and the 1968 Omnibus Crime Control and Safe Streets Act provided federal support to local law enforcement. Together, these laws created what Heather Thompson has called "the largest crime-fighting bureaucracy the nation had ever seen."[56]

To most observers, LEAA and the 1968 Safe Streets Act were clear evidence of a conservative, right-wing backlash against the civil rights movement and President Lyndon Johnson's Great Society. After all, Arkansas Senator John McClellan, a notorious anticommunist and civil rights opponent, was its chief sponsor. However, many liberal Democrats, including staunch civil rights supporters and those who believed poverty was a major cause of crime, were eager to prove their "tough on crime" bona fides by backing the new federal anticrime legislation. And despite his misgivings, Johnson signed both bills. After launching a presidential crime commission in 1965, he declared before Congress, "I hope that 1965 will be regarded as the year when this country began in earnest a thorough and effective war against crime."[57] Like many liberals, Johnson linked the fight against crime to his antipoverty program: "The war on poverty is a war against crime," he said.[58] But according to Richard Nixon, "The solution to the crime problem is not quadrupling of funds for any government war on poverty, but more convictions." Congress seemingly agreed and reauthorized the crime bill in 1970 with even more federal funding, leading to elevated arrest rates, backed-up court calendars, and crowded correctional facilities.[59]

Although concern over urban uprisings fueled support for national anticrime legislation, rural areas without race "riots" also received federal funds. Southern lawmakers, such as North Carolina Senator Sam Ervin, upheld the white South's historic commitment to states' rights and limited federal control by funneling funds directly to the states through block grants. In North Carolina, even state oversight was minimal. Regional policy boards had nearly free rein in allocating LEAA money. Moreover, few African Americans were appointed to the boards and they were totally absent in some areas of the state, despite federal requirements. As one report about LEAA's impact in North Carolina noted, "The lack of minority representation suggests that the LEAA program has served to extend discriminatory practices in the regions." But the federal dollars kept coming and in 1975, a year after Joan Little was denied CYO status, North Carolina boasted its largest LEAA grant ever (over $3 million). Ironically, a third of the money was directed to youth offender services. By 1979, when LEAA was disbanded, the federal government had distributed $7 billion to state and local governments to fight crime.[60]

Crime control, once considered primarily a state and local matter, now had unprecedented federal support. By providing financial inducements for state and local officials to increase their arrest, conviction, and sentencing rates, liberal reformers along with conservative politicians set in motion the nation's move toward mass incarceration and the prison boom, well before the War on Drugs was launched.[61] And the South led the way. According to Robert Perkinson, "The upswing in imprisonment began first and took hold most intensely in the South." Throughout the twentieth century, the South had imprisoned disproportionate numbers of its citizens, especially African Americans. But beginning in 1972, the regional imprisonment differential began to widen even more, and by 1980, it was 75 percent higher than the North's. "In aggregate terms, the South was locking up more than twice as many individuals as any other region," Perkinson noted.[62]

By the end of the 1970s, North Carolina boasted the highest per capita incarceration rate in the nation. Higher rates of imprisonment also brought higher costs and by 1975, the state ranked second in the percentage of its budget spent on crime.[63] Beaufort County was clearly on board with the new emphasis on crime. In the early 1970s, the county received state and federal funds for a new courthouse and jail. Despite the improved facilities, Joan Little spent countless hours locked in a five-by-seven-foot cell, with a toilet, a sink, and a twenty-seven-inch-wide cot. Without opportunities for exercise or any kind of rehabilitative activities, "Time inside the Beaufort County jail was still close arrest," a local attorney noted. "Ordinarily the situation was not tense, but the potential for violence was always present," he added ominously.[64]

Thus, Little's seven- to ten-year sentence, and potential fourteen- to twenty-year prison term, can be better understood within the context of discriminatory "tough on crime" policies of both liberal and conservative politicians *prior* to and *apart* from the War on Drugs. Her experience as a youthful delinquent and convicted felon is as significant as her rape-murder trial and the Free Joan Little campaign. This broader assessment of Joan Little's treatment reminds us that for every courtroom victory, there were scores of women—largely poor women of color—who did not fare so well. Little's acquittal of the murder charge should be celebrated, especially for what it reveals about the power of organized protest; for without the massive publicity and successful fundraising efforts, she may well have been convicted and executed. But our retelling of the Free Joan Little campaign can easily become a self-congratulatory morality tale that reinscribes pervasive stereotypes regarding Black womanhood. In effect, Joan the Jezebel becomes Joan the Victim-Survivor. The triumphalist narrative of "the strong, Black woman" within the context of the criminal justice system may be particularly insidious. It suggests, perhaps unwittingly, that if Joan Little, an impoverished, "disreputable" young woman, can find justice in a southern courtroom, then Jim Crow justice may well be a relic of the past.[65] Certainly, accounts of victory over discrimination, of perseverance in the face of adversity, are critical to a more accurate rendering of our past. But if we tell only the more celebratory, triumphant stories, we may risk creating iconic heroines and heroes rather than fully realized, even flawed human beings who did not always prevail.

In his closing argument in Joan Little's rape-murder trial, Jerry Paul compared Little to Rosa Parks. God had chosen both women "for a purpose," he insisted. Like Rosa Parks, Joan Little "was a hero," he told the jury. Like Parks, Little "stood up for what is right and she had the courage to come back and tell you about it," he said.[66] Paul may have exaggerated the similarities between Rosa Parks and Joan Little. But Little's more typical treatment within North Carolina's criminal justice system is at least as deserving of attention as her acquittal in the legendary rape-murder trial. As scholars and activists explore the roots of our contemporary carceral state, stories like Joan Little's, and those of other Black women who currently constitute the fastest-growing U.S. prison population, may well point us toward solutions to what has become the civil rights issue of the twenty-first century, the mass incarceration of brown and Black bodies, women and men alike. Indeed, despite the gains of the civil rights movement, the United States has the dubious distinction of incarcerating more people per capita than any other country in the world. In 2013, over seven million people were imprisoned or under correctional supervision, including more than one million women. Since 2000, Black women's rate of incarceration has declined by 35 percent. However, they are still over-represented in our nation's jails and prisons and are confined at more than twice the rate of white women. Moreover, the majority of all women are imprisoned for drug and property crimes.[67] Joan Little may have been no Rosa Parks, but we need and deserve a full accounting of her story. In so doing, we might better understand the deeper, longer history of Black women's criminalization and legal victimization.

NOTES

I would like to thank Joan Little for the hours she spent talking to me about her experiences. This is a revised and expanded version of an article that appeared in the Journal of African American History *in 2015.*

1 Exhibit A, Narrative Summary of Circumstances Surrounding Death, Hamilton Hobgood Papers, Southern Historical Collection, Wilson Library, University of North Carolina, Chapel Hill, NC (hereafter SHC). The Hobgood Papers were unprocessed when I initially consulted them, hence the lack of specificity in some references. Alligood was a farmer and ex–truck driver who worked as a night jailer. *Carolinian,* Aug. 23, 1975, 4.

2 *New York Times,* July 29, 1975, 12.

3 The statute was declared unconstitutional the following year. Fred Harwell, an attorney and journalist born in Little's hometown of Washington, NC, who attended the murder trial, claims she was never declared a fugitive outlaw. In a recent interview, Little said that she had not known about the statute and that she turned herself in because she wanted her story told, an argument made by historian Genna Rae McNeil. Little's memory may have shifted or her recollections may have been shaped by recent scholarship on the case, some of which she has seen. Harwell, *A True Deliverance: The Joan Little Case* (New York: Alfred A. Knopf, 1979), 81; Joan Little, interview by author, May 1, 2012, New York City; Genna Rae McNeil, "The Body, Sexuality, and Self-Defense in *State vs Joan Little,* 1974–75," *Journal of African American History* 93, no. 2 (Spring 2008): 235–261.

4 Ironically, in 1974 North Carolina responded to the U.S. Supreme Court's 1972 *Furman v. Georgia* decision (which struck down three death penalties as constituting "cruel and unusual punishment") by making the death penalty mandatory for all first-degree murder cases. In 1976, the Supreme Court struck down North Carolina's death penalty, and the state revised its statute again in 1977. No executions occurred in North Carolina between 1961 and 1984, but began again in 1984. For an overview of the death penalty in North Carolina, see Michael Radelet and Glenn Pierce, "Race and Death Sentencing in North Carolina, 1980–2007," *North Carolina Historical Review* 89, no. 6 (Sept. 2011): 2126, 2130–2134.

5 Angela Davis, "Joan Little: The Dialectics of Rape," *Ms.* magazine, May 1975, 49; Genna Rae McNeil, "'Joanne Is You and Joanne Is Me': A Consideration of African American Women and the 'Free Joan Little' Movement, 1974–1975," in *Sisters in the Struggle: African American Women in the Civil Rights-Black Power Movement,* ed. Bettye Collier-Thomas and V. P. Franklin (New York: New York University Press, 2001), 259–279.

6 See for example, McNeil, "Joanne Is You"; Danielle L. McGuire, *At the Dark End of the Street: Black Women, Rape, and Resistance—A New History of the Civil Rights Movement From Rosa Parks to the Rise of Black Power* (New York: Alfred A. Knopf, 2010); McGuire, "Joan Little and the Triumph of Testimony," in *Freedom Rights: New Perspectives on the Civil Rights Movement,* ed. McGuire and John Dittmer (Lexington: University Press of Kentucky, 2011), 191–223; Devin Fergus, *Liberalism, Black Power, and the Making of American Politics, 1965–1980* (Athens: University of Georgia Press, 2009); Christina Greene, "Gender, Black Power, Politics and the 1974–75 Free Joan Little Movement" (Paper presented at the annual conference of the Organization of American Historians, New York, NY, Mar. 28–31, 2008). The editors of a recent Black women's studies anthology also note the Joan Little story as an inspiration in their selection process. Stanlie M. James, Frances Smith Foster, and Beverly Guy-Sheftall, eds., *Still Brave: The Evolution of Black Women's Studies* (New York: Feminist Press, 2009), xx–xxi.

7 In the past decade, some prisoner advocates have pointed to the Free Joan Little campaign as a model for contemporary interracial coalitions. Minnie Bruce Pratt, "A Look Back at the Joann Little Case," Mar. 9, 2006, accessed Apr. 6, 2012, www.workers.org/

2006/us/joann-little-0316; "'Free Joan Little': Reflections on Prisoner Resistance and Movement-Building," Jan. 4, 2011, accessed May 11, 2012, www.usprisonculture.com/blog/2011/01/04/free-joan-little-reflections-on-prisoner-resistance-and-movement-building. However, prison activist Victoria Law decries high-profile cases such as Joan Little's because they detract attention from the far more numerous and serious incidents of intimate violence against women. Victoria Law, "Sick of the Abuse: Feminist Responses to Sexual Assault, Battering, and Self Defense," in *The Hidden 1970s: Histories of Radicalism*, ed. Dan Berger (New Brunswick, NJ: Rutgers University Press, 2010), 39; Law, "Resisting Gender Violence and the Prison Industrial Complex: An Interview with Victoria Law," *Angola 3 News*, Jan. 1, 2011.

8 Heather Ann Thompson, "Why Mass Incarceration Matters: Rethinking Crisis, Decline, and Transformation in Postwar American History," *Journal of American History* 97, no. 3 (Dec. 2010): 703–704; Kali Gross, "African American Women, Mass Incarceration, and the Politics of Protection," *Journal of American History* 102, no. 1 (June 2015): 25–33; Kali N. Gross and Cheryl D. Hicks, "Introduction—Gendering the Carceral State: African American Women, History, and Criminal Justice," *Journal of African American History* 100, no. 3 (Summer 2015): 357–365.

9 Little has given various explanations for the escape including fearing for her life and objecting to harsh prison treatment. More recently she explained that her mother's death, which occurred while Joan was incarcerated, and the need to look after her younger siblings propelled her escape. At the time, a psychiatrist maintained that she was suffering a delayed reaction to her mother's passing and was unable to respond to counseling in North Carolina due to her feelings about the prison system. *Black Panther* 17, no. 31 (Dec. 7, 1977): 7; *Jet Magazine*, June 28, 1979, 6; *New York Times*, Feb. 24, 1978, 16; Mar. 4, 1978, 5; May 10, 1978, 23; June 6, 1978, B4; July 13, 1978, A16; New York *Daily Challenge*, Jan. 26, 1978, 5; Feb. 24, 1978, 3; 9 Apr. 1978, 3; Joan Little interview by author, Oct. 26, 2013, New York City.

10 *Joan Little v. State of North Carolina*, Brief in Support of Motion to Dismiss the First Degree Murder Indictment, July 2, 1975, box 33, folder 348, Hobgood Papers; McGuire, "Joan Little," 207.

11 Of the 362 inmates executed in North Carolina between 1910 and 1961, 75 percent were African American; only two women were put to death, both African American. Chris Behre, Exhibit 2, "A Brief History of Capital Punishment in North Carolina," Office of Correction (Sept. 1973); "Inmates Presently Under Death Penalty," Aug. 20, 1974, Hobgood Papers. The 2009 Racial Justice Act allowed prisoners to use statistical evidence to prove racial bias in jury selection and death sentences, but North Carolina repealed the law in 2013. *New York Times*, June 5, 2013.

12 Several historians have explored black women's incarceration in earlier periods: Mary Ellen Curtin, "The 'Human World' of Black Women in Alabama Prisons, 1870–1900," in *Hidden Histories of Women in the New South* ed. Virginia Bernhard et al. (Columbia: University of Missouri Press, 1994), 11–30; Cheryl D. Hicks, *Talk with You Like a Woman: African American Women, Justice, and Reform in New York, 1890–1935* (Chapel Hill: University of North Carolina Press, 2010); Kali N. Gross, *Colored Amazons: Crime, Violence, and Black Women in the City of Brotherly Love, 1880–1910* (Durham, NC: Duke University

Press, 2006); Gail L. Thompson, "Special Report II: African American Women and the U.S. Criminal Justice System: A Statistical Survey, 1890–2009," *Journal of African American History* 98, no. 2 (Spring 2013): 291–303. See also Talitha L. LeFlouria, *Chained in Silence: Black Women and Convict Labor in the New South* (Chapel Hill: University of North Carolina Press, 2015) and Sarah Haley, *No Mercy Here: Gender, Punishment, and the Making of Jim Crow Modernity* (Chapel Hill: University of North Carolina Press, 2016).

13 Thompson, "Mass Incarceration," 703–734. Robert Perkinson contends that scholarly focus on the North's penal history has obscured the southern roots of mass incarceration. Perkinson, *Texas Tough: The Rise of America's Prison Empire* (New York: Henry Holt & Co./Picador, 2010) 4, 7–8.

14 Khalil Gibran Muhammad, *The Condemnation of Blackness: Race, Crime, and the Making of Modern Urban America* (Cambridge, MA: Harvard University Press, 2010); Gross, *Colored Amazons*.

15 Michelle Alexander, Distinguished Lecture Series, University of Wisconsin, Madison, WI, Mar. 3, 2013. James Forman Jr., "Racial Critiques of Mass Incarceration: Beyond the New Jim Crow," *NYU Journal of International Law and Politics* 87 (Apr. 2012): 21–69.

16 According to historian Chana Kai Lee, "Too often our study and research of black female historical figures yield depictions of yet another 'strong black woman.'" Political scientist Melissa Harris-Perry notes the danger in elevating these stories of triumph: ". . . the ideal of the strong black woman is impossible to maintain. Its insistence that black women can always make a way out of no way sets the stage for failure . . . and that failure can be used to rationalize continuing inequality." Lee, *For Freedom's Sake: The Life of Fannie Lou Hamer* (Urbana: University of Illinois Press, 1999), 180; Harris-Perry, *Sister Citizen: Shame, Stereotypes, and Black Women in America* (New Haven: Yale University Press, 2011), 189. See Michele Wallace, *Black Macho and the Myth of the Superwoman* (New York: Dial Press/Warner Books, 1979) for a critique of how Black women's presumed innate strength has been used to castigate them as domineering, emasculating matriarchs.

17 Beaufort County lost 10 percent of its Black population in the 1960s as African Americans left seeking better opportunities elsewhere. By 1980, the population of 40,000 was nearly 32 percent African American. Today the county's 47,000 residents are 26 percent African American, 66 percent non-Hispanic white, and 7 percent Latino. In 2012, one-fifth of county residents were at or below poverty. Louis Van Camp, *Beaufort County, North Carolina* (Charleston, SC: Arcadia Publishing, 2000), 7; U.S. Dept. of Commerce, U.S. Census Bureau: State and County Quick Facts, accessed Jan. 3, 2014, http://quickfacts.census.gov; *Beaufort County Land Use Plan*, N.C. Dept. of Natural and Economic Resources, N.E. Office (1976), accessed Jan. 10, 2014, www.gpo.gov/fdsys/pkg/CZIC-HD1291 343 B43; Beaufort County Census of Population and Housing 1980/Summary Tape File 3a (50), accessed Jan. 10, 2014, www.digital.ncdcr.gov/cdm/compundobject/collection/p15012co114/id/468/rec/160.

18 Harwell, *True Deliverance*, 22, 23, 26.

19 David Cecelski, *Along Freedom Road: Hyde County, North Carolina, and the Fate of Black Schools in the South* (Chapel Hill: University of North Carolina Press, 1994) 36, 182n21, 183n27, 185n70.

20 James Reston Jr., *The Innocence of Joan Little: A Southern Mystery* (New York: Quadrangle/Times Books, 1977), 13, 16, 18–19; Harwell, *True Deliverance*, 98–100. Reston was living and teaching in North Carolina and covered the murder trial for *Newsday*. Anita Earls, Emily Wynes, and LeeAnne Quatrucci, *Voting Rights in North Carolina, 1982–2006*, A Report by the Renew the VRA.org (Mar. 2006), 8, Appendix Section 7, 18.

21 Sheriff Davis resented the media's depiction of the county as a racist backwater. Davis and Paul quoted in Reston, *Innocence*, 68, 77; 13, 16, 18–19. Another journalist who covered the murder trial also refuted Davis's portrayal, claiming that the county "was dragging its feet" regarding "voting rights, jury service, public accommodations, school desegregation . . . and police brutality." Mark Pinsky, "The Innocence of James Reston, Jr.," *Southern Exposure* 6, no. 1 [n.d., c. 1977]: 40. Harwell, *True Deliverance*, 98–100. Little's lawyers secured a change of venue, moving her murder trial to Raleigh, in part by conducting a survey of potential jurors in Beaufort and surrounding counties that revealed widespread white racial prejudice. *State v. Joan Little*, Motion for Change of Venue, Mar. 14, 1975, Hobgood Papers; Raleigh *News and Observer*, Apr. 18, 1975, 32; May 2, 1975, 1.

22 Recent revelations suggest that Parks also may have been sexually abused by a white man. Her history of organizing against the rape of black women by white men began in the 1940s and in the 1970s she helped launch a Joan Little Defense Fund in her adopted city of Detroit. McGuire, "Joan Little," 203. See also Jeanne Theoharis, *The Rebellious Life of Mrs. Rosa Parks* (Boston: Beacon Press, 2013).

23 Joan Little, interview by author, May 1, 2012, New York City.

24 John Purcell, "North Carolina: Corrections and Juvenile Justice in a Rural State," *Columbia Human Rights Law Review* 187 (1973): 198, 202–203. Cheryl Hicks has shown that Black southern migrants in the North often turned to the courts to control and protect their "wayward" daughters. Hicks, *Talk with You*, 182–203.

25 Joan Little with Rebecca Ranson, "I Am Joan," *Southern Exposure* 6, no. 1 [n.d., c. 1977]: 42–47; Harwell, *True Deliverance*, 26–28; Reston, *Innocence*, 154–155.

26 *Joan Little v. State of North Carolina*, Summary of Indictment and Appeals, North Carolina Court of Appeals, May 19, 1975, box 1, folder 13, Reston Papers, SHC; Joan Little, telephone conversation with author, notes, Aug. 15, 2015.

27 Harwell, *True Deliverance*, 29; Little, telephone conversation, Aug. 15, 2015.

28 Joan Little, conversation with author, notes, Apr. 8, 2013, New York City. *Joan Little v. State of North Carolina*, Summary of Indictment and Appeals; Sheriff Davis's warrant for Little's arrest after her 1974 escape erroneously listed her age as twenty-five, which continued to be misreported in the local press. She was nineteen at the time of her arrest and conviction on the felony theft charges and twenty when she escaped from the Beaufort County jail. Otis E. Davis, Complaint for Arrest, Joan Little, Aug. 27, 1974, box 33, folder 345, Hobgood Papers. Washington (NC) *Daily News*, Sept. 10, 1974, 1.

29 Purcell, "Corrections and Juvenile Justice," 198, 202–203.

30 Reston, *Innocence*, 162, 105; Harwell, *True Deliverance*, 28; Raleigh *News and Observer*, Aug. 13, 1975, 10; Little interview, May 1, 2012. The lesbian charge was leveled during Joan's imprisonment in Women's Prison. For allegations of lesbianism in women's prisons, see Regina Kunzel, *Criminal Intimacy: Prison and the Uneven History of Modern American Sexuality* (Chicago: University of Chicago Press, 2008), 111–148.

31 Elaine Abelson, *When Ladies Go A-Thieving: Middle-Class Shoplifters in the Victorian Department Store* (New York: Oxford University Press, 1989), quoted in Hicks, *Talk with You*, 154. For changing conceptions of the "fallen woman" see Estelle B. Freedman, *Their Sisters' Keepers: Women's Prison Reform in America, 1830–1930* (Ann Arbor: University of Michigan Press, 1981). On the differential treatment of white immigrants and African Americans in the criminal justice system historically see Gross, *Colored Amazons*, 121–125, and Muhammad, *Condemnation of Blackness*, 271, 273–275. On Black women's vulnerability to theft charges see Gross, *Colored Amazons*, 34–35, 41–43, 54–55; on similar vulnerabilities of African American women in the South, see Tera Hunter, *To 'Joy My Freedom: Southern Black Women's Lives and Labor after the Civil War* (Cambridge, MA: Harvard University Press, 1997).

32 Gross, *Colored Amazons*, 155. See also Cynthia M. Blair, *I've Got to Make My Livin': Black Women's Sex Work in Turn-of-the-Century Chicago* (Chicago: University of Chicago Press, 2010).

33 Quoted in Reston, *Innocence*, 6. At the time of the trial, Bethea-Shields, then known as Karen Galloway, was the first black woman to graduate from Duke Law School. Karen Bethea-Shields, interview with author, Nov. 11, 2013, Durham, NC.

34 Little, "I am Joan," 42.

35 Little telephone conversation; Raleigh *News and Observer*, July 3, 1975, 40; Golden Frinks, Interview with Melynn Glusman, Jan. 1994, Edenton, NC, transcript in author's possession; Reston, *Innocence*, 53–55; McNeil, "The Body," 241; Harwell, *True Deliverance*, 143–146. Following Little's acquittal, Bethea-Shields lambasted Blacks who had failed to support her saying they "should hang their heads in shame." *Carolinian*, Aug. 23, 1975, 2.

36 Harwell, *True Deliverance*, 28; Reston, *Innocence*, 112–114.

37 McNeil, "The Body," 242; Fergus, *Liberalism*, 184.

38 "List" William Kunstler Papers, Unprocessed, Tamiment Library, New York University, New York, NY. *State of North Carolina v. Joan Little*, Superior Court File # 74- Cr-4176, Answer to Amendment to Defendant's Petition for a Writ of Prohibition, box 32, folder 343, Hobgood Papers. Harwell, *True Deliverance*, 29, 31–35, 49.

39 Joan still insists that Julius had nothing to do with the theft. Little interview, May 1, 2012; Little conversation, Apr. 8, 2013; Reston, *Innocence*, 157–158; Harwell, *True Deliverance*, 29, 31–35, 49.

40 Jerome changed his plea to guilty on the misdemeanor charge of possession of stolen merchandise and he was acquitted of the felony charges. In open court, the jury returned a verdict of guilty against Joan Little for three felonies of breaking, entry, and larceny; but both the bills of indictment as well as the clerk's certificate of court also showed that the jury had found her guilty of felonious possession. It is also unclear why she received two consecutive sentences when there were at least three felony convictions. This may have been just one of many problems with the trial. *Joan Little v. State of North Carolina*, Summary of Indictment and Appeals.

41 Bethea-Shields interview; *Southern Patriot*, Oct. 1975, 7. Using defendants against one another was a common prosecutorial tactic, but turning family members against each other was especially egregious and created strains within the Little family for decades. Joan's younger brother, Malcolm Williams, recalled repeated harassment in school where family members of the slain jailer worked. Little interview by author and conversation with Malcolm Williams, May 1, 2012, New York, NY; Little conversation, Apr. 8, 2013. For similar recent prosecution practices, see Alice Goffman, *On the Run: Fugitive Life in an American City* (Chicago: University of Chicago Press, 2014), 55–90.

42 The stolen items were discovered on Jerome's girlfriend, Melinda Moore, in Jerome's car and trailer, in the woods, and supposedly in Julius Rogers's "juke joint." According to Joan's attorneys, aside from Jerome's confession, the only evidence against Joan was an eyewitness who saw two women and a man outside one of the trailers; one of the women wore a coat similar to Joan's. *State of North Carolina v. Joan Little*, Superior Court File # 74- Cr-4176, Answer to Amendment to Defendant's Petition for a Writ of Prohibition; *State of North Carolina v. Joan Little*, Summary of Indictment and Appeals; *State of North Carolina v. Joan Little*, Defendant's Appellant Brief, North Carolina Court of Appeals, June 25, 1975, box 1, folder 12, Reston Papers; *State of North Carolina v. Joan Little*, Brief for the State, June 25, 1975, box 1, folder 11, Reston Papers; Little conversation, Apr. 8, 2013; Reston, *Innocence*, 157.

43 Reston, *Innocence*, 159. The prosecution's real target remains unclear. Rogers was questioned, but was never arrested or charged. During the felony theft appeal, the prosecution claimed that the state had a stronger case against Joan than Jerome. *State of North Carolina v. Joan Little*, Superior Court File # 74- Cr-4176, Answer to Amendment to Defendant's Petition for a Writ of Prohibition.

44 Reston, *Innocence*, 339; Raleigh *News and Observer*, Aug. 16, 1975, 1; Oct. 21, 1975, 1; "Little's Lawyer: Justice Was 'Bought,'" *Washington Star*, Oct. 20, 1975, A3, Clippings File, Hobgood Papers.

45 Discrepancies exist between Joan Little's court testimony and her recent recollections. In her 1974 confession, she testified that she and Jerome, together with Melinda and her brother Wilbur Moore, broke into the trailers and transferred all the loot, except the food, the TV, and the rifle (which she later said was a BB gun not a rifle) to Jerome's nearby trailer. In a 2013 conversation, Joan said she broke into only one trailer and speculated that perhaps Jerome and Melinda burglarized the other two trailers on their own. She confessed, she explained, because the theft was her idea and, as the older sister, she felt she should take responsibility. *Joan Little v. State of North Carolina*, Summary of Indictment and Appeals; Little conversation, Apr. 8, 2013; Joan Little, text message to author Apr. 8, 2013.

46 *Joan Little v. State of North Carolina*, Summary of Indictment and Appeals. In 1979, before North Carolina's Fair Sentencing Act was implemented, 49 percent of felons under the age of twenty-one were sentenced under CYO status. Susan Kelly Nichols, "Comments: Criminal Procedure—The North Carolina Fair Sentencing Act," *North Carolina Law Review* 60 (1981): 652n148; Table 1; 634–635; Reston, *Innocence*, 112.

47 *Joan Little v. State of North Carolina,* Summary of Indictment and Appeals; Bethea-Shields interview.

48 Martin quoted in Timothy B. Tyson, *Blood Done Sign My Name* (New York: Random House/Crown, 2004), 229, 231, 268–270; William H. Chafe, *Civilities and Civil Rights: Greensboro, North Carolina, and the Black Struggle for Freedom* (New York: Oxford University Press, 1981), 51, 58. Raleigh *News and Observer,* Jan. 1, 2013. When the Wilmington Ten finally were pardoned in 2012, four of the defendants had died and Chavis had spent almost four years in prison. The Charlotte Three was another racially tinged North Carolina case in the 1970s in which three African American civil rights activists were falsely convicted of arson. The case was similarly denounced for corrupt police and criminal justice practices, and its most prominent activist, Jim Grant, was sentenced to twenty-five years in state prison for burning a horse stable. Both the Wilmington and Charlotte cases also helped to fuel the creation of the North Carolina Prisoners Labor Union (NCPLU). For a first-hand account of the Oxford murder and the Wilmington Ten case by Ben Chavis, see Budd and Ruth Schultz, eds., *It Did Happen Here: Recollections of Political Repression in America* (Berkeley: University of California Press, 1989), 195–211; "NAACP Victory: The Wilmington 10 Pardoned," accessed Feb. 20, 2016, www.NAACP.org. Christopher Shutz, "The Burning of America: Race, Radicalism, and The 'Charlotte Three' Trial in 1970s North Carolina," *North Carolina Historical Review* 76, no. 1 (January 1999): 43–65; Donald F. Tibbs, *From Black Power to Prison Power: The Making of Jones v. North Carolina Prisoners' Labor Union* (New York: Palgrave Macmillan, 2012), 126–130. See also Dan Berger, *Captive Nation: Black Prison Organizing in the Civil Rights Era* (Chapel Hill: University of North Carolina Press, 2014).

49 James E. Bond, "Plea Bargaining in North Carolina," *North Carolina Law Review* 54 (1975–76): 830, 835. Nichols, "Comments," 634, 649. The American Bar Association adopted similar determinant sentencing guidelines in 1993, arguing that parole boards were often discriminatory and that prison failed to rehabilitate prisoners. Thomas Marvel and Carlise Moody, *The Impact of Determinant Sentencing Laws on Delay, Trial Rates, and Pleas Rates in Seven States,* National Institute of Justice, Report Prepared for the U.S. Dept. of Justice (Washington, DC, 2000). Prisoner advocates had long railed against "indeterminant" sentencing practices. However, sentencing reforms did not eradicate racial bias. Instead, "determinant" sentencing and mandatory minimums, such as the three-strikes rule, imposed rigid rules on the courts and left almost no room for judicial discretion. Coupled with discriminatory policing, arrest, and conviction rates, this "reform" led to longer sentences for prisoners of color. Michelle Alexander, *The New Jim Crow: Mass Incarceration in the Age of Colorblindness* (New York: The New Press, 2010, 2012), 89–93, 104–112.

50 *Females in the Department of Correction,* Legislative Commission, Report to the 1977 Assembly of North Carolina; Response to *Females in the Department of Correction,* NC Division of Prisons Interim Report of Legislative Research Commission, Nov. 12, 1976, North Carolina Collection, Wilson Library, University of North Carolina, Chapel Hill, NC. *Washington (NC) Daily News,* July 15, 1975; *Midnight Special,* Aug.–Sept. 1975, 5.

51 Nichols, "Comments," 631n4, 650, 655; Lawrence French, "The Incarcerated Black Female: The Case of Double Social Jeopardy," *Journal of Black Studies* 8, no. 3 (Mar.

1978): 324; Pat Bryant, "Justice vs. the Movement," *Southern Exposure* 8, no. 2 (Summer 1980): 36; Bethea-Shields interview. Among other grievances, the women protested working conditions in the prison laundry where nine of the ten worker-inmates were African Americans. They were forced to work eight hours a day without pay, in violation of a 1967 state law, and in temperatures that often reached 120 degrees. A federal investigation by the Occupational Safety and Health Association (OSHA) cited the Department of Corrections (DOC) for dangerous conditions in the laundry. Action for Forgotten Women, a Durham-based prisoner advocacy group, filed a federal lawsuit for redress against brutality suffered by the women strikers. In 1974, male inmates organized the North Carolina Prisoners Labor Union, the first in the South. In 1976, the NCPLU and two women from the Women's Prison strike filed a class action suit on behalf of all North Carolina inmates. *Southern Patriot*, Feb. 1975, 3; Apr. 1975, 8; Sept. 1975, 7; Oct. 1975, 4; Jan. 1976, 7; Apr. 1976, 7; *Midnight Special*, May 1975, 16; Tibbs, *From Black Power to Prison Power*. Victoria Law argues that scholars and activists alike have generally ignored prison protest by women, which was widespread. Law, *Resistance Behind Bars: The Struggles of Incarcerated Women* (Oakland, CA: PM Press, 2009), 13.

52 Nichols, "Comments," 63In4; French, "Incarcerated Black Female," 323, 326. By 2000, budgetary considerations had lowered the state's inmate population to thirty-first in the nation and second among southern states. Political scientist Marie Gottschalk notes that most prison costs are fixed and budget cuts frequently eliminate treatment programs, thus increasing recidivism rates and prison costs over the long term. Gottschalk, *The Prison and the Gallows: The Politics of Mass Incarceration in America* (New York: Cambridge University Press, 2006), 243.

53 Reston, *Innocence*, 112; French, "Incarcerated Black Female," 331, 333. The prison population was increasing during this period at about 100 inmates per month across the state. Nichols, "Comments," 65In146. U.S. Census, Table 48, North Carolina—Race and Hispanic Origin: 1970–1990, accessed Jan. 2015, www.census.gov/population/documentation.

54 By 2010, the state's prison population of 40,379 was 7 percent female and 57 percent African American; an additional 112,000 offenders were under criminal justice supervision, of which 24 percent were female and 45 percent were African American. North Carolina's Black population is just under 23 percent. DOC figures are not broken down by both race and gender making it difficult to determine the exact number of incarcerated Black women. "The Black Population: 2010," U.S. Census Bureau, Dept. of Commerce (Washington, DC, 2011), table 5, accessed Jan. 2015, www.census.gov/prod/cen2010/briefs/c2010br.

55 Some have argued that the impact of the baby boom was partially responsible for increased crime rates, while others pointed to the rise in Black unemployment. Although a spike in the crime wave occurred in the mid-1960s, including the homicide rate, these statistics have been widely debated by scholars; and FBI changes in tracking crime make comparisons difficult. Crime was counted quite differently after 1965, due largely to financial incentives for local law enforcement, particularly if they could demonstrate rising crime rates. In fact, crime waves had been at higher levels in U.S. history prior to the 1960s. Nichols, "Comments," 65In146. Thompson, "Mass Incarceration,"

727; Alexander, *New Jim Crow*, 41; Michael Flamm, *Law and Order: Street Crime, Civil Unrest, and the Crisis of Liberalism in the 1960s* (New York: Columbia University Press, 2005), 125–129. Compared with neighboring states, the Tarheel state had lower crime rates in every major category in the FBI crime report. Fergus, *Liberalism*, 140. For a discussion of how crime rates were racialized from 1890 to 1949, see Muhammad, *Condemnation of Blackness*.

56 Thompson, "Mass Incarceration," 730.

57 Flamm, *Law and Order*, 52–54; 132–141. Johnson quoted in Law, *Resistance Behind Bars*, 159. Jonathan Simon implicates Attorney General Robert Kennedy in his role in the Department of Justice for increasing federal involvement in crime. Simon, *Governing Through Crime: How the War on Crime Transformed American Democracy and Created a Culture of Fear* (New York: Oxford University Press, 2007), 49. Naomi Murakawa argues that "postwar racial liberalism"—i.e., the liberal push to modernize policing and create supposedly race-neutral penal policies beginning after World War II— inadvertently enhanced the notion of Black criminality and both strengthened and legitimized the modern U.S. carceral state. Murakawa, *The First Civil Right: How Liberals Built Prison America* (New York: Oxford University Press, 2014), 11–13.

58 Johnson quoted in Flamm, *Law and Order*, 47.

59 Nixon quoted in Katherine Beckett and Theodore Sasson, *The Politics of Injustice: Crime and Punishment in America*, 2nd ed. (Thousand Oaks, CA: Sage Publications, 2004), 52. Both the Senate and the House of Representatives, with Democratic majorities, wanted to increase LEAA funding to $750 million or even $1 billion, over Nixon's $480 million request, but settled on $650 million for the 1970–71 fiscal year. Howard E. Peskoe, "The 1968 Safe Streets Act: Congressional Response to the Growing Crime Problem," *Columbia Human Rights Law Review* 5 (1973): 69–116. See also Julilly Kohler-Hausmann, "Guns and Butter: The Welfare State, the Carceral State, and the Politics of Exclusion in the Postwar United States," *Journal of American History* 102, no. 1 (June 2015): 87–99, and Elizabeth Hinton, "'A War Within Our Own Boundaries': Lyndon Johnson's Great Society and the Rise of the Carceral State," *Journal of American History* 102, no. 1 (June 2015): 100–112.

60 Flamm, *Law and Order*, 115–120. When the bill was reauthorized in 1970, rural and suburban areas without racial disturbances—and with Republican majorities—also received funds; however, disproportionate funding went to riot control and organized crime under LEAA allocations. Peskoe, "The 1968 Safe Streets Act," 98–99; Purcell, "North Carolina: Corrections," 191–193; North Carolina Bar Association, "DOC Gets Largest LEAA Appropriation in Its History," Jan. 1975, box 74, folder 146, Hobgood Papers. U.S. Congressional Budget Office, *Law Enforcement Assistance Administration: Options for Reauthorization* (Washington, DC, 1979), xiii.

61 This is not to discount the impact of President Reagan's 1986 Anti-Drug Abuse Act or President Clinton's 1994 Violent Crime Control and Law Enforcement Act (which Clinton recently called a mistake before an NAACP audience). Both bills led to huge increases in the policing and imprisonment of disproportionate numbers of African Americans. Alexander, *New Jim Crow*, 48–58. *New York Times*, July 16, 2015, A16. Ironically, the 1994 bill also included the Violence Against Women Act.

62 Perkinson, *Texas Tough*, 302, 303.

63 Fergus, *Liberalism*, 140. In 2012, North Carolina spent $1.2 billion at a cost of $30,000 per inmate. "The Price of Prisons: North Carolina, Fact Sheet," Vera Institute of Justice, Center on Sentencing and Corrections (New York, Jan. 2012), accessed Jan. 2015, www .vera.org/priceofprisons.

64 Harwell, *True Deliverance*, 39–40, 42. Ironically, the arrest of civil rights activists in the South and the widespread perception of southern barbarism as a holdover from slavery led to reforms in southern more often than northern prisons during the 1960s and 1970s, despite similarly horrific prison conditions in both regions. However, improvements often meant modernizing, which did not necessarily humanize incarceration. Thompson, "Blinded by a 'Barbaric' South: Prison Horrors, Inmate Abuse, and the Ironic History of American Penal Reform," in *The Myth of Southern Exceptionalism*, ed. Matthew Lassiter and Joseph Crespino (New York: Oxford University Press, 2010), 74–51. On racialized penal practices in the South in an earlier period see, for example, Alex Lichtenstein, *Twice the Work of Free Labor: The Political Economy of Convict Labor in the New South* (New York: Verso, 1996); David Oshinsky, *Worse Than Slavery: Parchman Farm and the Ordeal of Jim Crow Justice* (New York: Free Press, 1996); and Mary Ellen Curtin, *Black Prisoners and Their World, Alabama 1865–1900* (Charlottesville: University Press of Virginia, 2000).

65 Violence, including sexual assault, against impoverished African American women remains a pressing problem, both in prison and in the larger society. For a recent work on this topic by a scholar/activist, see Beth E. Richie, *Arrested Justice: Black Women, Violence, and America's Prison Nation* (New York: New York University Press, 2012). See also Eleanor Bader, "Women Prisoners Endure Rampant Sexual Violence—Current Laws Not Enough," *Truthout*, Dec. 21, 2012, accessed June 2015, www.truth-out.org, and *The Sexual Assault to Prison Pipeline: The Girls' Story*, A Report by the Human Rights Project for Girls, Georgetown Law Center on Poverty and Inequality and the Ms. Foundation for Women (2015), accessed Nov. 2015, available at www.law.georgetown.edu/ go/poverty.

66 *State v. Joan Little*, Argument to the Jury by Mr. Paul, Aug. 14, 1975, box 1, folder 9, Reston Papers. *Chicago Defender*, Aug. 16, 1975, 1.

67 Despite a 2.8 percent decline in U.S. prisoners between 2009 and 2012, the United States still has the highest incarceration rate in the world. Thirty-eight percent of state and federal inmates are African American and 7 percent are female. "Incarcerated Women"; "Facts About Prisons and People in Prisons" (Jan. 2014) and "Trends in U.S. Corrections: Populations Under Control of the U.S. Corrections System, 1980 and 2013," The Sentencing Project (Washington, DC), accessed Oct. 2015, www.sentencingproject .org/doc/publications.

PART THREE RETHINKING
FEMINISM

7 ◆ GENDER EXPRESSION IN ANTEBELLUM AMERICA

Accessing the Privileges and Freedoms of White Men

JEN MANION

In 1856, a "Male Girl" was found working on the floor of the American Whip Company in Westfield, Massachusetts. The "Male Girl" was described as charming and suave—and therefore *convincingly* male. The account states, "She pretended to be a nice young man of 17, smoked strong cigars, was a successful beau among the young ladies, and acted her part as modern gentleman very well to all outside appearances."[1] People like the unnamed "Male Girl" aspired to pass and live as men for many reasons. Male attire offered greater safety to young people running away from home, walking the streets, or traveling alone.[2] Male attire made it easier to flirt with, charm, or seduce a woman for companionship, sex, or love.[3] Male attire offered entry to a diverse range of employment opportunities reserved for boys and men—and higher wages. Male attire allowed people to be seen as men and live their lives in a way that felt good to them. At a time when clothing was dramatically gendered, male attire was the first step that enabled many people designated female at birth to pass as men and experience the freedom that entailed—some for a moment, others for a lifetime.

Antebellum America was marked by the dramatic growth of social reform movements concerning a wide range of issues, from temperance and poor relief to abolition and women's rights. Debates over the inhumanity and viability of slavery raged as activists challenged the structural oppressions and everyday indignities faced by African Americans. The women's rights movement shed light on the hardships free women faced, including a devaluing of their domestic labor and low rate of pay for wage work as they fought for suffrage and citizenship, including the right to own property, to self-representation in court, and to enter into contracts. Those denied the legal, political, and social rights enjoyed by most white men became more organized, more vocal, and more resistant to white patriarchal authority in its many forms.[4] Countless women with varied motivations refused to wait for the laws to grant them freedom from enslavement, a living wage, or a political voice. Refusing femininity, domesticity, and submission, they changed their lives by changing the presentation of their gender.

While public debates over the meaning, constraints, and transformative potential of clothing focused on dress reform and its association with women's rights activists, other people pushed the limits of gender expression to more dramatic and unexpected ends by presenting themselves as men.[5] Those who sought to pass and live as men challenged fundamental assumptions of the relationship between gender roles and sexual difference. Upon being outed as people assigned the female sex at birth, this group demonstrated time and time again that they could do anything cisgender men could do, undermining justifications for restrictions on women's lives anchored in sexual difference.[6] In this respect, they carved out space for broader social acceptance of those women who sought an expansion of their legal and political rights *without* challenging the social distinctions of the sexes. But this was little consolation for those who had their identities, desires, and lives thwarted (and quite possibly ruined) when they were outed.

Gender as a category of historical analysis has forever transformed the writing of history.[7] Its most successful deployment has been part of an intersectional lens that interrogates race, class, and gender in dynamic combination to expose the production of power and difference.[8] And yet the radical possibility of gender's mutability and performativity has yet to be realized in historical research.[9] Judith Butler emphasized the relational aspect of her theory of gender performativity when she wrote, "One does not 'do' one's gender alone. One is always 'doing' with or for another, even if the other is only imaginary."[10] The views and judgments of others always play a role in shaping how a person feels about and/or acts in regard to their gender. Gender is always in the process of being done and given meaning. Given this temporality, the gender of any person is never static but rather in a constant state of becoming.[11] While this theory applies to everyone, it is most visible for those "who move away from the gender they were assigned at birth," which is how Susan Stryker defines the term "transgender."[12] Most significantly for this analysis, Stryker does not designate an "endpoint" that coincides with a transgender identity but rather opens a broad space that is defined chiefly by movement away. Lots of different people consciously rejected or moved way from expressions of gender that were deemed appropriate for their sex.

This essay aspires to bring together three distinct yet interrelated practices that made not only sexual difference but also racial identification and class status less stable than the historic record suggests: escaping enslavement by crossing gender and race, claiming more rights as women through reforming dress, and accessing the privileges and freedoms of white manhood by passing as men. In the antebellum era, reports of those wearing bloomers, pantaloons, or dressed from head to toe in male attire filled the pages of newspapers across the country.[13] There is much to learn from considering the shared and overlapping experiences of people who challenged the boundaries of prescribed gender norms for women in this early period.[14] Women's rejection of femininity was not explicitly associated with sexual deviance until the 1880s, when the emerging field of sexology pathologized and criminalized female masculinity.[15] If anything, white people who passed as men for work were treated with understanding and respect for decades. As abolitionists and women's rights activists challenged long-standing racial and gender hierarchies, however, those who challenged the constraints intended for their race, class, or gender received heightened scrutiny from policing authorities. The press, long a champion of gender crossers who were "discovered" to be women, also turned on them, as accounts once framed as celebratory human interest stories became fodder for the police report.

Dress reform was a contested part of the women's rights movement. Leading organizers including Susan B. Anthony, Elizabeth Cady Stanton, Lucy Stone, and Amelia Bloomer embraced the reform dress shortly after Elizabeth Smith Miller introduced the design at Seneca Falls, New York, in 1851.[16] For some, dress stood at the heart of women's suffering. Those who flouted convention by embracing bloomers—a shortened skirt with pants underneath—were taking a stand for an expansion of women's rights along with more flexible dress. This view was espoused by the National Dress Reform Association (NDRA) and defended repeatedly in *The Sibyl*, the movement's chief publication. One essay claimed that dress reform would bring about "a physiological reform, to elevate the weakened stamina of the race" that should be of far greater appeal than the more narrowly conceived movement for the vote.[17] But most women's rights advocates felt their platform was broader and more impactful than a simple call for changes in dress. Suffrage was seen as the end game—the ultimate way to ensure women could protect the other rights they were fighting for, such as greater access to education, a wider range of employment opportunities, better pay for all types of work, and the ability to divorce abusive husbands.[18]

Public debate over dress reform unearthed larger questions about the role of nature versus society in determining sexual difference.[19] Famed dress reformer Miss Weber advanced an essentialist view of sexual difference anchored in nature as a way to fortify her argument for greater social freedoms for women. Weber wrote, "Nature never intended that the sexes should be distinguished by apparel. The beard which she assigned solely to man is the natural token of his sex. But man effeminates himself, contrary to the evident purposes of nature, by shaving off his beard."[20] Man, not nature, anchored sexual difference in dress. Weber hoped to point out the patent arbitrariness of the socially prescribed distinctions between men and women. In her famous pamphlet, the American living in Brussels called for women to wear male attire as she herself did, at least "till they are married."[21] Opponents, however, expressed concern that dress reform would fundamentally transform women's relationship to both men and power. Miss Townsend wrote a lengthy essay about the state of women wearing "male attire" in which she claimed, "Among the schemes advocated by the female reformers of the present day, there is none more startling than that which aims at the overthrow of all distinctions in the costume of the sexes."[22] No one challenged the assumption that such alterations to women's dress would change their mobility, status, and opportunities. The fact that this idea was presumed on both sides confirms the importance of dress.

When women in reform dress entered the public sphere as advocates for abolition, women's rights, and temperance, the backlash against them was tremendous.[23] It was not long before newspapers were filled with criticisms of these alleged "masculine women" along with debates over what actually constituted masculinity. One essay defined the boundaries of women's proper behavior in the most narrow and punitive of ways, stating it was important that women remain illiterate, immobile, and helpless. But even a woman who succeeded in adhering to these restrictions could risk crossing the line into male territory if she dared to "be bold and confident in the

assertion of her opinions."[24] Negative reactions to women embracing a public role as speakers and advocates pushed the discourse around women's
dress and demeanor back even as the movement gained momentum.[25] One
need look no further than Catharine Beecher's famous attack on Frances
Wright, whom Beecher condemned because she was a "great masculine person" with a "loud voice" and "untasteful attire" who traveled and lectured
in mixed company.[26] Women's rights activists debated the origins and significance of so-called "feminine" traits. They defended women's expanded
rights and opportunities. They were criticized for trying to make women
more like men and for denouncing women's best qualities.

In response to such hostility, a growing number of reformers embraced a
view of women as essentially distinct from and weaker than men. The famed
radical Mary Gove Nichols echoed such a sentiment. In her defense of the
dress reform movement, she celebrated women who were weak and condemned those who were masculine: "Let the weak and timid rejoice. God
will have witnesses, if you are not strong enough to testify. Nor are bold,
masculine women wanted in this work, or women who will lay down their
worthless lives, for worthless and wicked fashions."[27] Though critiqued for
her own embrace of free love, Nichols had no qualms about policing her sisters who strayed from other aspects of feminine virtue that she embraced.[28]
Nichols and many others had no interest in blurring the social or cultural
distinctions between men and women.[29]

Universalist minister Edwin Hubbell Chapin, for example, argued for
women's equality and weakness in the same essay. He asserted clearly,
"Woman is simply the equal of man—nothing more, nothing less." Of
women's work, he declared, "Women's work will follow spontaneously
from woman's nature, and will accord with the qualities of her being. It
will not therefore be strong physical work, but where clean, delicate work
is needed, where emotion mingles with thought, it will be her work in
the future, and still more future opens into civilization. Woman's truest
work is of home and its sanctities."[30] Chapin's widely republished essay
promotes an essentialist view of sexual difference while advancing an
empty notion of "equality" that banished women from public life. But he
was clear on one thing: there was no place for masculine women: "It is
rather a fearful picture, to be sure, of a masculine woman, scheming in
Wall Street, or shouting in Tammany Hall."[31] Many champions of women's
political and legal rights (not to mention those opposed) shared Chapin's
outrage at such a sight.

The impact of the reform dress movement is difficult to assess. Some believe the dressing style was restricted to "only about one hundred prominent women" in the 1850s and that few working-class women would even have heard about it.[32] Others suggest that a broader range of women embraced the attire for "practical" reasons when working at home but did not wear it in public.[33] This distinction points to the significant racial and class dimensions of this debate in the first place. Leading African American activists such as Sojourner Truth and Frances Ellen Watkins Harper rejected the bloomer dress that their white colleagues and friends embraced. Consider Sojourner Truth's explanation for why she was not interested in trading in her dress for a short dress with pantaloons underneath: "An' I told 'em I had Bloomers enough when I was in bondage."[34] Truth's comment reveals dress reform not only offered nothing to advance the cause of Black freedom—the central "rights" issue for Black women—but it may have undermined Black women's claim to respectability, womanhood, and freedom.[35] Elite white women also questioned why their peers would want to embrace attire commonly associated with lower classes *and* the other sex. Editor Jane Grey Swisshelm—who stood in favor of women's rights but against dress reform—defended the value of distinction between the sexes and the classes: "Pantaloons are an emblem of servitude—were invented for the convenience of labor, and are suitable for masons, carpenters, &c., &c."[36] Swisshelm herself also criticized the conventions of women's clothing but was not willing to compromise distinctions of sex or class that would separate freeborn financially secure white women from poor working women or men.

It wasn't long before leading women's rights advocates gave up the reform dress in hopes of quelling their critics and expanding the appeal of their cause.[37] Stanton only lasted "two or three" years before giving into pressure from her friends and even her father.[38] Lucy Stone was more resolute than most but "with advancing years" she, too, abandoned reform dress. Amelia Bloomer—for whom the outfit was nicknamed—abandoned it as well. Bloomer reflected, "We all felt that the dress was drawing attention from what we thought of far greater importance—the question of women's right to better education, to a wider field of employment, to better remuneration for her labor, and to the ballot for the protection of her rights."[39] This decision was part of a larger campaign that sought to preserve social distinctions between men and women while advocating for some expansion of women's rights. Even Bloomer herself declared, "We do not advocate the same style of dress, altogether, for both sexes and should be sorry to see women dress just like men."[40] By allaying fears of white men from coast to coast that they might lose the privileges of their sex in domestic or public affairs, the movement for women's rights would live to fight another day. Traditional dress was donned.

While the phrase "masculine woman" was most commonly used as a slur against a woman who spoke publicly of political matters such as slavery or women's rights, this was not the group of people who actually embraced masculinity and the chance to present themselves as men. Those who crossed genders to live as men seldom gathered as leaders and organizers for social change but rather aspired to live anonymous, ordinary lives. They only made headlines when they were exposed as having been assigned the female sex at birth—something few willingly admitted.[41] The archive tells little about how gender crossers or passing men felt about their gender, making it difficult to ascertain parallels to a contemporary transgender identity. There are several reasons for this: One, reports were usually written about such people, not by them. Two, modern concepts such as gender identity or sexual orientation as expressions of an individual identity were not yet established.[42] We can speculate that what motivated *some* people to pass as men was not solely work or freedom or love but also a desire to be seen as and treated as a man—or as someone other than a woman.[43] There is one thing we know for sure: throughout the nineteenth century many people who were assigned the female sex at birth lived as men.

People with a range of desires, motives, and experiences have been lumped together under the category "cross-dresser."[44] This categorization not only elides distinctions within this diverse group but also reduces a serious, multifaceted, risky, and ongoing process—that of learning to pass as a man—into a simple, one-time act of acquiring and donning clothing. Many of these people embraced traits deemed masculine at the time—drinking, smoking, gambling, and flirting with women—as a means to bolster their likelihood of passing. Accounts contained a remarkable number of people who crossed genders to pursue work as men. Tales—both factual and fictitious—of girls and young women who went to sea working as cabin boys and common seamen were a staple of eighteenth-century Anglo-American culture.[45] Such accounts continued through the middle of the nineteenth century, though with lower frequency. A ship sailing out of Baltimore reported a "female sailor boy" who worked as a cabin boy on the schooner *St. Mary's.*[46] Another such story captured the entrepreneurial spirit of Ann

Johnson, who moved through a series of occupations in search of higher wages. For two months, Johnson drove the horse on a canal barge before going to work as a cabin boy at sea for $4 a month. Dissatisfied, Johnson inquired of the shipping master about a better opportunity, at which point he encouraged his cabin boy to pursue whaling. Johnson worked aboard a whaling ship from Nantucket for seven months before being discovered. The account of the incident emphasized that Johnson "never [shrank] from going aloft in the worst weather, or the darkest night" and was nineteen years old.[47] This framing served to quell any question about Johnson's willingness or ability to do work historically reserved for men.

Maritime work faded in prominence as the economy was transformed by urbanization, industrialization, and westward expansion—all inspiring new work opportunities. People passing as men took up diverse occupations including work as machine operators, clerks, errand boys, general laborers, cooks, and miners. One person who ran away at the age of twelve took the name George Moore Wilson and moved to Glasgow where they worked for years in a cotton factory. After courting and marrying a woman named Elizabeth Cummings, Wilson and Cummings together moved to New Jersey where Wilson worked in a mill. They moved again to New York where Wilson worked for a fur cap manufacturer.[48]

This range of jobs highlights the flexibility and diversity of wage-work opportunities for men during this period, while women's work options were increasingly constrained. This was caused by numerous forces, including an influx of European immigrants and a decline in available home work as factories dominated and drove wages down.[49] The transformation of needlework into wage labor had a negative effect on women's relation to the craft. No longer a vocation that women enjoyed in their homes, it became one of the least desirable occupations.[50] Poorer women had no choice but to continue to work for wages anyway. But by 1860, only 15 percent of all women were working for wages at a given time.[51] Changes in the production of men's clothes created more options for men (and gender crossers) as consumers while driving down women's wages. As early as the 1840s, there were two different categories of men's clothing stores in New York: clothiers' warehouses and tailors' establishments.[52] This raised anxieties for some who feared that men of lower classes could now pass themselves off as "gentlemen."[53] This development actually made it easier for anyone to acquire a suit of male attire, as mass-produced clothing was cheaper, more likely to be bought without a relationship to a tailor, and with little expectation that it would fit perfectly.

Awareness that women were paid poverty-level wages for their labor led to relatively sympathetic treatment in the press for those who pursued work as men. Consider this account written by a New York reporter about a gender crosser who worked as a cook for a group of loggers. The reporter noted the cook earned an average of $30 a month in this capacity, "having earned nearly as much in male attire, in six weeks, as she would have received in somebody's kitchen in St. Paul's for a whole year."[54] Another person, Catherine Craw, successfully passed as a man for three years before they were arrested at age nineteen for living and working in Oswego, New York, as an "errand boy" for a fruit dealer named Mr. Jones. Craw was described as honest, modest, and industrious. The article sympathetically states that Craw carried a knife for self-defense "should her sex ever have been discovered, and an attempt made to trifle with her honor."[55] An unnamed person was charged with vagrancy in New York City in 1856 solely for wearing male attire. Upon their arrest, they argued, "My hands are now as hard as any boy's who works, which I think is a sufficient guarantee that I get my living honestly . . . and I think that the public will agree with me in saying that I took the best course under the circumstances."[56] The fact that the New York reporter made the case for the person who went out west to work as a cook, that Craw's employer described them as honest, modest, and industrious despite the deceit, and that the person arrested on vagrancy charges felt confident that a general public would support the course of their life, all suggest a fair amount of recognition, understanding, and acceptance of this group's chosen path. Many coworkers, employers, witnesses, and reporters seemed to recognize the decision to cross genders and live as a man as rational and acceptable.

The terms on which a gender crosser received this support and sympathy, however, were rather narrow. As soon as the subject shifted from destitution or hard work to joyful adventures and frolicking good times, public attitudes shifted, too. This occurred when Charley of New Orleans was arrested at the age of nineteen after successfully passing as a man for four years. Charley was described as someone very comfortable and successful living as a man:

> When her fifteenth birthday rolled round she doffed her feminine and donned masculine attire. The change suited so well that she has never seen fit to change it since. She first offered her services as mess-boy on board of a Mississippi steamboat, and was on the up trip promoted to cabin-boy. She was for a

time employed in the latter capacity on board the ill-fated Jewess. She worked in New-Orleans for about two years, and made one or two voyages as a passenger from that city to this. . . . Charley says that she has maintained herself "like a man," without doing anything wrong, and feels an evident pride at the success with which she has carried out her masculine disguise.[57]

Charley gained further notoriety upon arrest by claiming to have palled around with another famous gender crosser from New York City, Emma Snodgrass, who was also arrested while in Boston "for donning the breeches." Like Charley, Snodgrass was good-looking and wore well-tailored clothes, so much so that they "applied for and obtained a situation as clerk at the clothing establishment of John Simmons & Co., Water-street."[58] Charley, it turned out, was too good at passing and took too much pleasure in the ways and freedoms of white men.

Accounts of people aspiring to access the privileges and freedoms of men share an unnamed racial assumption: the power of whiteness. As one scholar has argued, "In many instances, constructions of gender are about being white, being perceived to be white, or sometimes they are deeply ingrained in perceptions of beauty as white."[59] The striking absence of accounts of African Americans assuming male attire and personas to pass as men for work is evident. The meaning of this absence emerges when considered in the context of the constraints that existed on the freedom and mobility of all African Americans regardless of sex. African American men and women in transit were under serious scrutiny and suspicion, something Elizabeth Pryor refers to as the criminalization of black mobility.[60] This was only intensified by the passage of the Fugitive Slave Act in 1850 that authorized federal officers to enforce the rights and authority of slaveholders by punishing individuals who might help the enslaved escape in any way and thereby enabled the kidnapping and enslavement of an unknown number of free Blacks.[61] Black codes further restricted travel options, banning African Americans from first-class cars and forcing Black women to ride "in smoking cars or compartment cars with men of color and white men."[62] The intense surveillance of and restrictions placed on African Americans in this crucial period of American history cannot be overstated.

In this context, some African Americans who were assigned the female sex at birth turned to male attire to escape enslavement. There are many reasons why it was easier for Black men than Black women to run away or travel more generally.[63] Enslaved Black men had greater mobility because they were more commonly assigned work that involved transporting goods between markets and plantations. Enslaved women who worked indoors were less familiar with their immediate surroundings. Passing as a man would not only disguise the identity of a particular woman but also remove one trait likely to trigger suspicion.[64] When six African Americans were discovered aboard a ship heading from Virginia to the North, the lone woman was "dressed in male attire."[65] Incidents of this strategy are difficult to quantify but anecdotal evidence abounds.[66]

While the ability to pass as a man could serve as a gateway to freedom, it also affirmed long-standing racist views of Black womanhood.[67] Centuries of racial slavery advanced ideas about Black women that made it easy for whites to justify their ill treatment, from sexual abuse to segregation to the most physically demanding forms of labor.[68] Enslaved Black women were constantly judged for not living up to white ideals. Physical strength was held against them, as in the famous 1858 incident when Sojourner Truth was heckled and challenged to prove her womanhood by "show[ing] her breast to the women in the audience, who would report on her sex."[69] Those who decided to present themselves as men to escape slavery carried the weight of this dilemma: they would risk their own respectability—perceptions of their virtue and humanity—for freedom.

The great chronicler of the underground railroad William Still suggests that it was rather common for people to cross genders when escaping slavery: "Men disguised in female attire and women dressed in the garb of men have under very trying circumstances triumphed in thus making their way to freedom."[70] Still recorded numerous instances of the practice, including Clarissa Davis, who fled Virginia "dressed in male attire," and Nancy, who was threatened with rape by their master and thereby moved "to a death-struggle for her freedom, and she succeeded by dressing herself in male attire." Mary Millburn "alias Louisa F. Jones" escaped in male attire while Anna Marie Weems was only fifteen when named "Joe Wright" and dressed in male attire to prepare for traveling. These accounts affirm the role of gender in regulating the movement of African Americans, in both the North and South.[71]

One well-known account stands out above the rest because it challenges the boundaries of gender as well as those of race, class, and ability in one masterly performance that led from slavery to freedom.[72]

William and Ellen Craft represented all that was possible in manipulating gender roles, racial classification, and broader social expectations. Passing—a crucial way of understanding racial identity and social location—combined with crossing gender enabled Ellen to achieve this bold step. The couple devised a strategy whereby the light-skinned Ellen would present herself as a white man and attempt to pass as a slave master while her husband William would tend to her as a servant. A number of other manipulations were required to achieve the effect, including casting Ellen as partly disabled, hard of hearing, and unable to write. This would remove the expectation that she sign any documents and also justify her overreliance on her servant/slave assistant. They escaped from slavery in Georgia and arrived safely in Philadelphia, achieving freedom. Finally settled in Boston, William worked as a cabinet maker.[73] They eventually relocated to England amid threats from the Fugitive Slave Act of 1850, where they published their account. Their success compelled a heightened regulation of people crossing boundaries—especially from slavery to freedom—while also inspiring others to dare to escape.

The ability to pass as white was crucial to Ellen's gender crossing—for whiteness was the key to the privileges of manhood that so many white women sought.[74] As reported in an early account, Ellen Craft, who was "of very light complexion, disguised herself in male attire, and travelled from Macon to this city as a dashing youth from the South, with her husband, as her slave servant."[75] A more detailed account appeared a month later that fixated on Ellen's race: "no stranger would suspect from her appearance, that there was any colored blood in her veins." It also detailed their acquisition of male attire for her: "With his little gains he procured his wife a suit of male attire, piece by piece, as he could without exciting suspicion."[76] In a fictitious account of the Craft story in his novel *Clotel*, William Wells Brown describes an African American woman protagonist so light in complexion that it enabled her to pass not only as white but more importantly, as a white man.[77] Had Ellen and William been caught, the consequences would likely have been horrendous brutality and reenslavement. But their path to freedom was no Underground Railroad. Rather, it followed a course that accessed the privileges and freedoms of white manhood.

While the Crafts managed to successfully manipulate gender, race, class, and disability to escape slavery, they pulled off their tremendous trip in 1849. The Fugitive Slave Act of 1850 was a response to greater numbers of

African Americans escaping enslavement and led to heightened scrutiny of African Americans in public spaces. Those who passed as white men to enjoy freedom of movement and opportunity to work joined free African Americans in the eyes of the expanding police force as a threat not only to racial and gender hierarchies but also to social and moral order more generally. Numerous cities and municipalities expanded their anti-vagrancy legislation and added anti-cross-dressing provisions.[78] These policies targeted a range of people including those passing as men to work, those dressing as men for a night on the town, female impersonators, and sex workers. They aimed to enforce "gender normativity" in public spaces.[79] Those who passed and worked as white men came under greater scrutiny and were more likely to be punished for this transgression on the eve of the Civil War than ever before.[80] The regulation and punishment of those challenging racial and gender hierarchies had grave and lasting implications for American democracy, further clarifying that the promises of freedom, justice, and equality were reserved for the chosen few.

The lives of people presenting themselves as white men to travel, work, and live in antebellum America were given meaning through several important national discourses, from the fight for an expansion of women's rights to the low wages paid to free working women to the extensive restrictions placed on African Americans—enslaved and free. While African Americans designated female at birth who aspired to live and pass as men surely navigated this complex terrain of race, gender, and mobility, accounts of their lives in the antebellum period are scarce.[81] Narratives of people passing as men to escape enslavement all assert the category of woman was something only temporarily abandoned in pursuit of freedom, rather than a chosen way of life. The privileging of whiteness as the primary identity and vehicle for gender transgression both marginalizes gender crossers of other races and links the experience of gender crossing to distinct aspirations for the privileges and freedoms of white men. Though the long-standing Anglo-American tradition of quaintly celebrating the adventures of those who passed as men to work as sailors waned by the mid-nineteenth century, the role of whiteness in this journey persisted.[82]

Sympathetic accounts of poor people seeking to "make it" by passing as men after being abandoned by lovers or parents shared the pages with stories of those more daring who asserted a right to enjoy drinking, smoking, and finely tailored suits, and pursue the affections of women. The press played a complicated role, often mocking the women's rights movement while celebrating those who passed as men to pursue work. Phrases that joined the female sex with a male gender—such as "masculine-woman"— were used to attack women's rights activists claiming a public political voice. In reports about workers who were "outed" while passing as men, however, general descriptions and even phrases like "male-girl" ranged from titillating to neutral to celebratory; rarely were they entirely hostile.

There was a bitter irony to all this, not least because many women's rights activists were horrified by the prospect of getting rid of the distinctions between the sexes and spoke openly against those who embraced dress and behaviors that were socially designated for men. Crossing genders still cast one far beyond the realm of respectable sociality that even the most outspoken women's rights activists enjoyed. It was very much this respectable sociality that Susan B. Anthony, Elizabeth Cady Stanton, and Amelia Bloomer aspired to, one by one, as they rejected the controversial bloomer costume in favor of traditional dress. Though she once suggested that women would only achieve full equality and freedom if they dressed from head to toe in male attire, this was not something Elizabeth Cady Stanton herself would ever do.[83] These women knew they were different—more respectable and generally of a higher station—than those who would move around the country living as men and looking for work. Gender crossers went too far and would undermine the political movement's claims for an expansion of women's rights *as women*. But this view missed out on the bigger picture. Not only did gender crossers prove they could do anything that men did, but by demonstrating the dramatic lengths to which some people would go to claim the privileges and freedoms of white men, they made women's rights activists seem tame and reasonable. Women's rights advocates faced an uphill battle, failing to win even the franchise for women during Reconstruction. Few of them would think twice about the plight of those caught flagrantly violating the boundaries between the sexes and embracing a male persona, even though gender crossers and women's rights activists wanted the same thing: the privileges and freedoms enjoyed by white men.

NOTES

1 "A Male Girl," *Brother Jonathan*, June 14, 1856.

2 "Another Young Lady in Trowsers," *Brother Jonathan*, July 5, 1856; Patricia Cline Cohen, "Women at Large: Travel in Antebellum America," *History Today* 44, no. 12 (December 1994): 44–50; Elizabeth Stordeur Pryor, *Colored Travelers: Mobility and the Fight for Citizenship before the Civil War* (Chapel Hill: University of North Carolina Press, 2016).

3 Henry Fielding, *The Female Husband; or, the Surprising History of Mrs. Mary, alias Mr. George Hamilton, who was convicted of having married a young woman of Wells* (London, 1746); Jack Halberstam, *Female Masculinity* (Durham, NC: Duke University Press, 1998); Sharon Marcus, *Between Women: Friendship, Desire, and Marriage in Victorian England* (Princeton: Princeton University Press, 2007); Rachel Hope Cleves, "'What, Another Female Husband?': The Prehistory of Same-Sex Marriage in America," *Journal of American History* 101, no. 4 (2015): 1055–1081.

4 Nancy A. Hewitt, *Women's Activism and Social Change: Rochester, New York, 1822–1872* (Ithaca, NY: Cornell University Press, 1984); Lori D. Ginzberg, *Women and the Work of Benevolence: Morality, Politics, and Class in the Nineteenth-Century United States* (New Haven: Yale University Press, 1990); Nancy Isenberg, *Sex and Citizenship in Antebellum America* (Chapel Hill: University of North Carolina Press, 1998); Bruce Dorsey, *Reforming Men and Women: Gender in the Antebellum City* (Ithaca, NY: Cornell University Press, 2002); Anne M. Boylan, *The Origins of Women's Activism: New York and Boston, 1797–1840* (Chapel Hill: University of North Carolina Press, 2002); Lori D. Ginzberg, *Untidy Origins: A Story of Woman's Rights in Antebellum New York* (Chapel Hill: University of North Carolina Press, 2005). On patriarchy as a malleable force, see Judith M. Bennett, *History Matters: Patriarchy and the Challenge of Feminism* (Philadelphia: University of Pennsylvania Press, 2006); On the broader context of U.S. feminisms, see Nancy Hewitt, "Feminist Frequencies: Regenerating the Wave Metaphor," *Feminist Studies* 38, no. 3 (Fall 2012): 658–680.

5 Amy Kesselman, "The 'Freedom Suit': Feminism and Dress Reform in the United States, 1848–1875," *Gender and Society* 5, no. 4 (Dec. 1991): 495–510.

6 In contemporary terms, cisgender is a term commonly used for those whose gender identity is in alignment with the sex they were designated at birth. Also see Finn Enke, *Transfeminist Perspectives in and beyond Transgender and Gender Studies* (Philadelphia: Temple University Press, 2012).

7 Joan Wallach Scott, "Gender: A Useful Category of Historical Analysis," *American Historical Review* 91, no. 5 (Dec. 1986): 1053–1075; Denise Riley, *Am I That Name: Feminism and the Category of "Women" in History* (New York: Palgrave Macmillan, 1988); Judith Butler, *Gender Trouble: Feminism and the Subversion of Identity* (New York: Routledge, 1996).

8 Dozens of important books have embraced this approach. For example, see Kathleen M. Brown, *Good Wives, Nasty Wenches, and Anxious Patriarchs: Gender, Race, and Power in Colonial Virginia* (Chapel Hill: University of North Carolina Press, 1996); Nancy A. Hewitt, *Southern Discomfort: Women's Activism in Tampa, Florida, 1880s–1920s*

(Champaign: University of Illinois Press, 2001); Jennifer Morgan, *Laboring Women: Reproduction and Gender in New World Slavery* (Philadelphia: University of Pennsylvania Press, 2004).

9 Joan Wallach Scott, "Some More Reflections on Gender and Politics," in *Gender and the Politics of History* (New York: Columbia University Press, 1999), 199–222; Jeanne Boydston, "Gender as a Question of Historical Analysis," *Gender & History* 20, no. 3 (Nov. 2008): 558–583.

10 Judith Butler, *Undoing Gender* (New York: Routledge, 2007), 1.

11 Also see Gayle Salamon, *Assuming a Body: Transgender and Rhetorics of Materiality* (New York: Columbia University Press, 2010).

12 Susan Stryker, *Transgender History* (Berkeley, CA: Seal, 2008).

13 We might begin to consider the place of kinship or even brotherhood within the "sisterhood" of women's and gender history, as sisterhood has always been problematic. See Nancy A. Hewitt, "Beyond the Search for Sisterhood: American Women's History in the 1980s," *Social History* 10, no. 3 (Oct. 1985): 299–321.

14 This is an important connection because of the vocal arguments by some radical feminists who accuse transgender people of perpetuating sexism and undermining women's equality. It is sexism, however, that anchors attacks on cisgender women, transwomen, and transmen, albeit differently. Transwomen are mocked and not trusted for giving up male privilege to become women while transmen are denied the privileges of manhood and ridiculed as really being women. This argument was first made of homophobia and sexism in Suzanne Pharr, *Homophobia: A Weapon of Sexism* (Inverness, CA: Women's Project, 1988).

15 Lisa Duggan, *Sapphic Slashers: Sex, Violence, and American Modernity* (Durham, NC: Duke University Press, 2001); Regina Kunzel, *Criminal Intimacy: Prison and the Uneven History of Modern American Sexuality* (Chicago: University of Chicago Press, 2008).

16 Carol Mattingly, *Appropriate[ing] Dress: Women's Rhetorical Style in Nineteenth-Century America* (Carbondale: Southern Illinois University Press, 2002), 40.

17 "A criticism on a 'Criticism,'" *The Sibyl—For Reforms*, July 15, 1856. Also see Gayle V. Fischer, *Pantaloons and Power: A Nineteenth-Century Dress Reform in the United States* (Kent, OH: Kent State University Press, 2001), 118.

18 Dexter C. Bloomer, *Life and Writings of Amelia Bloomer* (Boston, 1895), 70; Ellen DuBois, *Feminism and Suffrage: The Emergence of an Independent Women's Movement in America, 1848–1869* (Ithaca, NY: Cornell University Press, 1978); Judith Wellman, *The Road to Seneca Falls: Elizabeth Cady Stanton and the First Women's Rights Convention* (Champaign: University of Illinois Press, 2004); Sally McMillen, *Seneca Falls and the Origins of the Women's Rights Movement* (New York: Oxford University Press, 2008); Lori Ginzberg, *Elizabeth Cady Stanton: An American Life* (New York: Hill and Wang, 2010); Lisa Tetrault, *The Myth of Seneca Falls: Memory and the Women's Suffrage Movement, 1848–1898* (Chapel Hill: University of North Carolina Press, 2014).

19 For more on the role of biology in debates over sexual difference, see Thomas Laqueur, *Making Sex: Body and Gender from the Greeks to Freud* (Cambridge, MA: Harvard University Press, 1990); Alice Domurat Dreger, *Hermaphrodites and the Medical*

Invention of Sex (Cambridge, MA: Harvard University Press, 1998); Elizabeth Reis, *Bodies in Doubt: An American History of Intersex* (Baltimore: Johns Hopkins University Press, 2009).

20 "A Champion of Woman's Rights," *Hartford Daily Courant*, Dec. 6, 1850.

21 "Untitled," *International Monthly Magazine of Literature, Science & Art*, July 22, 1850.

22 "Women in Male Attire," *Holden's Magazine*, Mar. 1, 1850.

23 Fischer, *Pantaloons and Power*, 101.

24 "Masculine Women," *Mirror of the Times*, Mar. 22, 1851; *New York Organ*, June 15, 1850.

25 Also see Carolyn Eastman, *A Nation of Speechifiers: Making an American Public After the Revolution* (Chicago: University of Chicago Press, 2009).

26 Catherine E. Beecher, *Letters on the Difficulties of Religion* (Hartford, CT, 1836), 23.

27 Mary S. Gove Nichols, "Dress Reform," *Water-Cure Journal*, Jan. 1, 1853.

28 Patricia Cline Cohen, "The 'Anti-Marriage Theory' of Thomas and Mary Gove Nichols: A Radical Critique of Monogamy in the 1850s," *Journal of the Early Republic* 34, no. 1 (Spring 2014): 1–20.

29 Fischer, *Pantaloons and Power*, 83.

30 This view of women's physical distinctions and presumed inferiority inspired a generation of radical Quakers "to reconsider the very nature of sex roles," something those raised in more egalitarian rural villages had previously not faced. See Nancy Hewitt, "Feminist Friends: Agrarian Quakers and the Emergence of Women's Rights in America," *Feminist Studies* 12, no. 1 (Spring 1986): 45.

31 "Woman and Her Work," *Sibyl*, May 1, 1858; "Woman and Her Work," *Spiritual Age: Devoted to Rational Spiritualism & Practical Reform*, Jan. 22, 1859; "Woman and Her Work," *Ark*, Mar. 1, 1859; "Woman and Her Work," *Agitator*, Feb. 15, 1859.

32 Einav Rabinovitch-Fox, "[Re]Fashioning the New Woman: Women's Dress, the Oriental Style, and the Construction of American Feminist Imagery in the 1910s," *Journal of Women's History* 27, no. 2 (Summer 2015): 18. Also see Nan Enstad, *Ladies of Labor, Girls of Adventure* (New York: Columbia University Press, 1999), 30.

33 Fischer, *Pantaloons and Power*, 134.

34 Mattingly, *Appropriate[ing] Dress*, 110.

35 Mattingly also pointed out that Harriet Tubman favored the bloomer. On the politics of respectability, see Evelyn Brooks Higginbotham, *Righteous Discontent: The Women's Movement in the Black Baptist Church, 1880–1920* (Cambridge, MA: Harvard University Press, 1993); Michelle Mitchell, *Righteous Propagation: African Americans and the Politics of Racial Destiny after Reconstruction* (Chapel Hill: University of North Carolina Press, 2004).

36 Mattingly, *Appropriate[ing] Dress*, 51.

37 Fischer, *Pantaloons and Power*, 122.

38 Bloomer, *Life and Writings*, 70.

39 Ibid., 70.

40 Ibid., 78.

41 The author has consciously chosen the gender-neutral singular pronouns "they/them/their" in reference to those who crossed gender and/or passed as men. While uncommon, this usage is technically grammatically correct. See *Oxford English Dictionary*. Direct quotes will retain the pronouns as they appeared in print.

42 See Michel Foucault, *The History of Sexuality*, trans. Robert Hurley (New York: Vintage, 1990); David Halperin, *How to Do the History of Homosexuality* (Chicago: University of Chicago Press, 2002).

43 We might now describe some people with those feelings as transgender. Pathbreaking work in transgender history includes Leslie Feinberg, *Transgender Warriors* (Boston: Beacon Press, 1996); Joanne Meyerowitz, *How Sex Changed: A History of Transsexuality in the United States* (Cambridge, MA: Harvard University Press, 2004); Susan Stryker, *Transgender History* (Berkeley, CA: Seal Press, 2008).

44 Important scholarship on cross-dressing includes: Marjorie Garber, *Vested Interests: Cross-dressing and Cultural Anxiety* (New York: Routledge, 1991); Vern L. Bullough and Bonnie Bullough, *Cross Dressing: Sex and Gender* (Philadelphia: University of Pennsylvania Press, 1993); Daniel Cohen, *"The Female Marine" and Related Works: Narratives of Cross-Dressing and Urban Vice in America's Early Republic* (Amherst: University of Massachusetts Press, 1998); Peter Boag, *Re-Dressing America's Frontier Past* (Berkeley: University of California Press, 2011).

45 Dianne Dugaw, *Warrior Women and Popular Balladry 1650–1850* (Cambridge: Cambridge University Press, 1989).

46 "News and Pickings," *Weekly Symbol & Home Magazine*, Oct. 16, 1847.

47 "A Romance of the Ocean," *Spirit of the Lakes & Boatmen's Magazine*, May 1, 1850; Also printed in "What Is Talked About," *Literary World*, Jan. 19, 1850.

48 *Atkinson's Saturday Evening Post*, Aug. 27, 1836.

49 Alice Kessler-Harris, *Out to Work: A History of Wage-Earning Women in the United States* (New York: Oxford University Press, 1982), 60; Chris Stansell, *City of Women: Sex and Class in New York, 1789–1860* (New York: Knopf, 1986), 105.

50 Mary Jo Buhle, "Needlewomen and the Vicissitudes of Modern Life: A Study of Middle-Class Construction in the Antebellum Northeast," in *Visible Women: New Essays on American Activism*, ed. Nancy A. Hewitt and Suzanne Lebsock (Urbana: University of Illinois Press, 1993), 149. Also see Marla R. Miller, *The Needle's Eye: Women and Work in the Age of Revolution* (Amherst: University of Massachusetts Press, 2006).

51 Kessler-Harris, *Out to Work*, 46.

52 Michael Zakim, *Ready-Made Democracy: A History of Men's Dress in the American Republic, 1760–1860* (Chicago: University of Chicago Press, 2003), 70.

53 Ibid., 120.

54 "A Female Adventurer," *Moore's Rural New-Yorker*, July 16, 1853.

55 "In Men's Apparel. Catherine Craw Has Been Arrested in Oswego, N.Y." *The Liberator*, Aug. 7, 1857.

56 "Items," *Circular*, Mar. 20, 1856.

57 "An Unfeminine Freak—a Girl in Man's Clothes," *New York Daily*, Mar. 14, 1856.

58 *New York Daily Times*, Nov. 30, 1852.

59 Salvador Vidal-Ortiz, "Whiteness," *Transgender Studies Quarterly* 1, no. 1–2 (Summer 2014): 264–266.

60 Stordeur Pryor, *Colored Travelers*.

61 Anthony J. Sebok, "Judging the Fugitive Slave Acts," *Yale Law Journal* 100, no. 6 (Apr. 1991): 1835.

62 Barbara Welke, "When All the Women Were White, and All the Blacks Were Men: Gender, Class, Race, and the Road to *Plessy*, 1855–1914," *Law and History Review* 13, no. 2 (Autumn 1995): 269–271 and 276.

63 Michael P. Johnson, "Runaway Slaves and the Slave Communities in South Carolina," *William and Mary Quarterly* 38, no. 3 (July 1981): 418–441; Deborah Gray White, *Ar'n't I a Woman? Female Slaves in the Plantation South* (New York: Norton, 1985); Billy Smith and Richard Wojtowicz, "Advertisements for Runaway Slaves, Indentured Servants, and Apprentices in the *Pennsylvania Gazette*, 1795–1796," *Pennsylvania History: A Journal of Mid-Atlantic Studies* 54, no. 1 (Jan. 1987): 34–71; Stephanie M. H. Camp, *Closer to Freedom: Enslaved Women and Everyday Resistance in the Plantation South* (Chapel Hill: University of North Carolina Press, 2004); Robert M. Owens, "Law and Disorder North of the Ohio: Runaways and the Patriarchy of Print Culture, 1793–1815," *Indiana Magazine of History* 103, no. 3 (Sept. 2007): 265–289.

64 As Deborah Gray White illustrated, Black women "had to consider how conspicuous a lone black woman or group of black women would be in a countryside infrequently traveled by such humanity." White, *Ar'n't I a Woman?*, 72–76.

65 "Slaves Attempting to Escape," *Frederick Douglass' Paper*, June 22, 1855.

66 One study from Mississippi suggests that only 2 of 225 sought to escape slavery by wearing "clothing of the opposite gender." Matthew C. Greer, "Bundles, Passes, and Stolen Watches: Interpreting the Role of Material Culture in Escape," *Southern Studies: An Interdisciplinary Journal of the South* 21, no. 1 (Spring/Summer 2014): 88.

67 Barbara McCaskill argues, "Audiences might consider Ellen's mannish disguise as mere proof of the assumption that all African women occupy an intrinsically attenuated, oppositional relationship with the classification 'woman.'" Barbara McCaskill, "'Yours Very Truly': Ellen Craft—The Fugitive as Text and Artifact," *African American Review* 28, no. 4 (Winter 1994): 517; Also see McCaskill, *Love, Liberation, and Escaping Slavery: William and Ellen Craft in Cultural Memory* (Athens: University of Georgia Press, 2015).

68 Jennifer Morgan, "'Some Could Suckle Over Their Shoulder': Male Travelers, Female Bodies, and the Gendering of Racial Ideology, 1500–1770," *William and Mary Quarterly* 54 no. 1 (Jan. 1997): 167–192; Black women joined both free and enslaved Black male laborers in Maryland and Pennsylvania doing arduous work on the railroad. See Patricia A. Reid, "Margaret Morgan's Story: A Threshold between Slavery and Freedom, 1820–1842," *Slavery and Abolition* 33, no. 3 (Sept. 2012): 363.

69 Nell Irvin Painter, *Sojourner Truth: A Life, a Symbol* (New York: Norton, 1996), 139.

70 William Still in Barbara McCaskill, "Yours Very Truly," 509.

71 William Still, *Still's Underground Rail Road Records: With a Life of the Author* (Philadelphia, 1886), 60, 185, 460, 558.

72 Amani Marshall, "'They Will Endeavor to Pass for Free': Enslaved Runaways' Performances of Freedom in Antebellum South Carolina," *Slavery and Abolition* 31, no. 2 (June 2012): 161–180.

73 "Fugitive Slave Romance," *Church Advocate*, Nov. 15, 1850.

74 In March of 1837, a twenty-year-old white woman posed as a white male slave master while trying to help a young man of twenty-four who was enslaved by her aunt escape. This white woman laid claim to the privileges and freedoms of white manhood in order to facilitate freedom for a Black man. The plan required a manipulation of gender to thwart a powerful legal and social system predicated on African American enslavement and female inferiority. The magnitude of this challenge weighed on her as she came under suspicion when they stopped at a public house on their way north and she confessed. "An Elopement," *The Liberator*, Mar. 24, 1837.

75 "First Fugitive Slave Cases in Boston," *Hartford Daily Courant*, Oct. 28, 1850.

76 "William and Ellen Craft," *Portland Pleasure Boat*, Nov. 28, 1850.

77 Suzanne Bost, "Fluidity without Postmodernism: Michelle Cliff and the 'Tragic Mulatta' Tradition," *African American Review* 32, no. 4 (1998): 675. The story was celebrated in the *Juvenile Anti-Slavery Series* and "adorned with an excellent likeness of the heroine Ellen Craft, in the male attire in which some years ago, accompanied by her husband as a servant, she effected her wonderful escape from the far southern slave state of Georgia." "Notice: Juvenile Anti-Slavery Series," *The Anti-Slavery Advocate*, April 1857.

78 The earliest places to adopt anti-cross-dressing provisions included: Columbus, Ohio (1848); Chicago, Illinois (1851); Wilmington, Delaware (1856); Newark, New Jersey (1858); and Charleston, South Carolina (1858). William N. Eskridge Jr., *Gaylaw: Challenging the Apartheid of the Closet* (Cambridge, MA: Harvard University Press, 1999), appendix A2.

79 Clare Sears, *Arresting Dress: Cross-Dressing, Law, and Fascination in Nineteenth-Century San Francisco* (Durham, NC: Duke University Press, 2015), 18 and chapter 2.

80 Amy Dru Stanley, "Beggars Can't Be Choosers: Compulsion and Contract in Postbellum America," *Journal of American History* 78, no. 4 (Mar. 1992): 1265–1293.

81 New research by C. Riley Snorton promises to add to this conversation.

82 Tales of the eighteenth-century British soldier Hannah Snell and American Revolutionary hero Deborah Sampson, for example, were reprinted countless times in the press. See Alfred F. Young, *Masquerade: The Life and Times of Deborah Sampson, Continental Soldier* (New York: Knopf, 2004).

83 Isenberg, *Sex and Citizenship*, 54.

8 • WHEN A "SISTER" IS A MOTHER

Maternal Thinking and Feminist Action, 1967–1980

ANDREA ESTEPA

In 1970, Shulamith Firestone, in what was probably her genera-tion's most radical critique of traditional motherhood, argued that women would not be truly liberated unless they were able to cede responsibility not only for child-rearing but also for childbearing. "Until the decision not to have children or not to have them 'naturally' is at least as legitimate as traditional childbearing, women are as good as forced into their female roles," Firestone wrote.[1] Her proposal to liberate women from pregnancy and childbirth through artificial reproduction was one that even many femi-nists found extreme, but the problem that Firestone was addressing—how to undermine the widely held assumption that because women gave birth, they should be primarily or solely responsible for the care and upbringing of children—weighed heavily on the minds and hearts of many in the wom-en's movement. For example, Lourdes Benería, a graduate student, daycare activist, and mother of two young children when she read Firestone's *The Dialectic of Sex*, disagreed strongly with the book's position on pregnancy (Firestone described it as "barbaric," while Benería found it "a wonder-fully rich experience" and "would not have wanted to miss it"[2]), but she did wonder:

> Why was it, that women were assumed to be responsible for domestic work and childcare? And why should we (women) have to be grateful when men merely "helped"? . . . I remember the first time that the difference between child bearing and child rearing (that wonderful distinction in the English language) became so vivid to me. Yes, women carried babies in their wombs

and we had breasts to nurse them, but there was nothing biological about the association of women with child rearing and domestic work. Biology was not destiny![3]

Despite their differing positions on pregnancy and childbirth, both Firestone and Benería were rejecting a set of cultural ideals and social norms that restricted women's opportunities and experiences by suggesting that once a woman became a mother, her children should (and would) be her primary and exclusive concern. This was not a new position for those committed to gender equality. That women's lives should not be limited to or constrained by having children had long been an article of faith among American feminists. At the end of the nineteenth century Elizabeth Cady Stanton, herself a mother of seven, referred to the roles of "mother, wife, sister, daughter" as "incidental relations of life" that should not place any limitations on one's "rights and duties as an individual, as a citizen, as a woman."[4] During the mid-twentieth century women members of the Communist Party USA—"the most radical feminists of the antifeminist 1950s," according to Kate Weigand—challenged the party leadership to recognize the burden of the double shift experienced by wives and, especially, mothers and the limitations this placed on their ability to attend meetings and remain politically active.[5] In 1963, Betty Friedan's groundbreaking *The Feminine Mystique* argued that women could not be fulfilled by marriage and children alone—they needed "something more" and society would only benefit from the "more" wives and mothers like herself were capable of offering.[6]

What developed specifically within the context of the women's liberation movement of the 1960s and 1970s, I argue, was an activist identity that grew out of the intersection of feminism and motherhood. In this chapter, I identify a cohort of feminist activists who *chose* to have children at a time when the institution of motherhood was being subjected to intense critical scrutiny by the very movement they were helping to build. They wanted to have and raise children, but as adherents to the belief that women needed to be liberated from narrowly defined gender roles and expectations, they rejected the cultural ideal of motherhood as both all-consuming and completely fulfilling. Through their feminist activism and their practice of mothering, they strove to transform both the "institution" and the "experience" of motherhood in the United States.[7] Their political agendas and activist identities were shaped as much by their experience of motherhood as by their feminist convictions. They became or remained active in the women's liberation movement not *in spite* of their motherhood but, at least in part, *because* of it. The personal reflections of Benería and the other women under discussion here suggest that some committed radical and socialist feminists were actively and self-consciously engaged in an effort to integrate feminism and motherhood, and that they saw the roles of mother and women's liberationist as "ideologically compatible" to use sociologist Rhoda Lois Blumberg's phrase.[8] In this way, they were different from feminist forebears like Stanton and Friedan, who appear to have compartmentalized their activist and family responsibilities. (The women's liberation generation of mothers had more in common with the mid-century Communist women who sought "an end to the separation of 'personal' and 'party' life."[9]) Also, while Stanton and Friedan focused on giving women access to public roles outside the home, the radical feminists of the 1960s and 1970s also sought to transform marriage and the family by demanding that the social and economic value of domestic and caretaking labor be recognized, that men also be expected to do it, and that children be raised to consider both housework and paid labor outside the home as gender-neutral activities.

While some radical feminists argued that there was no room in the life of a women's liberation activist for children[10]—at least not until after the revolution—for Benería and others this position was as abhorrent as the belief that women could be nothing more than or other than mothers. "I enjoyed deeply every stage and every step of motherhood. . . . I still feel angry when I remember how it seemed as if I had to apologize for being a mother," Benería recalls.[11] Alice Wolfson, a women's health and reproductive rights activist in Washington, D.C., says she "was always extremely committed to my mothering and felt strongly that I would not sacrifice my kids to my politics."[12] And Heather Booth, a founding member of the Chicago Women's Liberation Union and the Jane abortion service, says, "Our children are our future. My kids are a center of my life and concern."[13]

Feminists like Benería, Wolfson, and Booth viewed their mothering not only as a source of personal fulfillment, as these quotes suggest, but also as an expression of their feminism. They believed that the way they raised their children would play an integral part in transforming a sexist society into a non-sexist society.[14] And they believed that a society transformed by feminism was in the best interests of children as well as women. Furthermore, the way they framed the significance of issues like day care, early childhood socialization, educational reform, reproductive rights, and welfare rights fused feminist and maternal concerns. Although they did not join together to form an organization of feminist mothers, I argue that these women did comprise a previously unrecognized cohort within the larger women's liberation movement. All the women I discuss here considered themselves radical or socialist feminists during the late 1960s and early 1970s. They had similar activist histories and shared certain values, beliefs, priorities, goals, and life experiences. As feminist-mother-activists, they played a significant role in building and shaping grassroots organizations and institutions around the country that specifically addressed the needs and concerns of parents and children.

Yet feminist mothers as a group get short shrift in many of the classic surveys of the second wave.[15] The major works of historical writing on motherhood during the period that Alice Echols identifies as the high-water mark of radical feminism (approximately 1967–1975) focus on ideas, rhetoric, and discourse.[16] They make it clear that there was a lot of feminist thinking about motherhood, but feminist activism by or on behalf of mothers is rarely addressed, in spite of the fact that some of the women who are consistently identified as movement founders and leaders were themselves mothers.[17] This gap in the historiography has had the unintended consequence of lending support to the popular image of the "second wave" feminist as uninterested in (if not antagonistic toward) motherhood and children. Perhaps this is because, in both history and popular memory, the efforts of the women's movement to reconceive motherhood, familial relationships, and childcare arrangements have been overshadowed by its commitment to reproductive rights in general, and the decriminalization of abortion, in particular. The fact that legal access to abortion continues to be both controversial within and central to mainstream American political debates may explain why it has become the issue most associated with the women's liberation agenda. The fight for accessible, affordable day care, on the other hand, has received so little attention that feminists are sometimes criticized for ignoring the needs of working mothers, in particular.[18] The result is that the women's liberation generation is depicted as being primarily concerned with avoiding or escaping motherhood as opposed to transforming it. That was certainly not the case for the radical and socialist feminists who are my subjects here. These women sought to change the institution of motherhood from within, through their practice of mothering as well as through community organizing, protest, and the establishment of alternative institutions.

The exception to the rule, the rare piece of scholarship on this period to focus on the attitudes and experiences of grassroots activists regarding motherhood, is M. Rivka Polatnick's article comparing two feminist "small groups"—one comprising Black women, the other white women.[19] Polatnick made the widely influential argument that Black feminists were more likely to view motherhood as a source of strength and power, while white feminists were more likely to view it as an impediment to achieving their personal and political goals. "As a young woman in the late 1960s, I had internalized an attitude from my radical feminist circles that becoming a mother meant getting mired in women's oppression," Polatnick writes. "By the early 1980s I had experienced a trend in white feminism toward revaluing motherhood."[20] The basic premise of Polatnick's argument has merit—given that many young white feminists of the time had grown up with stay-at-home mothers, and internalized fears of becoming trapped in the feminine mystique's "comfortable concentration camp."[21] As Ruth Rosen has argued, the generation gap that developed between white baby boomers and their parents was gendered: young men of the New Left could reject their fathers' politics and definitions of success without rejecting fatherhood; it was a more difficult task for their female peers to envision a life that integrated marriage and motherhood with social and cultural revolution.[22] Black feminists of this generation were more likely than their white counterparts to have mothers who worked outside the home, who were openly struggling against racism and sexism, and who were respected by their families and communities for their efforts.[23] But Polatnick's article, despite its small sample of subjects, has contributed to the invisibility in the scholarly literature of white feminists who "valued children, gave high priority to their care and education, and considered political work with children a vital contribution to social change," qualities that Polatnick associates exclusively with Black feminists prior to the 1980s. As Rosalyn Baxandall has written, "the daycare and prochildren's activities" of predominantly white women's liberation groups "are often erased from the historical record." While "[s]ome groups, mainly separatists who advocated a total separation from patriarchal institutions, were hostile to mothers and children, especially male children . . . this was far from the norm" among even radical feminists.[24] In this chapter, I will address that erasure by focusing primarily on white participants in the women's liberation movement who focused their activism on issues that were important to them as feminist mothers.

Lauri Umansky, in the one historical monograph on feminism and motherhood during this period, largely accepts, and expands upon, Polatnick's analysis, placing it in the context of the Black Nationalist movement's pro-natalism and the admiration and respect expressed by Black feminist writers for their own mothers. "An African American feminist pro-mother voice rings clear, early on," Umansky writes, "articulating many of the sentiments and concerns that white feminists would later endorse."[25] Although Umansky acknowledges that "the negative critique of motherhood, never hegemonic within feminism, has achieved an exaggerated reputation," her reference to white feminists coming to share the perspective of Black feminists "later," suggests that she, like Polatnick, associates the development of a pro-motherhood tendency within white feminism with the ascent of cultural feminism, and works like Jane Alpert's "Mother Right," which celebrated women's "difference" from men and reframed motherhood as a source of women's power, rather than a site of oppression.[26]

This is not to say that there was widespread agreement among white feminists about how their organizations should respond to motherhood or, for that matter, to the actual mothers in their midst. In many women's groups, a split developed between mothers and nonmothers, based on divergent interests and priorities. Dana Densmore, a founder of Boston's radical feminist group Cell 16, "didn't want to sit around with housewives concerned with getting more help with childcare." She was looking for "comrades who were ready for revolution."[27] Conversely, when Jane Lazarre went to the first meeting of a women's group comprised largely of her husband's female classmates at Yale Law School, she realized "the students lived in a world miles away from my own."[28] Lazarre did not return; instead she went home and made a flyer that read, "Tired of being somebody's mother or somebody's wife? Come . . . talk about your real feelings. Women's group forming."[29] As the text of her sign suggests, it was how mothers were perceived that was the primary source of Lazarre's frustration, not her young son. In a similar vein, Sara Evans recalls that "How do we create new ways to raise children, for ourselves and for society?" was the question that motivated the activities of her North Carolina–based women's liberation group. In the introduction to her book *Tidal Wave*, Evans describes how, in the late 1960s, her women's group organized a childcare cooperative, began writing and publishing nonsexist children's books, and started a preschool. "Several younger women split off to form their own CR group because they found our focus on childcare socialization not 'relevant' to their immediate interests," Evans recalls. "For Group 22, however, partly because most of us had, or were about to have children, and partly because we had a high concentration of sociologists, the ways that children 'learn' to be female or male became the focus. In many other consciousness-raising groups, women talked about and thought through their own socializations. Instead, we were determined to *do* it differently and to make it possible to liberate children from the constraints of cultural prescription."[30] Nancy Hawley was a mother of two and active participant in a number of women's organizations in Boston, including the socialist feminist group Bread and Roses and the women's health collective that produced the feminist classic *Our Bodies, Ourselves,* when she wrote an essay tracing her evolution as a feminist. In it, she stated, "I'm for . . . working on specific projects that are things we all need (women's clinic, round the clock community-controlled childcare facility, a free, experimental school, etc.) and that can be models of women working together to build something that meets our real needs, the needs of our children."[31] Like Evans and Group 22 in Chapel Hill, Hawley and her Boston "sisters" were identifying problems women—and mothers, in particular—faced in their local communities and then creating programs and institutions that would provide solutions in the form of new products and services.

Evans, Hawley, and the others I've mentioned believed their feminist activism was going to improve life for their children and for future generations as well as for themselves and other women. As Hawley suggests in the passage above, feminist mothers believed that their needs and those of their children were intertwined. They did not believe that their desires had to go unfulfilled in order to satisfy the demands of their children, or vice versa. They believed that transforming gender roles, family structures, and educational and childcare institutions would create a social context in which mothers would have the time and freedom to pursue interests other than their offspring, while requiring other adults to take on a share of the responsibility and demands of caretaking. Although I focus here on individuals and organizations based in and around a few major cities—Boston, Chicago, Los Angeles, New York, and Washington, D.C.—similar efforts could be found all over the country, as evidenced by articles and advertisements in the feminist press of the era. The national scope of the activism of feminist mothers and their allies can be seen, for example, in the pages of *The New Woman's Survival Catalog,* published in 1973 by a six-woman collective with contributions from women in twenty-one cities, including Baltimore, Pittsburgh, Atlanta, Detroit, New Orleans, Kansas City, and Albuquerque. The hefty, broadsheet-sized paperback allotted about 15 percent of its pages to a chapter entitled, "Children," which was devoted to short articles and resource listings that addressed single motherhood, working mothers, day care, sexism in education and children's books, and "liberating young children from sex roles."[32]

Following their belief that "the personal is political," some feminist mothers of the era began their campaigns for women's and children's liberation at home, by demanding that fathers take on a much greater share of the work of caretaking. The belief that men needed to take increased responsibility for child-rearing, and that it was "important for . . . children to see that men can be sensitive to their needs," was widely held and publicized.[33] The writer Alix Kates Shulman, who was already married and the mother of two when she became active in the women's movement in the late 1960s, noted that before having children, she and her husband both worked outside the home and shared domestic responsibilities in a way she found relatively fair and equitable. After their children were born, however, she gave up her job to care for them and found that there was both much more to do around the house and that she was doing nearly all of it. "Once we had children," Shulman wrote, "we totally accepted the sex-roles society assigns." Household maintenance, which had once been "beautifully uncomplicated," had become "a tremendous burden."[34] Angry and frustrated, but also buoyed by the burgeoning women's movement, Shulman wrote a modest proposal called "A Marriage Agreement," although "A Parenting Agreement" would have been an even more accurate title, given that its central focus was the feminist demand that fathers share childcare equally with mothers. In it, she listed all the tasks involved in taking care of her home and children. She gave it to her husband and demanded that he begin doing 50 percent of that labor if he wanted their marriage to survive. Shulman published the piece in a small women's magazine in 1970, and over the next couple of years it was reprinted in increasingly more mainstream and widely read publications: from *Ms.* to *Redbook*.[35] Clearly she had touched a nerve.

Shulman's initial motivation for writing "A Marriage Agreement" was to advocate for a more equitable division of household labor across gender lines, in order to free more time for her (and other wives and mothers) to pursue activities and interests aside from their domestic responsibilities. But she soon "came to see domestic equity not only as simple justice but as one means of transforming society by reforming the rearing of the young."[36] After Shulman and her husband began following the agreement she discovered that she wasn't the only one who benefited from the new system. As a result of spending more time together, her husband

and children became closer: "After only four months of strictly following our agreement, our daughter said one day to my husband, 'You know,
Daddy, I used to love Mommy more than you, but now I love you both
the same.'"[37] Her original article ends on this sweet note, suggesting that
the adoption of the "Marriage Agreement" was a success. What Shulman
did not acknowledge at the time was that the childcare issue was not the
only challenge her marriage faced when she wrote the essay. She and her
husband were considering divorce before it was published and although
the "Agreement" alleviated some of the tensions in their marriage, other
conflicts went unresolved. The couple divorced three years after the
piece's initial publication. Concerned that her marriage's "failure" would
be blamed on the "Agreement," Shulman hoped that its readers, especially
its critics, wouldn't find out.[38]

Shulman's article was extremely controversial and widely debated but
it definitely captured a common experience, as feminists who had children saw their lives completely transformed by motherhood, while their
children's fathers appeared to come through relatively unchanged and
unscathed. Jane Lazarre recalls a struggle similar to Shulman's over childcare responsibilities in her household. She wrote, addressing her husband:
"I simply couldn't live that motherwife life—you saw that; I was desperate.
I needed you to help me. *Help me*, not just support me; not on Sundays and
special occasions, *Help me*, all the days and nights, *raise our child with me*."[39]

To institutionalize the sharing of childcare duties, Lazarre and her husband made a schedule and chart of duties, comparable to what Shulman
had done. It took two years for Lazarre to feel that they had achieved real
equality in parenting. Lazarre writes she knew this had happened when she
had to ask her husband if their son had gotten his polio booster shot. "I was
happy for days" after that, she recalls. She also saw, as Shulman had, a new
intensity to the bond between her husband and son. Lazarre was "proud
that Benjamin wants to be held by his daddy as much as his mommy, that
either of us will do for him," she writes.[40]

Most radical and socialist feminist mothers believed that such individual
transformations, while necessary, were insufficient, particularly for women
heading single-parent households, or for families where all the adults
worked full time, outside the home. All mothers, they believed, should have
access to affordable, safe, well-run daycare centers, twenty-four hours a day,
seven days a week—whether or not they had supportive partners, relatives,
or friends. Through building cooperative daycare centers and advocating

for policies and funding that would support publicly run childcare facilities, they strove to create new options for themselves while also addressing a broader question of personal and political concern: how could they transform the institution of motherhood so that women who chose to have children would not have to give up all other interests and pursuits to do so? Day care was a significant part of the answer, even for a woman like Lazarre, who came to consider her husband a real partner in raising their child. She recalls being "struck with the suddenness of the changes in me, the tripled confidence I felt in my ability to be a 'good mother' and still live a life that was similar to the life I always had in mind" after she placed her son in a "good daycare center, a place where Benjamin loved to go every day . . . which, therefore, freed me from the guilt of leaving him."[41] But Lazarre did not just "leave" her son at day care—she got involved in a cooperatively run center, built and operated by parents who hired the teachers who looked after their children.

For the majority of activists I discuss here, day care was not just a place to park their children while working or going to school or attending a meeting. It was a key component of the process of socializing their children and they wanted what happened there to reflect their values. In their 1970 position paper, "On Day Care," Louise Gross and Phyllis MacEwan elaborated on the potentially transformative role of day care, not just for mothers, but for society as a whole. Gross and MacEwan advocated using day care to help liberate children from gender-role stereotyping by hiring equal numbers of male and female caregivers and designing curricula that introduced children of both sexes to a wide variety of activities and tasks. In a model daycare center, they wrote, both boys and girls would be "given opportunities to cook, play with dolls and trucks, sew, build with blocks, wash clothes and dishes, dress up as doctors, firemen and women, construction workers, and other interesting occupations."[42]

Feminist mothers found day care to be an appealing issue for a variety of reasons. For women who worked outside the home, especially single mothers, it offered a practical solution to an immediate problem; for women who kept their motherhood in the closet when participating in other feminist activities, daycare groups were a place where they could be "out" about their concerns as mothers (where, as Rachel Brown Cowan, a New York–based mother of two, put it, she could discuss "bedwetting and chickenpox as well as politics and poverty"); for those interested in working in a multiracial, cross-class environment, day care was an issue that resonated with women from a variety of racial, ethnic, and socioeconomic backgrounds; for women who believed that transforming a sexist society would require new approaches to the way children were educated and socialized, day care was a way to keep rigid and outdated ideas about gender roles from being passed on to the next generation.[43] Day care was not a priority simply because it would free women from some of the burdens of child-rearing but because, if done right, it would help them raise a generation of "little people" free of constricting assumptions about gender. As Gross and MacEwan concluded, "While recognizing that day care is essential for women's liberation, the authors want the movement to further recognize that day care is essential for the liberation of children. . . . The struggle for day care centers needs to be considered a people's liberation issue, not a women's issue."[44]

Because most of the feminist mothers I am discussing here began their activist careers in the civil rights movement and New Left, day care also resonated as an issue that attracted women from a variety of socioeconomic backgrounds, enabling them to build organizations, coalitions, and alliances that were multiracial and economically diverse.[45] As legal historian Deborah Dinner points out, advocates in the late 1960s and early 1970s envisioned day care as a universal right, rather than a social program targeted primarily to low-income families, or an individual option, where quality and reliability of service would vary based on ability to pay. This theoretical foundation "encouraged working-class and middle-class, African American and white, radical and liberal feminists to identify shared policy interests and to form coalitions on both the local and national levels."[46] Heather Booth recalled proudly that the Action Committee for Decent Daycare (ACDC) in Chicago was a "wonderful multi-racial direct action organization" that brought together Black and white women, mothers and daycare workers, all of whom felt the group was addressing their needs.[47] Lourdes Benería was active in the Columbia University Day Care Coalition, which, after "many sit-ins, demonstrations, petitions, and negotiations with the university administration and the City of New York," won control of a Columbia-owned building, which they dubbed The Children's Mansion. The resulting daycare program was, she recalled, "a truly multicultural institution, with children from different social and economic backgrounds . . . nurtured by feminist politics and persistent work among the parents."[48]

The work of building a daycare center involved picketing and lobbying, as well as painting walls, developing curricula, and hiring staff. In New York, Chicago, Los Angeles, and other cities, building codes and child protection

laws made it difficult for collectively run grassroots programs to pass government inspections. Ruth Beaglehole, a preschool teacher who helped
start a daycare program in a working-class neighborhood in Los Angeles,
acknowledged that "state and city codes are protective of children; they
have closed down a lot of bad places," but found that government officials
were unwilling to negotiate with or make exceptions for a group of parents
"with little or no money" that "had taken all reasonable precautions" and
provided "adequate supervision" for the children in their care. Beaglehole's
group lobbied city and state officials, attended city council meetings, and
met with the city attorney. In response, the city council called for a review
of the codes in question and established an advisory board that included
community people as well as construction and safety experts.[49] In Chicago,
ACDC faced similar challenges. At the beginning of its campaign for "free,
24 hour, client controlled childcare," the group "found the city licensing for
child care was designed to support two large contractors and not women
and their children. We had to make 32 stops to get a city license, if we could
get it at all."[50] ACDC set aside its initial plan of opening a daycare center and
instead focused on getting the city to revise its licensing laws for childcare
facilities, provide funding for day care, and put a group of parents and daycare operators in charge of oversight of childcare facilities. Heather Booth
recalls that eight months of community organizing, pressuring politicians,
and attracting media attention resulted in a big win: "1) A child care licensing review board to revise the city childcare code to make it more children
and family friendly; 2) it would be composed 50% of parents and 50% of
childcare operators; and 3) we won $1 million of city funds for childcare—
which in [the early 1970s] was real money."[51] In New York, Rosalyn Baxandall's center, Liberation Nursery, fought the city administration over
"stringent, outdated rules," like the requirement that food be served on
china plates, rather than paper. In retrospect, she acknowledged that "some
of the rules—like hiring trained teachers and providing a certain amount
of space per child—make sense, but at the same time, we were so eager to
expand women's access to cheap, convenient day care that we could only see
the regulations as making community-controlled day care impossible for
those in need."[52]

The popular notion that radical feminists were antimotherhood likely
stems in part from their passionate support for reproductive freedom, particularly the right to abortion. But feminist mothers believed reproductive
rights were necessary not only to liberate women by giving them control

over when (or whether) to have children, but also to guarantee that every child would be a "wanted child" and, hence, lessening the number of children who suffered from neglect, abuse, abandonment, or abject poverty. Alice Wolfson recalled that her group, D.C. Women's Liberation, began by focusing on abortion as "a key issue" but quickly developed a broader reproductive rights agenda. "Because D.C. was and is a black city, very early on it became clear that [we] could not address abortion in isolation from the issues of sterilization abuse and population control," she wrote. Her group organized a picket line at the publicly funded D.C. General Hospital to protest the disproportionate number of Black women who "were being maimed and dying from botched illegal abortions." That same day, she saw a group of interns and residents, also picketing, in protest of "the deplorable conditions at the hospital." As a result, Wolfson realized, "we could not see abortion as a single issue but were going to have to make the connections to other women's health issues."[53]

D.C. Women's Liberation forged an alliance with the local welfare rights group and "together we worked on the issues of abortion, sterilization abuse, and numerous other health concerns affecting poor women and children in the city." Wolfson credits her "growing awareness of the interconnection of the issues of race and gender" for turning her into what she calls a "health feminist."[54] Becoming the mother of a son at the same time that separatist ideology began to dominate her organization also played a part. When told that to remain part of her women's group she would have to give up her son, Wolfson recalled, "I instinctively knew that these women were not going to make a revolution that I—or anyone—would want to be a part of, if the only way we could become a part of it was to give up our male children. . . . While I opted out of this part of the women's movement, I continued with my women's health work."[55]

If Wolfson's group was hostile to motherhood, at least when it involved male children, other feminist organizations were entirely comfortable with and supportive of mothers. Ironically, one of these was Jane, the Chicago abortion service. In her book, *The Story of Jane*, Laura Kaplan describes a baby shower for the group's founder. Two of the other guests were also pregnant at the time. Kaplan writes, "There was nothing unusual in this group of middle-class, college-educated white women celebrating an impending birth except these women were ardent feminists and most of them were abortion counselors. . . . Here they were, a group of women, many of them mothers, some of them ecstatically pregnant, who were more committed than ever to each woman's right to make that important decision herself—when and whether to bear a child."⁵⁶ The Black feminist group studied by Polatnick also believed that you didn't have to be antimother or antichild to support reproductive rights: for them, access to "birth control meant they could be better mothers and teachers to the children they and their neighbors already had."⁵⁷

Like Wolfson and the members of the Mount Vernon Group, the mothers who were active in Jane saw reproductive rights, women's health, and being able to care for the children you *did* have as part of a continuum. Two members of the group had had children before they were ready. They joined Jane so "no other woman would have to bear a child she did not want," as one of them put it.⁵⁸ Another Jane member, a twenty-six-year-old mother of two, was suffering from lymphatic cancer but her doctor refused her request to be sterilized because he thought she was "too young." Another Jane counselor, desperate to *have* a child, was furious at her lack of control over what was happening to her as she sought fertility treatments. All these women were appalled by the way the male-controlled medical profession had been able to determine their fates. "I identified with those on the other side who didn't want to be pregnant," the woman seeking fertility treatments recalled. "I felt they should have the same control over their bodies that I needed."⁵⁹

When two of the service's abortion counselors became pregnant at the same time, the group debated whether pregnant women should be allowed to counsel clients and decided they should. They believed that a "woman who needed an abortion today might have had a child the previous year or would choose to next year." One woman who got an abortion through Jane later recalled that during her counseling session, "Charlotte's kids were crawling all over the place and I thought that was real nice—a woman who had two kids and did that. It made it seem more like a part of everything, not real bizarre."⁶⁰ The feminist "mothers of the service," as one Jane member called them, shared an article of faith, that "women should have babies when they want them and abortions when they need them."⁶¹

Alice Wolfson has described her health advocacy work as having "concreteness" and achieving "tangible results," qualities that "seemed to protect that part of the movement from the extremism that existed in other places."⁶² Another commonality shared by these feminist mothers was that they gravitated toward institution building and service provision, forms of activism that were sometimes criticized by other women's liberationists for not being revolutionary enough. For example, some members of the

Chicago Women's Liberation Union thought the Jane abortion service was "not [a] radical activity but merely reformist social service work." They saw Jane as "a Band-Aid that might help a few women but did not further or reflect the social goals they envisioned."[63] But concrete short-term goals, whether providing abortions, creating more daycare slots, or improving conditions at publicly funded hospitals, appealed to women with immediate survival needs and may help explain why groups like Action Committee for Decent Childcare in Chicago, the D.C. Women's Liberation/Welfare Rights Alliance, and the Columbia University Daycare Coalition were able to build organizations with economically and racially diverse memberships.

The fusing of feminist and maternal concerns into a single activist agenda was not without its challenges during the early years of the women's liberation movement. A number of feminists who were mothers at that time have acknowledged in retrospect that they downplayed or even hid the fact that they had children in certain movement contexts because they feared being ostracized. Some felt their decision to have children was attacked by other feminists, others that it simply went unacknowledged, that *as mothers*, they were invisible. Some have admitted that in certain feminist circles they felt the need to hide or downplay their involvement in their children's lives and, especially, the pleasure they took in being mothers. But none of these women rejected feminism, or feminist activism, as being incompatible with motherhood. They may have left a particular group or rejected a particular strain of feminist thought, but they found or built activist organizations that were both ideologically and practically compatible with their practice of motherhood and based on a worldview that was both feminist and maternalist in orientation. Alice Wolfson speaks for many of them when she writes, "My life and options as a feminist were forever changed by [my son's] birth . . . [but I] remained a committed feminist throughout."[64]

NOTES

This article is dedicated to Nancy A. Hewitt—teacher, mentor, friend—and to the mothers who are my "sisters": Lizzie Olesker, Barbara Solow, Abigail Norman, Mary Helen Berg, Joan Jubela, and Loretta Chan. For reading and commenting on earlier versions of this piece, my great thanks to Dorothy Sue Cobble, Rosalyn Baxandall, Linda Gordon, Stephanie Gilmore, Martin Meeker, Annie Valk, Jacki Castledine, and Leslie Brown. The research for this project was funded, in part, by a grant from the Radcliffe Center for Advanced Study and benefited from the assistance of the staff of Radcliffe's Schlesinger Library.

1 Shulamith Firestone, *The Dialectic of Sex* (New York: Farrar, Straus and Giroux, 1970), 182.

2 Firestone in ibid., 180. Lourdes Benería, "In the Wilderness of One's Inner Self: Living Feminism," in *The Feminist Memoir Project: Voices from Women's Liberation*, ed. Rachel Blau DuPlessis and Ann Snitow (New York: Three Rivers Press, 1998), 260.

3 Ibid., 259.

4 Elizabeth Cady Stanton, "Solitude of Self. Address Delivered before the Committee of the Judiciary of the United States Congress, Monday, January 18, 1892," accessed Aug. 30, 2015, http://www.nps.gov/wori/learn/historyculture/solitude-of-self.htm.

5 Kate Weigand, *Red Feminism: American Communism and the Making of Women's Liberation* (Baltimore: Johns Hopkins University Press, 2001), especially chapter 4. Quote appears on xii.

6 Betty Friedan, *The Feminine Mystique* (New York: W. W. Norton, 1963), 18.

7 This distinction was first articulated by Adrienne Rich in *Of Woman Born: Motherhood as Experience and Institution* (New York: W. W. Norton, 1986, 1995).

8 Rhoda Lois Blumberg, "White Mothers as Civil Rights Activists: The Interweave of Family and Movement Roles," in *Women and Social Protest*, ed. Guida West and Rhoda Lois Blumberg (New York: Oxford University Press, 1990), 166–179.

9 Weigand, *Red Feminism*, 67.

10 Dana Densmore of Boston's Cell 16 was one example. She is discussed later in the text and cited in note 27 below.

11 Benería, "In the Wilderness of One's Inner Self," 260.

12 Alice Wolfson, "Clenched Fist, Open Heart," in *The Feminist Memoir Project*, ed. Blau DuPlessis and Snitow, 280.

13 Becky Kluchin and Gina Caneva, "Heather Booth: Living the Movement Life," *CWLU Herstory Project*, accessed Aug. 28, 2015, http://www.cwluherstory.org/heather-booth-living-the-movement-life.html.

14 Some feminists whom my subjects would have identified as part of the "liberal" wing of the movement shared their interest in nonsexist child-rearing. For example, *Ms.* magazine published a regular feature called "Stories for Free Children," which rejected the gender-role stereotyping of characters that was common in children's literature of the time. "Thirty Years of *Ms.*," *Ms.* magazine, accessed Nov. 24, 2015, http://www.msmagazine.com/dec01/thirty.asp. The (child-free) actress Marlo Thomas's multimedia passion project *Free to Be . . . You and Me*, released in 1972, was another liberal feminist intervention that challenged the sexism inherent in so much of the popular culture targeted to children. For analysis of the production, content, and impact of the *Free to Be* television special, book, and album by scholars and participants, see Lori Rotskoff and Laura L. Levitt, eds., *When We Were Free to Be: Looking Back at a Children's Classic and the Difference It Made* (Chapel Hill: University of North Carolina Press, 2012).

15 The ambivalence that many young feminists felt about the prospect of having children during the early years of the movement received much more attention than the feelings and experiences of women who were mothers in works including Alice Echols, *Daring to Be Bad: Radical Feminism in America 1967–1975* (Minneapolis: University of

Minnesota Press, 1989) and Ruth Rosen, *The World Split Open: How the Modern Women's Movement Changed America* (New York: Penguin Books, 2000).

16 Echols, *Daring to Be Bad*. The sole historical monograph on the intersection of feminism and motherhood during this period is Lauri Umansky, *Motherhood Reconceived: Feminism and the Legacies of the Sixties* (New York: New York University Press, 1996). The other key work on "second wave" feminist thinking on motherhood is Ann Snitow, "Feminism and Motherhood: An American Reading," *Feminist Review* 40 (1992): 32–51. Snitow analyzes feminist writing on motherhood published from 1963, when *The Feminine Mystique* appeared, through 1990. The feminist activism of women who were mothers or around issues of particular concern to mothers is not a focus of either work. Sociologist Jo Reger has written about the relationship of "motherhood and feminism in a social movement context" but her research focuses on members of two chapters of the liberal feminist National Organization for Women during the 1980s and 1990s, a very different political and cultural climate than that of the 1960s and 1970s. Jo Reger, "Motherhood and the Construction of Feminist Identities: Variations in a Women's Movement Organization," *Sociological Inquiry* 71 (2001): 85–110.

17 Rosalyn Baxandall, Heather Booth, and Alix Kates Shulman are three prominent examples. Many radical feminists of this period eschewed being identified by gender-specific terms such as "wife" and "mother" or having their positions on issues interpreted through lenses they considered essentialist; historians of their movement may have shared this perspective. One notable exception to this trend in the historiography is Judith Ezekiel, *Feminism in the Heartland* (Columbus: Ohio University Press, 2002). In her study of feminist activism in Dayton, Ohio, Ezekiel not only identifies "large numbers of mothers" in the movement but discusses how her subjects' personal lives influenced their activities and positions on issues.

18 For a surprising example (in that it is articulated by a self-described feminist), see Karen Nussbaum, "Where the Women's Movement Failed," *MAKERS*, accessed Nov. 25, 2015, http://www.makers.com/moments/where-women%E2%80%99s-movement -failed.

19 M. Rivka Polatnick, "Diversity in Women's Liberation Ideology: How a Black and a White Group of the 1960s Viewed Motherhood," *Signs* 21, no. 3 (1996): 679–706.

20 Ibid., 683.

21 Friedan, *Feminine Mystique*, 425.

22 Rosen, *The World Split Open*, 38–40.

23 See Patricia Hill Collins, *Black Feminist Thought: Knowledge, Consciousness, and the Politics of Empowerment*, 2nd ed. (London and New York: Routledge, 2000); Patricia Hill Collins, "Shifting the Center: Race, Class, and Feminist Theorizing about Motherhood," in *Mothering: Ideology, Experience, and Agency*, ed. Evelyn Nakano Glenn, Grace Chang, and Linda Rennie Forcey (London and New York: Routledge, 1994), 45–66; and Dorothy Roberts, "Race, Gender, and Mothers' Work," *Social Politics* 2, no. 2 (1995): 195–207.

24 Rosalyn Baxandall, "Re-Visioning the Women's Liberation Movement's Narrative: Early Second Wave African American Feminists," *Feminist Studies* 27, no. 1 (2001): 234.

25 Umansky, *Motherhood Reconceived*, 5.

26 Ibid., 16; Jane Alpert, "Mother Right: A New Feminist Theory," accessed Aug. 30, 2015, http://library.duke.edu/digitalcollections/wlmpc_wlmms01022/.

27 Dana Densmore, "A Year of Living Dangerously: 1968," in *The Feminist Memoir Project*, ed. Blau DuPlessis and Snitow, 74.

28 Lazarre, *The Mother Knot*, 46.

29 Ibid., 64.

30 Sara M. Evans, *Tidal Wave: How Women Changed America at Century's End* (New York: The Free Press, 2003), 11.

31 Nancy Hawley, Untitled Document, Rochelle Ruthchild Papers, Box 1, Folder 12, Schlesinger Library, Rutgers Institute for Advanced Study.

32 Kristen Grimstad and Ruth Bayard Smith, eds., *The New Woman's Survival Catalog* (New York: Berkeley Publishing, 1973), 108.

33 Ibid. This relates to my use of the term "maternal thinking" in the title—an oblique reference to the ground-breaking work of philosopher Sara Ruddick, specifically her idea that "maternal thinking arises out of actual child-caring practices," and is a social, rather than a biological, development. Ruddick argues that men as well as women can be maternal thinkers. Although Ruddick's writing on this subject did not begin to appear until 1980, after most of the events and publications discussed here, I believe the feminist mothers I study would have agreed.

34 Alix Schulman [*sic*], "A Marriage Agreement," *Up from Under* 1, no. 2 (Aug./Sept. 1970): 5. Available online at http://jwa.org/feminism/shulman-alix-kates (accessed Aug. 27, 2015).

35 Ibid. A version of Shulman's piece was even slated to run in *Life* magazine, but the venerable weekly ceased publication shortly before it was scheduled to appear.

36 Alix Kates Shulman, "A Marriage Disagreement, or Marriage by Other Means," in *The Feminist Memoir Project*, ed. Blau DuPlessis and Snitow, 284.

37 Shulman, "A Marriage Agreement," 6.

38 Ibid.

39 Lazarre, *The Mother Knot*, 97.

40 Ibid., 98.

41 Ibid.

42 Louise Gross and Phyllis MacEwan, "On Daycare," Ruthchild Papers, Box 2, Folder 38, Schlesinger Library, Rutgers Institute for Advanced Study.

43 Rachel Brown Cowan and Jane Lazarre White, "Dialogue: It's All Right to Be a Mother," Charlotte Bunch Papers, Box 2, Folder 37, Schlesinger Library, Radcliffe Institute for Advanced Study.

44 Gross and MacEwan, "On Daycare."

45 Umansky, *Motherhood Reconceived*, 5.

46 Deborah Dinner, "The Universal Childcare Debate: Rights Mobilization, Social Policy, and the Dynamics of Feminist Activism, 1966–1974," *Law and History Review* 28, no. 3 (2010): 578–579.

47 Kluchin and Caneva, "Heather Booth."

48 Benería, "In the Wilderness of One's Inner Self," 257–258.

49 Ruth Beaglehole, "Ventures in Daycare," in *The New Woman's Survival Catalog*, ed. Grimstad and Smith, 95.

50 Heather Booth, "Chicago Women's Liberation Union: If We Organize We Can Change the World. But Only if We Organize!" (Paper presented at "A Revolutionary Moment: Women's Liberation in the late 1960s and early 1970s," a conference organized by the Women's, Gender, and Sexuality Studies Program at Boston University, Mar. 27–29, 2014), accessed Aug. 30, 2015, http://www.bu.edu/wgs/files/2013/10/Booth -Chicago-Women%E2%80%99s-Liberation-Union-If-we-organize-we-can-change-the -world-but-only-if-we-organize.pdf.

51 Ibid.

52 Rosalyn Baxandall, "Catching the Fire," in *The Feminist Memoir Project*, ed. Blau DuPlessis and Snitow, 217–218.

53 Wolfson, "Clenched Fist, Open Heart," 269–270.

54 Ibid., 278.

55 Ibid., 276–278.

56 Laura Kaplan, *The Story of Jane: The Legendary Underground Feminist Abortion Service* (Chicago: University of Chicago Press, 1995), 48.

57 Polatnick, "Diversity in Women's Liberation Ideology," 687.

58 Kaplan, *The Story of Jane*, 74.

59 Ibid., 18.

60 Ibid., 135.

61 Ibid., 132.

62 Wolfson, "Clenched Fist, Open Heart," 278.

63 Kaplan, *The Story of Jane*, 45.

64 Wolfson, "Clenched Fist, Open Heart," 278.

9 ✦ CONTESTED GEOGRAPHY

The Campaign against Pornography and the Battle for Urban Space in Minneapolis

KIRSTEN DELEGARD

Between 1970 and 1977, millions of Americans made virtual visits to Minneapolis thanks to *The Mary Tyler Moore Show*, which beamed images from Nicollet Mall into living rooms across the country. The popular prime-time television show opened each week with Mary striding through the city's parks and downtown, stopping only to throw her hat in the air in a fit of exuberance. This moment—which became one of the most memorable scenes in television history—gave vicarious pleasure to viewers who cheered her ability to walk unaccompanied and unmolested in public.[1] Her bold claim to urban space cast Minneapolis as a site of liberation for women who sought to realize hopes and dreams outside of traditional marriage and motherhood.

This opening sequence belied the reality of life in Minneapolis, where a majority of women found they could not move through public spaces without harassment. Just as *The Mary Tyler Moore Show* went off the air in 1977, women in the Powderhorn and Central neighborhoods mobilized to remake the urban environment in this residential area of the city where the proliferation of pornographic bookstores and movie theaters had created a streetscape that was toxic for women. Empty storefronts had provided the foundation on which a pair of local entrepreneurs built what one local newspaper called an "empire of smut." The Alexander brothers had sensed opportunity in the wake of loosening obscenity laws and the rise of "porno chic," which brought sexually explicit films like *Deep Throat* to mainstream movie theaters.[2] In the late 1960s, the Alexanders began building an adult

entertainment district along Lake Street, once a vibrant commercial corri-
dor for a residential section of the city. Between 1977 and 1986, residents
fought to push these businesses out of South Minneapolis. This essay tells
the sometimes heartbreaking story of their campaign, which has been both
forgotten and misremembered. It shows the challenges of creating an inclusive urban environment and the pitfalls for progressive activists of making
common cause with police and city officials.

The neighborhood women took aim at the Alexander brothers and their
male customers, whom they blamed for making the commercial backbone
of their neighborhood into a public space hostile to women. But their real
struggle was with decades of urban renewal policies that had created a gendered streetscape that was overwhelmingly male. Working in a moment
of heady feminist possibility—it was the era of *Free to Be You and Me* and
the year of the National Women's Conference—these women articulated a
politics of place. They illuminated the gender hierarchies that structured the
geography of their everyday lives, connecting the shape of the built environment with the oppressive street climate for women and girls. They objected
to the new urban economy that had taken root in the wake of suburban-
ization and construction of the freeways, which made their neighborhood
into the domain of men seeking anonymous sexual encounters with one
another as well as women in the sex trade. Over the course of the decade,
their frustration with being harassed in public blossomed into a movement
that made Lake Street into contested geography.[3]

Like the women in Finn Enke's groundbreaking history of second-wave
feminism in the Upper Midwest, these activists did not identify primarily
as feminists in the early years of their campaign. Instead, they articulated an
attachment to place. But it was a landscape that was already shaped by politics. This section of South Minneapolis was home to the Amazon bookstore
(the longest-running feminist bookstore in the country) and the Women's
Coffeehouse, which brought feminists from all over the region together on
Friday and Saturday nights to dance, theorize, and organize.[4] The stretch of
Lake Street that became the center of the pornography district bordered the
Powderhorn neighborhood, known in some circles as "Dyke Heights" for
its high concentration of visible and politically engaged lesbians. Powder-
horn was the epicenter of the loose network of activists affiliated with the
Lesbian Feminist Organizing Committee (LFOC), an organization started
by Karen Clark, who used this coalition to win election to the Minnesota
House of Representatives in 1980. She was one of the first open lesbians

to be elected to office in Minnesota.[5] This social geography shaped these neighborhood activists, who seamlessly integrated feminist analysis and critiques of urban renewal into a bid for local control of neighborhood public spaces. They were comfortable "enacting feminism" to intervene on Lake Street to make it more welcoming to women and girls.[6]

By 1983, despite years of protests, lobbying, and advocacy, the neighborhood activists had made little headway in their battle with pornography purveyors. Hoping to find an innovative way to break a frustrating impasse, they solicited assistance from Andrea Dworkin and Catharine MacKinnon, two nationally known feminist theorists who were visiting the city to teach a class at the University of Minnesota law school.[7] The pair had been working together for years to develop their argument that pornography scripted women's oppression. At the invitation of these local activists, they moved from the classroom into city hall. There, they presented their analysis to local elected officials, who commissioned them to write an amendment to the city's already expansive civil rights ordinance that would recast pornography as a violation of women's civil rights; opponents viewed the measure as a de facto ban on pornography.[8]

The intervention of Dworkin and MacKinnon changed the terms of debate about pornography in Minneapolis, transforming a struggle over public space into a major skirmish in what became known as the "sex wars." Media from around the world watched the city council approve the Dworkin and MacKinnon ordinance during the winter of 1983–84. The measure was vetoed by Mayor Donald Fraser.[9] But Dworkin and MacKinnon were able to use the ensuing publicity storm to jump-start their national crusade. The ordinance they wrote in Minneapolis would later be considered for adoption by cities from Los Angeles to Cambridge, Massachusetts.[10]

In the years since the "sex wars," antipornography activism has been omitted from synthetic narrative accounts of second-wave feminism or even autobiographical accounts like that written by Minnesota feminist Arvonne Fraser, who ultimately dismissed the debates over pornography as peripheral to the quest for women's liberation.[11] Instead, the story of Dworkin and MacKinnon and their ordinance has been documented by critics and opponents who viewed the movement against pornography as a perversion of feminism or an unholy alliance between feminist sexual puritans and the Christian Right.[12] The Minneapolis ordinance has been remembered as one chapter in a binary battle between "sex-positive" and antipornography feminists.

This narrow focus on the pornography ordinance has obscured the campaign that laid the groundwork for this measure to be considered. This essay recount this history from the vantage point of the people who first raised concerns about the way that adult entertainment businesses were changing their neighborhoods. Later debates about pornography and its implications for feminist theory or First Amendment legal precedent have obscured the original concerns of these protesters, who sought to create public spaces that served the people—especially the women and girls—who lived in the city.[13] Rooting this protest in place and time helps to resituate this activism on a continuum of political work inspired by second-wave feminism that includes Take Back the Night marches and self-defense clinics.[14] And it shows the perils of calling on police for assistance. Greater police presence in the bookstores did little to curb the harassment of women and made a site of sexual liberation into a danger zone for men exploring their attraction to other men.

THE GENDERED STREETSCAPE

The grassroots campaign against pornography in Minneapolis centered on Lake Street, which began as an ordinary commercial thoroughfare that connected the city's ritzy lake district to the Mississippi River. Lake Street was not downtown but uptown, the place where early twentieth-century residents of the city's leafy streetcar suburbs could find the necessities of life. The growth of the streetcar system in the city spawned a series of small shopping "centers" that bound together the mostly working-class Scandinavian enclaves that bordered Lake Street. This local economy began to erode in 1928 with the construction of a huge Sears Roebuck complex at the corner of Chicago Avenue and Lake Street.[15] Hailed as a sign of the street's vitality as a retail center, the complex functioned like a postwar suburban shopping mall, drawing customers from a wide area who appreciated the convenience of parking their automobiles in the store's vast parking lot. But by the end of World War II, even the presence of this behemoth retailer did little to quell concerns that Lake Street— like all urban shopping districts—was imperiled. City leaders sought to rescue their communities from obsolescence by remaking shopping districts that were first constructed to be navigated on foot or by streetcars to accommodate the automobile.[16]

In Minneapolis, planners and political leaders embraced urban renewal with gusto.[17] They flattened 40 percent of the downtown to rid themselves of the largest skid row in the region.[18] They traded streetcars for buses.[19] And they worked assiduously to relieve traffic congestion and provide ample parking, two key dictates of the decade's urban renewal orthodoxy. These preoccupations prompted the city to transform Lake Street. First they pulled up the streetcar tracks. Then they repaved, widened, and illuminated the street with hundreds of fluorescent fixtures, in the hope of creating what was known at the time as a "Great White Way." Planners in Minneapolis took their cues from national experts, who argued that these measures were necessary to ensure that white, middle-class women would feel comfortable patronizing urban shopping districts like those along Lake Street.[20]

Despite these massive efforts, women shoppers did abandon Lake Street, unless they were looking for a new car. Dotted by gas stations and drive-ins, the street boasted seventy-four automobile dealers at the most impassioned moment of the American love affair with the car.[21] And thanks to the repaving and widening project, the street became a magnet for *American Graffiti*–style drag racers, who cruised the avenue until the wee hours every night, staging impromptu contests of speed and vying for the attention of female pedestrians.[22] Urban renewal had redrawn the sexual geography of the neighborhood, making a neighborhood shopping street into an arena for masculine sexual competition. And the results would prove especially devastating for the women who remained in the neighborhood.

Lake Street would have been a perfect case study for urbanist Jane Jacobs, who was derided as a "crazy housewife" when she launched a frontal attack on the masculine-dominated urban planning orthodoxy with her claim that planners did not understand how cities actually worked.[23] "Traffic arteries, along with parking lots, gas stations, and drive-ins, are powerful and insistent instruments of city destruction," she asserted, prophetically, in 1961.[24] Lake Street had been refashioned into an area of what Jacobs called "in-between" density: "too low for cities, too high for suburbs. . . . The common fate of such districts nowadays is to be abandoned by people with choice."[25] This is exactly what happened to Lake Street. By 1967, when the new freeway through South Minneapolis bypassed this commercial thoroughfare, the "Great White Way" of the 1950s had come to resemble a dead end. The population of the adjacent neighborhoods had dropped; the poverty rate had spiked; the number of businesses plummeted.[26] Just as Mary Tyler Moore was making television history, a new era was dawning in this section of South Minneapolis. And it would not inspire women to stop on the sidewalk to throw their hats in the air.

THE PORN DISTRICT ON LAKE STREET

The neighborhood's newly empty storefronts created an opening for a pair of local entrepreneurs, Ferris and Edward Alexander, whom the FBI called the "largest smut dealers in the Midwest."[27] For more than two decades, the brothers ran an empire of bookstores and movie theaters that stretched across Minnesota. They seized the opportunity presented by declining property values. As an attorney for the city observed, "Whenever you find a neighborhood in decline, those guys come in to give it the kiss of death."[28] In 1969, they bought the Rialto Theater on Lake Street. Once a destination for family movie-goers, the theater began screening movies like *I Am Curious Yellow* and *Deep Throat*. Soon they opened a bookstore next to the theater; this became the nexus of a growing adult entertainment district. These businesses attracted prostitutes and drew men who were looking for sex from across the metropolitan area.[29]

The South Minneapolis porn district had none of the neon flash of famous sex districts like Times Square in New York. The drab storefronts of the Alexander businesses seemed designed to be unobtrusive. But they were a powerful presence in the neighborhood, changing the environment on the surrounding streets. According to Alderman Mark Kaplan, the bookstores and movie theaters made "men from the suburbs" think that Lake Street was a "free-fire zone" when it came to women.[30] A sympathetic newspaper reporter asserted that this kind of business inflamed "patrons with lust." Pornographic images emboldened customers to "think they can say anything to a woman standing outside as if she's an extension of the bookstore atmosphere and not just someone waiting for the bus to take her to a job that has nothing to do with prostitution, sadomasochism, or bestiality."[31] According to activist Linda Wejcman, the men who patronized these establishments were constantly "hustling women in the neighborhood."[32] Any woman on the street—but especially African American women—were assumed to be prostitutes by men who followed them, sometimes masturbating in public. No one escaped sexual taunts and comments. Men shouted: "Lean on me." And "Hey, baby, I like my meat well-seasoned."[33]

The Alexanders had their defenders, who asserted that this sexual banter was nothing new for Lake Street, which had been known for its cruising culture since the muscle car days.[34] But the women who mobilized in the late 1970s felt that the growth of a concentrated pornography district changed the atmosphere in this section of the city. Jacqui Thompson explained: "When I stand on 4th Avenue and Lake Street and wait for a bus, it makes me uncomfortable."[35] Thompson and other women felt like outsiders in the neighborhood they called home. Grown women no longer felt free to walk these streets. And mothers forbade their daughters from going to McDonald's, a favorite hangout for neighborhood teens.[36] Women who ventured out on to the street in this section of South Minneapolis were assumed to be either sexually suspect or sexually vulnerable. Images of growing female autonomy and feminist possibility stood in stark contrast to the realities of this neighborhood, where the streetscape was ruled by Victorian-era gender conventions.[37] At a moment when feminists were working to make city streets safer and more welcoming for women, the growth of this commercial pornography district made this hostile terrain for women.

In 1977, a group of residents organized Neighborhood Fightback, which focused on calling attention to deteriorating conditions along Lake Street. After these activists organized a picket line outside one of the neighborhood bookstores, the city responded sympathetically, passing a zoning law that outlawed the operation of adult bookstores and theaters within five hundred feet of churches, schools, or residential areas.[38] But this injunction proved short-lived. The Alexander brothers sued the city and won.[39]

"BROWSING" THE BOOKSTORES

In 1979, neighborhood activists regrouped in the wake of this unfavorable ruling. Linda Wejcman—who had been a part of Neighborhood Fightback and would later be elected to the Minnesota House of Representatives—convened a strategy session at her house near Lake Street. The six women in attendance decided that they would forget picketing in favor of a new strategy that they called "browsing." The women decided to make weekly visits to the bookstores on Lake Street where they were courteously confrontational, "standing behind customers, watching customers watch the quarter movies" and "greeting people at the door" (see figure 9.1). Like temperance activists in the nineteenth century, they understood how the mere presence

FIGURE 9.1 In the latter half of the 1970s, neighborhood activists in Minneapolis organized to stop the proliferation of adult entertainment businesses around their homes. Local women decided to stake a claim to the public spaces along Lake Street by paying weekly visits to these businesses, which catered exclusively to men. This photo shows Linda Wejcman, Liz Anderson, Cathy Blacer, Jacqui Thompson, and Becky Anderson on Lake Street. (Photographed by Meg McKinney on July 28, 1979, for the *Minneapolis Tribune*. Used with the permission of John Wareham and the *Minneapolis Star Tribune*. © Minneapolis Star Tribune. All rights reserved.)

of women disrupted an all-male environment.[40] In a nod to popular under-standings of sexual respectability, "browsers" dressed as though they were on their way to an afternoon of bridge. Later they wryly dubbed one of their groups a "sewing circle." This time-tested strategy created a tension that embarrassed customers who visited the bookstores in search of an exclu-sively masculine milieu.[41] Their goal, according to Jacqui Thompson, was to make the men in the stores feel like the women on the street. "It makes the people in the stores uncomfortable and that's the point," she explained.[42]

Their protest was effective. Clerks responded to this incursion by telling the women to leave and then calling the police. As one man declared: "It just doesn't look right to have a bunch of women standing in here."[43] This bold challenge to the sexual geography of the bookstores was disruptive enough to be illegal, according to one of the lawyers representing the Lake Street pornographers. "These people are weird," declared attorney Thomas Burke, who asserted that their desire to embarrass men interested in pornography indicated mental instability and a need for greater male supervision. "If my mother did this, I'd have her put away."[44]

None of these women were arrested or sent to jail. And in these early years of mobilization against the porn industry in Minneapolis, these activ-ists had little interest in the theoretical implications of pornography or ques-tions of sexual morality or even the images of women in the media. This activism was about claiming urban space. Activist Liz Anderson asserted that "we were careful to take no position on the content of the material, but rather to focus on neighborhood blight."[45] The Lake Street activists were fol-lowing the lead of other feminists at the time who fought male hegemony in the halls of power and on the "ground of everyday life."[46] Their efforts made the porn district on Lake Street into one of many "contested spaces" during the 1970s, when feminists used all kinds of street theater and direct action to challenge exclusionary and threatening practices that inhibited women's ability to move freely in public or to have full access to restaurants, bars, or parks.[47]

These women looked at the pornography businesses through the lens of class and gender, calling on fellow citizens to resist capitalist efforts to shape both sexuality and the city. They took aim at both the store owners and the patrons, whom they perceived to be wealthy professionals who worked downtown and lived in the suburbs. "You'd see them park their big cars and come in in their nice suits," Wejcman said. "We knew they weren't from this neighborhood because the only people around here with big cars are the pimps. Most of them work downtown but don't go to the stores down there because they don't want to run into somebody who might know them. So they stop out here on their way home to the suburbs."[48] Activists like Wejcman saw both of these groups to be profiting from the exploitation of these struggling neighborhoods, where people were determined to reestablish some modicum of local control after decades of top-down development efforts.

WHO USED THE BOOKSTORES?

For most neighborhood activists, wealthy, heterosexual men from the suburbs were the villains in this drama. Yet this narrative of urban exploitation glossed over a critical point that would prove contentious as the protests intensified. Many of the men who were patronizing the bookstores and movie theaters were seeking sexual encounters with other men. The bookstores—perceived as a pathological presence by women in the neighborhood—served as a critical community space for men wanting to explore same-sex desire without publicly identifying as gay. The establishments owned by the Alexanders were known for encouraging male "cruising"; employees cut "glory holes" in the plywood sheets that separated the viewing cubicles in these bookstores. This allowed men in adjoining booths to have sex through the wall, without ever seeing one another.[49] This grim-sounding arrangement met the needs of "closeted" gays, according to gay activist Robert Halfhill, who explained that "since most gays are still closeted, bookstores are one of the few places most of us can meet."[50] The situation was hardly ideal, gay activist and editor Tim Campbell admitted, conceding that bookstore sex was not "good sex . . . but it's better than none at all."[51] If stores, as Jane Jacobs observed, make "an urban neighborhood a community," these businesses had redrawn the geography of belonging in this stretch of South Minneapolis.[52] Lake Street presented a landscape of sexual harassment and humiliation for women; but it offered a site of sexual liberation for men grappling with their attraction to other men. According to Campbell, the street's bookstores made possible the gay rights movement that was taking shape in Minneapolis.[53]

To draw attention to their concerns, antipornography activists in the Lake Street neighborhoods recruited city council members, police officers, and journalists to do guided "tours" of adult bookstores and movie theaters.[54] Police responded to the resulting pressure. But the nature of their reaction illuminates the perils of demanding assistance from law enforcement. The officers deployed to the bookstores were animated by the conventional priorities of the "morals squad," which had been created to monitor sex workers and sexual dissenters. Stationed on Lake Street, police did little to improve the street climate for women. Instead, under the leadership of Chief Tony Bouza, who had fixated on the "glory holes" during his tour of the district with neighborhood activists, they focused their attention on the men who were using the bookstores to have sexual encounters with other men.[55]

In a long-running sting operation that used officers to encourage male patrons to initiate sexual contact in bookstores and movie theaters, police arrested 3,500 men for "indecent conduct" between 1979 and 1985.[56] "This movement against pornography bookstores has had a terrible effect on the gay community," gay activist Robert Halfhill testified to the city council in December 1983. The arrests sparked homophobic police brutality against the targeted men, leading to many injuries and at least one suicide. "We had a police officer beat a gay up," Halfhill recounted, "and he said, 'you mother fucking faggot, if I ever see you around here again they will find you in the river and your own mother won't be able to recognize you.'"[57]

Gay activists tried to make common cause with the neighborhood activists. "We agree on goals," Campbell asserted. "I would like to see queer bashing stopped, I would like to see sexual assault against women stopped."[58] And antipornography activists were frustrated by the police. "The problem," neighborhood activist Liz Anderson told Bouza, "is not the gays in the bookstores. What can we do about the women being hassled on the streets around the bookstores?"[59] But these two groups were unable to forge an alliance to press the police department for change. Instead, the campaign against the bookstores deepened already bitter divides between gay men and lesbian women, who were angry with the men who were using the bookstores, which they felt were harmful to women. "I'm sick of defending faggots, child sex, bathroom arrests, and pornography," one woman asserted.[60] And gay men were enraged by what they viewed as an unwillingness to listen to their grievances about police abuse and public space. "Dworkin can take her campaign against pornography and shove it up her wazoo," Campbell proclaimed. "Dworkin is far more dangerous to women than all the porn stores in the universe."[61] By the early 1980s, the grassroots antipornography campaign in Minneapolis had opened rifts in the gay and lesbian community that would prove difficult to heal in the years that followed.

By 1983, antipornography activists had reached a stalemate. The city had failed to close down the Alexander brothers, who had a virtual monopoly on pornography sales in Minnesota. Neighborhood activists continued to hound city hall and the police, who ignored complaints of street harassment in favor of a campaign against men who had "public sex" in adult movie theaters and bookstores. It was at this point that Andrea Dworkin and Catharine MacKinnon entered the story. And the chronology of the events that followed is well known.[62]

Dworkin and MacKinnon seemed to offer a way to clear the political logjam. After years of refining their analysis of pornography as the root of women's oppression, they could offer neighborhood activists a new weapon for their battle with the local adult entertainment conglomerate. They met with the Neighborhood Pornography Task Force, which had been organized in response to the success of the Alexander lawsuit, providing them with new language and logic for making their case. The group asked Dworkin and MacKinnon to speak before the city's zoning committee. Neighbors figured they had nothing to lose. "Dworkin has an idea? Is it a good one? Who knows? Let's see," one resident recalls thinking.[63] "This time we're trying to be innovative," the president of the Powderhorn neighborhood association proclaimed. "This zoning is a bunch of malarkey and gets nowhere. So we're going to approach it from the standpoint that pornography is really violence against women."[64]

On October 18, 1983, Dworkin and MacKinnon directed the zoning committee to forget about regulating pornography. Pornography was more than an affront to decency. It was a crime against women, a violation of their civil rights. Pornography, MacKinnon asserted, was "a form of discrimination on the basis of sex," which Minneapolis already prohibited.[65] What was needed, they argued, was a measure that would give women harmed by pornography an avenue for redress.[66] Dworkin and MacKinnon were immediately hired to write the new ordinance.

The city's history gave special resonance to MacKinnon's "civil rights approach" to pornography. Under the leadership of an ambitious mayor named Hubert Humphrey, the city had been one of the first in the nation to adopt a civil rights ordinance prohibiting racial and religious discrimination in the late 1940s.[67] Over the years this ordinance had been expanded to include age, marital status, disability, and sex. And in 1974, Minneapolis was one of the first big cities to amend its ordinance further to protect lesbians, gays, and transsexuals.[68] The city perceived itself as a citadel of civil rights, which made it a friendly proving ground for Dworkin and MacKinnon's paradigm-shifting attack on patriarchy. Though it was later deployed for conservative purposes, the MacKinnon and Dworkin ordinance took root in the fertile terrain of progressive intentions.[69] This strategy was precedent-breaking yet familiar, offering an opportunity for the city to reaffirm its commitment to social justice. "Let's light a candle for Hubert Humphrey and pass this. We'll send a message to the purveyors of pornography that an era has ended when women can be denied their rights," city council member Walter Dziedzic told the *Star Tribune*.[70]

On December, 30, 1983, the Minneapolis city council approved the Dworkin/MacKinnon ordinance in a seven-to-six vote.[71] But six days after the city council cast its historic vote, the measure was vetoed by Mayor Fraser, described by one reporter as a "feminist by philosophy and by voting record." Fraser used the language of the Minnesota Civil Liberties Union to argue that the measure would never pass judicial review.[72] Dworkin and MacKinnon did not linger in the city to contribute to the debate that continued to rage until the Supreme Court declared bans on pornography to be unconstitutional in 1986.[73]

Six months after the pornography ordinance was vetoed by Fraser, Wejcman complained that "we still have the bookstores, we still have the prostitutes, we still have people being hassled on the street." She begged the city to take some action. "After seven years, we are a little desperate and the Federal Government won't send us any Sherman tanks."[74] Neighborhood activists like Wejcman found themselves caught in the crossfire after the MacKinnon ordinance. The question of pornography was so overwhelming for one young woman that she made the decision to douse herself with gasoline and set herself alight in a downtown Minneapolis bookstore that had a section of pornographic magazines. Ruth Christensen left a letter that explained that her self-immolation in Shinder's bookstore was necessary since she could "no longer accept living" in a society where "men do not want to end the degradation and exploitation of women." This realization prompted her "to take my life and to destroy the persons who have destroyed me."[75]

No other women made so public their despair. But by the summer of 1984, many of the neighborhood activists felt betrayed and abandoned. Those who had shared personal stories found themselves stigmatized. Threatening phone calls and letters had forced others to move, leaving behind the neighborhoods they had fought to preserve.[76] While some local women joined Dworkin and MacKinnon's national crusade, others found themselves burned by the political firestorm that consumed the city in the wake of their proposal, which did nothing to change the built environment that had become so toxic for women.[77]

When activists began their campaign against the pornographic bookstores and movie theaters in their neighborhood in 1977, they were driven by the desire to repair an urban space that had been damaged by decades of federally funded urban renewal policies. Their neighborhood, they felt, had been abandoned by those with power and money. But they had claimed this space and they wanted everyone—but especially women—to feel welcome in the public venues surrounding their homes. This simple goal proved impossible to attain. Neighborhood women were relentless. But their protests, lobbying, and policy-making proved ineffectual. They faced a deteriorating climate for small businesses in an increasingly impoverished part of the city. And they were working against a pair of wealthy pornographers with the economic resources to fund endless legal challenges. Moreover, by enlisting the police in their efforts, they unwittingly intensified homophobic violence in this contested space. This created rifts that are still evident in the progressive political landscape of Minneapolis.[78] This is perhaps the most enduring legacy of this political mobilization.

Visit Lake Street today and no signs of the earlier struggle remain. A parking lot sits on the site of the notorious Rialto Theater and the nearby Avalon has been transformed into the acclaimed Heart of the Beast Theater, known for politically and community-engaged puppetry. The bookstores and video rental stores disappeared with the advent of the Internet; men now have myriad venues for exploring their attraction to other men. A new generation of immigrants has established small businesses that have brought foot traffic back to the street. There is nothing in the physical environment to remind us of when Lake Street was a pornography district. And no physical marker is necessary. But we need to remember the power of this place, which inspired a deep commitment to a vision of a progressive metropolis that could ensure full citizenship for everyone. Central to this dream was the utopian ideal that women and girls should be able to walk freely through public space without fear of misogynistic violence.

NOTES

This essay developed in conversation with a generous group of readers: Jacqueline Castledine, Anne Valk, Leslie Brown, Jacquelyn Hall, Jacquelyn DeVries, Michael Lansing, Kate Bjork, Linda Janke, Peter Hennigan, James Eli Shiffer, Kevin Ehrman-Solberg and Lizzie Ehrenhalt. I am so grateful for their insights and editing.

1 One of the most famous sequences in television history, MTM's walk has inspired endless parodies and homages, many of which have been recorded on YouTube. "The Top 100 Moments in Television," *Entertainment Weekly*, Feb. 19, 1999; "Minneapolis Bestowing Immortality on a Sitcom Tam-Tosser," *New York Times* (hereafter *NYT*), Dec. 26, 2001.

2 See "Pornography in Minnesota" series in the *Minneapolis Star* (hereafter *Star*), Nov. 17, 18, 19, 20, 21, 1975; "Pornography: A Twin Cities Status Report," *Star*, Apr. 10, 1972, 1B; "Ferris Alexander: Patriarch of Porn," *St. Paul Pioneer Press* (hereafter *PP*), Jan. 26, 1986; Mike Kaszuba and Lynna Williams, "Police and City Attorney at Odds over Porno Case," *Star*, Aug. 20, 1980; Dennis Cassano, "Alexander Brothers Launch New Plan," *Minneapolis Tribune* (hereafter *Tribune*), Jan. 9, 1981, 1B; "Patriarch of Porn" series, *PP*, Jan. 26, 1986; Kevin Ehrman-Solberg, "The Battle of the Bookstores and Gay Sexual Liberation in Minneapolis" (Senior Honors Thesis, History Department, Augsburg College, 2014). For a discussion of how changing obscenity laws allowed pornographic films like *Deep Throat* to achieve mainstream box office success nationally in the early 1970s see Ralph Blumenthal, "Porno Chic: 'Hard-Core' Grows Fashionable—and Very Profitable," *NYT*, Jan. 21, 1973; and Thomas Borstelman, *The 1970s: A New Global History from Civil Rights to Economic Inequality* (Princeton: Princeton University Press, 2012).

3 I borrow this terminology and concept from A. Finn Enke, *Finding the Movement: Sexuality, Contested Space, and Feminist Activism* (Durham, NC: Duke University Press, 2007). See also Georgina Hickey, "The Geography of Pornography: Neighborhood Feminism and the Battle against 'Dirty Bookstores' in Minneapolis," *Frontiers: A Journal of Women's Studies* 32, no. 1 (2001): 125–151. For other examples of spatial analysis in feminist history see Jessica Ellen Sewell, *Women and the Everyday City: Public Space in San Francisco, 1890–1915* (Minneapolis: University of Minnesota Press, 2011); Sarah Deutsch, *Women and the City: Gender, Space, and Power in Boston, 1870–1940* (New York: Oxford University Press, 2000); and Mary Ryan, *Women in Public* (Baltimore: Johns Hopkins University Press, 1990).

4 Enke, *Finding the Movement*; Stewart Van Cleve, *Land of Ten Thousand Loves: A History of Queer Minnesota* (Minneapolis: University of Minnesota Press, 2012).

5 Van Cleve, *Land of Ten Thousand Loves*, 91–92, 244–246.

6 Enke, *Finding the Movement*, 2, 5.

7 Paul Brest and Ann Vandenberg, "Politics, Feminism, and the Constitution: The Anti-Pornography Movement in Minneapolis," *Stanford Law Review* 39, no. 607 (Feb. 1987): 607–661; Hickey, "The Geography of Pornography"; Donald Alexander Downs, *The New Politics of Pornography* (Chicago: University of Chicago Press, 1989).

8 See original ordinance in Box 2, The Records of Organizing Against Pornography (OAP), Minnesota Historical Society (MHS).

9 For a sense of the global media attention given this local debate see "Minneapolis Rights Attack on Pornography Weighed," *NYT*, Dec. 18, 1983, 22; Ellen Goodman, "Porn Ordinance in Shaky Law," column from the *Boston Globe* reprinted in the *Star Tribune* (hereafter *ST*), Jan. 14, 1984, 8A; Martha S. Allen, "Letters, Calls Pour in As Mayor Ponders Antipornography Rule," *ST*, Jan. 5, 1984, 1A; "Liberal Mayor 'Hurt' by Attacks over Civil Rights," *USA Today*, July 27, 1984; Eleanor J. Bader, "Porn Wars Raging in Legislatures and Courts," *Guardian*, Dec. 19, 1984; David Ruhenstein, "Pornography Law Splits Minneapolis," *In These Times*, Jan. 16–24, 1984, 5–6; "Minneapolis Gets a Statute on Smut," *NYT*, Dec. 31, 1984; "Mayor of Minneapolis Vetoes Measure to Ban Pornography," *NYT*, Jan. 6, 1984; Claudia Waterloo, "Fighting Porn and Other Plagues on Women," *Wall Street Journal*, Jan. 27, 1984.

10 Lisa Duggan and Nan Hunter, eds., *Sex Wars: Sexual Dissent and Political Culture* (New York: Routledge, 1995); Downs, *The New Politics of Pornography*; Brest and Vandenberg, "Politics, Feminism, and the Constitution."

11 Sara Evans, *Tidal Wave: How Women Changed America at Century's End* (New York: Free Press, 2003); Gail Collins, *When Everything Changed: The Amazing Journey of American Women From 1960 to the Present* (New York: Little, Brown, 2009). This debate is briefly mentioned in Estelle Freedman, *No Turning Back: The History of Feminism and the Future of Women* (New York: Ballantine Books, 2002), 270–272; and Ruth Rosen, *The World Split Open: How the Modern Women's Movement Changed America* (New York: Viking, 2000), 191–194; Arvonne Fraser, *She's No Lady: Politics, Family, and International Feminism*, ed. Lori Sturdevant (Minneapolis: Nodin Press, 2007).

12 Brest and Vandenberg, "Politics, Feminism, and the Constitution"; Downs, *The New Politics of Pornography*; Catharine MacKinnon and Andrea Dworkin, *In Harm's Way: The Pornography Civil Rights Hearings* (Cambridge, MA: Harvard University Press, 1997); Duggan and Hunter, *Sex Wars*; Pamela Butler, "Sex and the Cities: Re-evaluating 1980s Feminist Politics in Minneapolis and St. Paul," in *Queer Twin Cities: Twin Cities GLBT Oral History Project*, ed. Michael David Franklin, Larry Knopp, Kevin P. Murphy, Ryan Patrick Murphy, Jennifer L. Pierce, Jason Ruiz, and Alex T. Urquhart (Minneapolis: University of Minnesota Press, 2010), 203–239.

13 Kathryn Abrams, "Sex War Redux: Agency and Coercion in Feminist Legal Theory," *Columbia Law Review* 95 (1995): 304–376; Brest and Vanderberg, "Politics, Feminism, and the Constitution"; Downs, *The New Politics of Pornography*.

14 This essay belongs to a growing body of work that revisits antipornography activism. Claire Bond Potter, "Taking Back Times Square: Feminist Repertoires and the Transformation of Urban Space in Late Second Wave Feminism," in "Calling the Law into Question," ed. Andy Urban and Amy Tyson, special issue, *Radical History Review* 113 (Apr. 2012): 67–80; Butler, "Sex and the Cities"; Hickey, "The Geography of Pornography." For links in Minneapolis between antipornography feminism and Take Back the Night see Box 2, OAP.

15 Judith A. Martin and David A. Lanegran, *Where We Live: The Residential Districts of Minneapolis and Saint Paul* (Minneapolis: University of Minnesota Press, 1983), 17.

16 Alison Isenberg, *Downtown America: A History of the Place and the People Who Made It* (Chicago: University of Chicago Press, 2004), 168–173.

17 Judith A. Martin and Antony Goddard, *Past Choices/Present Landscapes: The Impact of Urban Renewal on the Twin Cities* (Minneapolis: University of Minnesota Press, 1989); John R. Borchert, *Legacy of Minneapolis: Preservation amid Change* (Bloomington, MN: Voyageur, 1983); Martin and Lanegran, *Where We Live*.

18 Joseph Hart and Edwin C. Hirschoff, *Down and Out: The Life and Death of Minneapolis's Skid Row* (Minneapolis: University of Minnesota Press, 2002); David Rosheim, *The Other Minneapolis, or The Rise and Fall of the Gateway, the Old Minneapolis Skid Row* (Maquoketa, IA: Andromeda Press, 1978); James Eli Shiffer, *The King of Skid Row: John Bacich and the Twilight Years of Old Minneapolis* (Minneapolis: University of Minnesota Press, 2016).

19 John W. Diers and Aaron Isaacs, *Twin Cities by Trolley: The Streetcar Era in Minneapolis and St. Paul* (Minneapolis: University of Minnesota Press, 2007).

20 Isenberg, *Downtown*, 166–171.

21 John S. Adams and Barbara J. Van Drasek, *Minneapolis/St. Paul: People, Place, and Public Life* (Minneapolis: University of Minnesota Press, 1993), 115.

22 This history is based on a series of oral histories conducted by the Lake Street Council. See "Brad Herring Remembers Drag Racing on Lake Street," accessed Apr. 21, 2015, https://www.youtube.com/watch?v=gKTn6wlyLFw; "Bill Nelson, Oral History of Lake Street," accessed Apr. 21, 2015, https://www.youtube.com/watch?v=vOfo5V72QdI 15.

23 Alice Sparberg Alexiou, *Jane Jacobs: Urban Visionary* (New Brunswick, NJ: Rutgers University Press, 2006), 57–67.

24 Jane Jacobs, *The Death and Life of Great American Cities* (New York: Random House, 1961), 338.

25 Ibid., 357.

26 Hickey, "The Geography of Pornography," 128.

27 FBI file, Feb. 10, 1969, General Investigative Division. My thanks to Dave Kenney for requesting and sharing this file. See also "Pornography in Minnesota" series in *Star*, Nov. 17, 18, 19, 20, 21, 1975; "Pornography: A Twin Cities Status Report," *Star*, Apr. 10, 1972, 1B; "Ferris Alexander: Patriarch of Porn," *PP*, Jan. 26, 1986; Mike Kaszuba and Lynna Williams, "Police and City Attorney at Odds over Porno Case," *Star*, Aug. 20, 1980; Dennis Cassano, "Alexander Brothers Launch New Plan," *Tribune*, Jan. 9, 1981, 1B; "Patriarch of Porn" series, *PP*, Jan. 26, 1986; Ehrman-Solberg, "The Battle of the Bookstores."

28 Brest and Vandenberg, "Politics, Feminism, and the Constitution," 608–609.

29 Butler, "Sex and the Cities," 208; Hickey, "The Geography of Pornography"; Brest and Vandenberg, "Politics, Feminism, and the Constitution."

30 Ruth Hammond, "Porn Arouses Neighborhood Passion," *Tribune*, Jan. 31, 1981, Pornography subject file, Minneapolis collection, Hennepin County Central Library (HCLB).

31 Ibid.

32 Interview by Georgina Hickey, June 15, 2008, quoted in "The Geography of Pornography," 130.

33 Hammond, "Porn Arouses Neighborhood Passion"; Tom Sorensen, "'Browsing' Is the Weapon Women Use to Attack Neighborhood Pornography," *Tribune*, July 28, 1979,

1B; David Carr, "Come Tour with Me: Pornography on Parade," *Twin Cities Reader*, Sept. 28, 1983, 4; Helen Robinson and Ann Stumme, "Adult Bookstores in Minneapolis," *Star*, Aug. 4, 1977, Pornography subject file, HCLB.

34 Hammond, "Porn Arouses Neighborhood Passion."

35 Sorensen, "'Browsing' Is the Weapon." See also testimony of Wanda Laurence, Session II, Public Hearings on Ordinances to Add Pornography as Discrimination Against Women, Dec. 12, 1983, Box 2, OAP.

36 Hammond, "Porn Arouses Neighborhood Passion"; Sorensen, "'Browsing' Is the Weapon"; Helen Robinson and Ann Stumme, "Adult Bookstores in Minneapolis," *Star*, Aug. 4, 1977, Pornography subject file, Minneapolis collection, Hennepin County Central Library.

37 For a description of these conventions see Enke, *Finding the Movement*, 6; Judith R. Walkowitz, *City of Dreadful Delight: Narratives of Sexual Danger in Late-Victorian London* (Chicago: University of Chicago Press, 1992).

38 Sorensen, "'Browsing' Is the Weapon"; "The 7th Annual Urban Journalism Workshop Reports on Adult Bookstores in Minneapolis," *Star*, Aug. 4, 1977; "City Loses Lawsuit on Adult Bookstore," *ST*, Apr. 28, 1979, Pornography subject file, HCLB.

39 Margaret Zack, "Adult Business Zoning Law Challenged," *ST*, June 26, 1981, Pornography subject file, HCLB.

40 Bessie Scovell, *A Brief History of the Minnesota Women's Christian Temperance Union from Its Organization, September 6, 1877 to 1939* (Minneapolis–St. Paul, MN: Bruce Publishing Company, 1939).

41 This strategy was also employed by cold war peace activists. See Jacqueline Castledine, *Cold War Progressives: Women's Interracial Organizing for Peace and Freedom* (Urbana: University of Illinois Press, 2012) and Andrea Estepa, "Taking the White Gloves Off: Women Strike for Peace and 'the Movement' 1967–73," in *Feminist Coalitions: Historical Perspectives on Second-Wave Feminism in the United States*, ed. Stephanie Gilmore (Urbana: University of Illinois Press, 2008).

42 Sorensen, "'Browsing' Is the Weapon"; Downs, *The New Politics of Pornography*, 54.

43 Sorensen, "'Browsing' Is the Weapon."

44 Ibid.

45 Quoted in Downs, *The New Politics of Pornography*, 54.

46 Enke, *Finding the Movement*, 7.

47 Ibid.; Georgina Hickey, "Barred from the Barroom: Second Wave Feminists and Public Accommodations in US Cities," *Feminist Studies* 34, no. 3 (Fall 2008): 382–408.

48 Sorensen, "'Browsing' Is the Weapon."

49 Many thanks to Kevin Ehrman-Solberg for sharing his groundbreaking work with me. Much of the discussion that follows draws on his insights and research. Oral history of Tim Campbell by Kevin Ehrman-Solberg, Augsburg College Honors Thesis Project, in the possession of the author. Quote from Ehrman-Solberg, "The Battle of the Bookstores." See also testimony of Tim Campbell and Robert Halfhill, Session II, Public Hearings on Ordinances to Add Pornography as Discrimination Against Women, Dec. 12, 1983, Box 2, OAP.

50 Ehrman-Solberg, "The Battle of the Bookstores." Quote is from Statement of Robert Halfhill, the Hearing on Ordinances to Add Pornography as Discrimination, Before the Pornography Task Force Committee, Minneapolis City Council, June 7, 1984, Box 2, OAP.

51 Ehrman-Solberg, "The Battle of the Bookstores." Quote is from Tim Campbell, "Bookstore Sex: Therapy Is the Answer: Who Should Get It?" *GLC Voice*, Jan. 7, 1985.

52 Alexiou, *Jane Jacobs*, 57.

53 Tim Campbell, "Dworkin Is the Real Woman Killer," *GLC Voice*, Dec. 5, 1983, 3.

54 Jim Parsons, "City Officials Visit Adult Bookstore," *ST*, Sept. 23, 1983; David Carr, "Come Tour with Me, Pornography on Parade," *Twin Cities Reader*, Sept. 28, 1983, Pornography Subject File, HCLB.

55 Carr, "Come Tour with Me."

56 Ehrman-Solberg, "The Battle of the Bookstores." See also "Police Escalate Gay Harassment," *MCGLR: Lesbian/Gay Newsbriefs*, Dec. 14, 1979, HQ 75, Pamphlet Collection, MHS.

57 Quote is from testimony of Robert Halfhill, Session II, Public Hearings on Ordinances to Add Pornography as Discrimination Against Women, Dec. 12, 1983, Box 2, OAP.

58 Quote is from testimony of Tim Campbell, Session II, Public Hearings on Ordinances to Add Pornography as Discrimination Against Women, Dec. 12, 1983, Box 2, OAP.

59 Ehrman-Solberg, "The Battle of the Bookstores." Quote is from Robert Halfhill, "DFL, Bouza in Heated Exchange over Vice," *Gaily Planet*, Nov. 19, 1980.

60 Quote is from Jill (no surname given) in "Pride Group Snubs Lesbians, Boycott Called," *Equal Time*, June 2, 1982.

61 Tim Campbell, "Dworkin Is the Real Woman Killer," *GLC Voice*, Dec. 5, 1983, 3.

62 Brest and Vandenberg, "Politics, Feminism, and the Constitution"; Downs, *The New Politics of Pornography*; MacKinnon and Dworkin, *In Harm's Way*; Duggan and Hunter, *Sex Wars*; Butler, "Sex and the Cities."

63 Wizard Marks, resident of the Central neighborhood. Oral history by Georgina Hickey quoted in "The Geography of Pornography," 135.

64 Jim Parsons, "Protest Equates Porno, Violence," *ST*, Sept. 29, 1983, Section 2, OAP.

65 Brest and Vandenberg, "Politics, Feminism, and the Constitution," 615.

66 Downs, *The New Politics of Pornography*, 55; Brest and Vanderberg, "Politics, Feminism, and the Constitution"; Hickey, "The Geography of Pornography."

67 Enke, *Finding the Movement*; Randy Stoecker, *Defending Community: The Struggle for Alternative Redevelopment in Cedar-Riverside* (Philadelphia: Temple University Press, 1994); Robert Roscoe, *Milwaukee Avenue: Community Renewal in Minneapolis* (Charleston, SC: History Press, 2013); Hickey, "The Geography of Pornography"; Jennifer A. Delton, *Making Minnesota Liberal: Civil Rights and the Transformation of the Democratic Party* (Minneapolis: University of Minnesota Press, 2002), 93–159; Tim Thurber, *The*

Politics of Equality: Hubert H. Humphrey and the African American Freedom Struggle (New York: Columbia University Press, 1999), 23–48.

68 Van Cleve, *Land of 10,000 Loves*, 83; Delton, *Making Minnesota Liberal*, 93–159.

69 This history helps to debunk the myth that antipornography crusaders were all puppets of the Christian Right. It underscores Claire Bond Potter's assertion that "feminist anti-pornography politics were not conservative, nor is it credible that these radical women became conservatives without being aware of it." Potter, "Taking Back Times Square," 68.

70 Quote from Emily Warren, "Radical Feminism in Political Action: The Minneapolis Pornography Ordinance," case study, Center on Women and Public Policy 2005, accessed Mar. 1, 2016, http://lgi.umn.edu/centers/wpp/women-centered_nonprofits/case_studies/radicalfeminisminpoliticalactiontheminneapolispornographyordinance.html.

71 "Council Passes Pornography Law," *ST*, Dec. 31, 1983, front page.

72 David Carr, "Fraser Vetoes: Pressure's Still On," *Twin Cities Reader*, Jan. 11, 1984, 4–5.

73 Downs, *The New Politics of Pornography*; Brest and Vandenberg, "Politics, Feminism, and the Constitution."

74 Testimony of Linda Wejcman, Task Force Hearing on Ordinances to Add Pornography as Discrimination Against Women, Thursday, June 7, 1984, 66–67, Box 2, OAP.

75 "Text of Ruth Christensen's Letter," *PP*, Apr. 12, 1984, 78.

76 Brest and Vandenberg, "Politics, Feminism, and the Constitution," 654.

77 For a sense of the all-consuming nature of this controversy see editorials and letters to the editor in the *Star Tribune*. For example: "A Dangerous Anti-Pornography Ploy," *ST*, Dec. 28, 1983; "Fraser Should Veto Anti-Porn Ordinance," *ST*, Jan. 4, 1984, Clipping file, Pornography, Minneapolis History Collection, HCLB Special Collections; Mike Kaszuba, "Hallway Full of People Awaited Word of the Ordinance's Fate," *ST*, Jan. 6, 1984; Randy Furst and Jim Parsons, "Groups Plot Strategy for Antipornography Fight," *ST*, Jan. 7, 1984.

78 Van Cleve, *Land of Ten Thousand Loves*, 245–246; Butler, "Sex and the Cities," 220–226.

10 ◆ REMEMBERING TOGETHER

Take Back the Night and the Public Memory of Feminism

ANNE VALK

In a 2011 interview, Andrea, a student, described her anticipation of the upcoming Take Back the Night in Hamilton, Ontario. The yearly event in Hamilton took a form common to many communities: a rally energized participants for an all-woman nighttime march. Walking, chanting, and waving signs, marchers demonstrated their anger and called for action to reduce incidents of sexual violence; male allies clapped and showed their support from the sidelines. Andrea enthused about the gathering: "I was thinking about this—this is the 30th year, it's been 30 years of women working their asses off to put this event together, confronting violence against women. It's really exciting and awesome to be a part of it." Her interviewer, another member of the Hamilton committee, concurred, indicating the importance to her of "celebrat[ing] how many generations of women have been involved in this event, have participated in this struggle, and are still wanting to be part of the event . . . daughters, mothers, grandmothers!" When published on a blog maintained by the Hamilton organizing committee, Andrea's comments helped to build anticipation and ground the march and rally in a tradition of women's organizing.[1]

As Andrea noted, Take Back the Night (TBTN) has a long history. Started during feminism's so-called "second wave," it endured into the "third wave" and beyond.[2] This longevity makes it historically and culturally significant within the context of modern feminism. Along with bridging generations, TBTN has connected communities geographically. Since the 1970s, TBTN, or "Reclaim the Night," the common appellation outside the United States, has been a worldwide phenomenon. That TBTN not only continues but has spread across borders is all the more remarkable given that the event always has been organized at the local level.

This chapter examines TBTN's history as a representation of feminist movement culture. Over the past forty years, TBTN organizers have generated reams of posters and flyers, written press releases and articles, designed and printed T-shirts and banners, and invented chants and traditions. Now preserved in the form of recurrent practices, newspaper articles, social media posts, online photograph displays, and, more rarely, in formalized archival collections of organizing committees, these materials document TBTN's history. Such movement culture created by TBTN organizers and expressed through the annual event mobilizes participants in the moment and sustains TBTN over time.[3]

Public memory has been a self-conscious and central aspect of TBTN's movement culture.[4] Always and inevitably selective, public memory preserves, produces, and perpetuates a shared history that becomes "an active resource on which current discussion and action draw."[5] In her study of feminist collective memory, Maria Grever identified three categories of memory-based resources: ritualized memory in the form of commemorations, traditions, and icons; frozen memory comprising monuments, symbols, and other material forms; and continued memory expressed through written texts and formalized institutions.[6] For activists, the useable past expressed in such forms aims to promote their political interests and mobilize other supporters to their cause. Sara Evans articulated such a motivation when she argued in 1983: "the feminist movement, like any democratic social movement, will build its vision of the future—implicitly or explicitly—on some vision of the past. Having a history is an essential prerequisite to claiming the right to shape the future." Nancy Hewitt has similarly emphasized that the construction of feminist history has been both a political and an academic project. Feminists in the 1970s, for example, turned to archives to resurrect evidence of women's past accomplishments, experiences, and tribulations in order to further their analyses and advance a vision for social change. That activity has continued, with later feminist generations seeking from movement history ways of "improving upon, not just building on, the wave(s) that preceded them."[7]

Collective remembrance shapes TBTN in at least two ways. First, an archive of symbols and ritual practices forms the strands that connect participants across time and place. This archive includes both tangible objects and inherited rituals that compose "the material through which political agendas are performed."[8] In the 1970s, events in one city inspired similar events elsewhere, as activists watched and learned from each other. Later organizers incorporated TBTN's own history into their calls for continued participation. Largely celebratory and self-referential, the archive calls up a tradition of women's collective action and places TBTN at its center. Second, TBTN events explicitly make public the memories of individual participants and individual assaults as a way to understand violence and its impact. Weaving in references to women's and feminist history, as well as incorporating personal recollections, TBTN asks participants to remember together as a means to build community today for the sake of making change in the future.[9]

TBTN's incorporation of history and memory, however, obscures many changes in the event and the larger movements of which it is a part. In its early years, TBTN organizers looked to the past to help them understand and broadly contextualize violence against women. Gradually, noisy demonstrations to reclaim the streets were replaced by more somber commemorative gatherings, often held on college and university campuses. Turning TBTN from protest to tradition, organizers increasingly stressed the history and memories of victims and survivors and celebrated the resilience demonstrated by survivors and activists alike. TBTN still generates pride and spurs action but through its selective uses of memory and history TBTN obscures any critique of its own methods and erases more radical possibilities for change. By looking at the history of TBTN, this article suggests new ways to think about narratives of modern U.S. feminism and, especially, how feminists have mobilized history and memory to support their activism.

ORIGIN STORIES

TBTN emerged in conjunction with the 1970s' and early 1980s' movement to combat violence against women. It formed a mass action arm of this broader effort, using collective protest to complement and expand the work of rape crisis centers and battered women's shelters, institutions which often coordinated the event. TBTN built on consciousness raising and rape speak-outs, examining personal experiences to understand the "rape culture" that pervaded patriarchal societies, past and present. Speak-outs also aimed to lessen the shame that silenced women from talking about sexual assaults and to challenge the pervasive sense that rape victims were responsible for their attacks. In this context, TBTN contributed to feminists' work to make publicly visible women's anger about sexual violence and to leverage pressure for changes in law and public policy.[10]

The more specific origins of Take Back the Night are hard to trace.[11] This difficulty is not surprising given that most events generally have been planned at the local level with minimal coordination across sites. Moreover, most early events did not use the Take Back the Night name. Despite this ambiguity, activists have sought to ground TBTN in history as a way to assert its validity and to celebrate its endurance. Whether displayed on websites, hidden in organizational records, incorporated into event announcements, or conveyed via media accounts, most materials recount a transnational origin story that traces back to protests in Europe in the mid-1970s. For example, a Temple University website traces TBTN to the International Tribunal on Crimes Against Women in Brussels in March of 1976.[12] In contrast, others point to protests across Germany in April 1977 hurriedly organized in response to serial rapes reported in West Berlin.[13] Penning a "Short History" of TBTN in September 1978, members of the Boston Coalition to Take Back the Night recalled that the inspiration for their first event, held only the previous month, came from reading in a British women's newspaper about a demonstration in London the previous year.[14] In the United States, many organizers highlight a 1975 protest following a violent murder in Philadelphia, and a 1977 antiviolence rally organized by the Pittsburgh Alliance Against Rape. At that gathering, activist Anne Pride recited a poem titled "Take Back the Night"; her poem was reprinted and is credited with birthing the name now associated with the annual event.[15] Still other histories, however, associate the movement's start with a November 1978 San Francisco conference against pornography. The publication that resulted from the conference, titled *Take Back the Night: Women on Pornography*, not only took up the TBTN name but also took credit as the first use of that slogan.[16]

Even without an agreed-upon origin story, activists have relied on narratives about TBTN's past to explain its purpose. References to TBTN's lineage appeared in materials produced in the 1970s for public promotion and in internal documents created for activists. An article from Boston's *Gay Community News* titled the "History of Take Back the Night," for instance, appeared in 1978 at the time of the city's first march. Similarly, posters and flyers mark anniversaries, such as the poster from Springfield, Massachusetts, in 1993 (see figure 10.1). And now websites and blogs typically dedicate pages to tracing TBTN's roots.[17]

FIGURE 10.1 Poster from the Third Annual Take Back the Night March, Springfield, Massachusetts, 1993. (Courtesy of the Arise for Social Justice Records, Sophia Smith Collection, Smith College.)

Especially when recounted in the media and promotional materials, the act of tracing TBTN's past has established credibility for the event and for the larger issues it addresses. In addition, notes about lineage reveal points of inspiration and personal and political connections between women in various places. For activists, culling through old meeting minutes and preparing a history of their local movement provided a way to track evolving partnerships and ideas, and to reflect on successes and challenges. These organizational histories revealed activists' awareness that when they coordinated TBTN they were making history and, as such, that history should be documented for the future. They also intended these accounts to be immediately useful to their own organizing. A 1983 history of TBTN in New York City explained, for instance, that "the earliest marches focused primarily on the issue of rape; each year that focus has been redefined and expanded to include more and more of what we, as women, consider to be the violences [sic] in our lives." Their multi-page document charted an expanding coalition that organized the yearly event, their changing relationship to city officials, growing access to resources helpful to coordinate and publicize TBTN, and TBTN's involvement in affiliated events including a conference on crime and social justice and protests against U.S. military intervention in South America and the Caribbean.[18]

Along with showing networks within a single location, references to lineage in TBTN's nascent years illuminated direct connections between different sites. Activists reached out to organizers in other locations, seeking advice and resources to help them get started. Women's newspapers and newsletters facilitated sharing by reporting regularly on events across the country and printing letters from activists. For instance, in 1979, women in Gainesville, Florida, appealed to readers of *off our backs* for "advice on publicity, legal problems, mistakes, and successes."[19]

Through such communications, organizers began to accumulate an archive of materials and knowledge that passed from one place to another. This practice supplied advice and direction to those organizing TBTN. Moreover, by linking activists and locales and ensuring that events in various places shared some similarities, the archive helped form a community around TBTN. Examples from Boston demonstrate how these links shaped subsequent marches in tangible and intangible ways. When organizing the city's first march in August 1978, the Boston coalition consulted activists in Pittsburgh, London, and D.C.—all sites of recent TBTN events. These conversations helped the Boston coalition determine whether to seek police permits, how to publicize the event, if they should allow men to join the protest, and what route their march should take, among other logistical matters. In addition, Boston activists drew substantially from a set of demands and principles written and distributed by D.C. organizers at their first TBTN, only months earlier.[20] The resulting statement produced by Boston women

FIGURE 10.2 Image used to promote 1978 inaugural Take Back the Night in Boston, Massachusetts. This identical design featuring a hand and stars appeared three months later on materials advertising events in another city, Northampton, Massachusetts. (Courtesy of Northeastern University Libraries, Archives and Special Collections Department.)

addressed specific city and state issues and incorporated many demands that overlapped with Washington. These included:

Women have the right to be on the streets when we choose, where we choose, and with whom we choose without being subject to attack or threat.

Women have a right to fight back against the violence directed towards us by all reasonable means necessary.

Women have the right to access to self defense.

No man has the right under any circumstance to abuse, physically or emotionally, any woman. We call for community censure of violence: individuals and groups taking responsibility for reporting, criticizing, breaking into, and ending violence against women wherever it occurs.

Women have the right to control our own bodies, and our own sexuality.
We reclaim the right to determine our own sexual and social identities.

Economic independence for women is a necessary factor in realizing our
right to self determination and enabling us to stop being victims of men's and
institutional violence.[21]

The archive of knowledge and materials that has passed from place to
place also includes visual images. In Massachusetts, for instance, an identical graphic image appeared in materials that publicized the inaugural
TBTN events in Boston in August and Northampton in November. Figure
10.2 shows the hand-drawn depiction of a woman's hand reaching for stars
and the moon and encouraging women to "unite" and "take back the night"
featured on pamphlets distributed in both locations. The archive does not
reveal how this design traveled from one place to another, but given the
technology of the time, it is likely that a hard copy would have passed from
hand to hand.[22]

Like the graphic that passed from Boston to Northampton, other symbols and icons used to promote TBTN have been transmitted across place
and time. These graphics have created and perpetuated a shared visual
vocabulary that references feminist culture as well as the history of TBTN
itself. Activists in western Massachusetts described some of these desired
characteristics. According to minutes from a 1989 meeting, after agreeing
on a slogan—"power in the moonlight, women take back the night"—the
group specified that its poster should include:

a representation of a lunar cycle with women of various colors, abilities, etc.
inside of the circle or a semicircle of lunar cycles with a woman underneath
each phase with uplifted arms, drawing upon the power of the moon, alone,
yet with other women—here also the women represented would not all be
the same image. *Please enlist the aid of graphic designers* for the graphics to
accompany the slogan and stress the above requirements for diversity in representation of women along with the lunar imagery.[23]

In addition to recurrent images of women, often dancing or in motion,
other objects repeat, such as the moon, stars, and raised fists or hands
extended skyward. Posters feature the color purple prominently. An image
depicting a hand grasping a crescent moon, for example, appeared on
materials that Boston organizers used to promote their 1978 TBTN. Their

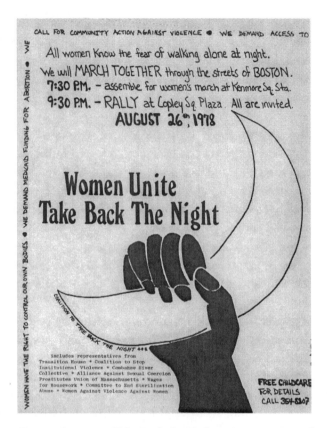

FIGURE 10.3 Poster advertising Take Back the Night in Boston, Massachusetts. The design components on this poster often were incorporated into materials used at other places and times. (Courtesy of Northeastern University Libraries, Archives and Special Collections Department.)

graphic was drawn by hand with details about the rally surrounding it (see figure 10.3).

Thirty-five years later, virtually identical images of a hand clutching a crescent moon appeared on a purple background in two separate posters, one from McMaster University in Hamilton, Ontario, and the other from Northeastern Illinois University. Along the bottom a row of logos indicated organizational sponsors, accessibility, and social media contacts. The technology used to produce and reproduce the posters has changed but the dominant iconography remains the same.[24] The TBTN Foundation, established in 2001, also adopted a crescent moon as its logo. The TBTN Event Manual, available on the foundation's website, contains many examples of

event posters and explains the meaning of such symbols to a new generation of activists:

> Consider using colors that are symbolic. For example, in the TBTN Logo, our
> moon represents our night sky, where we seek to shed the light of hope and
> healing for survivors and awareness. The purple of our font color represents
> our support of survivors of domestic, sexual, and dating violence. Black rep-
> resents the dark night to be reclaimed by survivors, and white embodies the
> light and energy of our cause and the many that stand with us.[25]

Almost certainly, activists who participated in TBTN in the 1970s and
1980s played a role in creating the TBTN Foundation's logo. And it is possible that young activists from Ontario visited the university library in
Boston where the 1978 materials are held. As Kate Eichhorn has argued,
for young activists born after the 1980s the act of mining the mimeo-
graphed and published work of second-wave feminists to create zines and
other print culture is an integral part of their "knowledge making, cultural
production, and activism."[26] Whether deliberate, such as logos developed
under the TBTN Foundation's guidance, or unconscious, these icons nod
to TBTN's own history while the use of recurrent designs suggests the
vitality of an archive of symbols that continues to circulate among feminists. Sharing a library of materials, signs, information, and ideas became
an important method for building a movement against violence against
women and creating a sense of community that spanned from one location and one generation to another.

RECOVERING MEMORIES

TBTN relies on individual and collective memory in many forms to
inspire and shape collective action. Of course, the notion of "taking *back*"
(or "*re*claiming") the night implicitly references the past. By suggesting an
unnamed era when women could safely walk the streets after dark, TBTN
evokes longing for an unspecified, more egalitarian past. TBTN also references the past in more explicit ways. In the 1970s, organizers incorporated historical figures and events into their programs and activities. At
the first Reclaim the Night gathering in Manchester, England, part of a
country-wide movement in November 1977, activists rallied at the foot of

a statue honoring Queen Victoria to call for an end to rape.[27] While the British monarch could have ambiguous meaning, other historical references were more direct. In Boston the first TBTN took place on August 26, 1978, a date that marked the fifty-eighth anniversary of the passing of the women's suffrage amendment to the Constitution. Boston activists chose the date for its convenience. Mentioning it in media coverage, they also appreciated its historical significance. The 1981 TBTN in Washington, D.C., similarly recalled the history of women's fight for the vote when the D.C. Area Feminist Chorus performed "March of the Women," written by a British suffragist.[28]

Scholars have noted that second-wave feminists often looked to suffragists as forerunners to their movement, particularly those militant activists who used hunger strikes and civil disobedience to demand the vote.[29] Thus the Boston and D.C. programs linked TBTN to a history of women's political activism. Organizers of the inaugural TBTN in Northampton, Massachusetts, made this link clearly in materials justifying their gathering: "Our action to TAKE BACK THE NIGHT becomes part of a long herstory of resistance to this violence which maintains control over our lives."[30] With this statement, Northampton organizers invoked the past to call attention to a long history of men's violent oppression of women, as well as women's prolonged struggle for safety.

Historical references also helped organizers understand the causes of sexual violence and contextualize the problem. At one of the earliest TBTN events in the United States, held in 1977 in Pittsburgh, Anne Pride wrote and read a so-called "memorial" invoking numerous women in whose honor activists would reclaim the night, including:

> Factory girls burned to death when their factory door was locked to keep them at their machines
> The women victims of all men's wars
> The women of Bangladesh, raped and abandoned . . .
> Our Native American sisters, raped and ravaged by the great white heroes of the New Frontier
> William Calley's victims at My Lai
> The silent women of Nanking—raped by the thousands by Japanese soldiers in 1937

She also named a host of individuals including Joan of Arc, Kitty Genovese, and several women murdered in or near Pittsburgh in the months before

that city's march. By naming women who died because of industrial acci-
dents, war, imperialism, and religious persecution, Pride framed sexual
violence as another expression of male supremacy and women's economic,
political, and social subordination.[31]

Similarly, the Boston organizers who planned their first gathering wrote
a historical skit about Mary Dyer, found guilty of witchcraft in the seven-
teenth century and hanged on Boston Common. "Violence against women
is not new," the script proclaimed, describing the continuity between
"labeling women who deviated from their traditional roles as witches" in
medieval Europe and colonial Massachusetts and contemporary harassment and attacks on women.[32] Like the Boston protest, other TBTN events
in the 1970s associated feminists with witches; rather than calling up the
murder of suspected witches or characterizing witches as malevolent, these
references suggested positive connections between present-day activists
and earlier women who were persecuted for defying social expectations.
Reclaim the Night events in cities in Europe in 1977 and 1978, for instance,
coincided with the celebration of Halloween, including one event in the
Netherlands where "1,500 women dressed as witches marched with music
and torches." This gathering followed others in West Germany scheduled
the previous year for Walpurgis Night, "a traditional German witches' holiday."[33] Whether intended to celebrate women's resistance and strength or to
explain the more troublesome constancy of violence against women, the
inclusion of witches, suffragists, and other historical references established
a continuum of women's struggle from the sevententh century to TBTN.

By the early 1980s the history TBTN celebrated most often was its
own. Using visual and textual references to past TBTN events, organizers
established the movement's place and importance in the ongoing struggle
against sexual violence. For many participants, the act of attending TBTN
became a way to partake in family and personal rituals while rekindling
friendships and recalling the events of prior years. "At every TBTN I
see people that I only see at the march," one organizer remarked. Others remembered accompanying their parents to the annual rally or eagerly
waiting to be old enough to go. In reminding participants of TBTN's history and their own role in that history, the annual event conveys wom-
en's strength, endurance, and resilience. As one long-time participant in
Hamilton, Ontario's march explains, since it began in 1979, TBTN has
moved from a protest to "a celebration of women's strengths."[34] With this
transition, specific details about the issues, agendas, programs, and even

conflicts that characterized earlier events began to disappear, however. At the same time, the history that activists shared largely focused on superficial aspects of TBTN's history—graphic representations used in posters, for instance, and on individual memories.

This shift from protest to celebration coincided with other changes in commemorative practices and in the TBTN movement. The silent vigils launched by the Mothers of the Plaza de Mayo in Argentina, and the Vietnam Veterans Memorial and the AIDS Memorial Quilt in the United States represented new memorial forms that merged political action, personal memory, and collective mourning.[35] The AIDS Quilt inspired the Clothesline Project, which, since 1991, has been become intertwined with TBTN, although it was originally intended as a one-time display. The Clothesline Project aims to create a tangible exhibit that raises awareness of violence against women and gives survivors and friends and family members another way to express some of the pain of their experiences. Now more than five hundred Clothesline projects have begun with an estimated fifty to sixty thousand shirts that often are displayed in conjunction with TBTN events.[36] Like these other observances, TBTN honors victims but its main impact remains with the living, who can sustain a connection between past and present, among participants, victims, and survivors through the act of remembering together. By reading names of victims, creating opportunities for survivors to tell their stories, and constructing artifacts of remembrance, TBTN organizers hope to raise awareness for individuals who believe they have suffered alone and offer opportunities for collective healing.

TBTN also has incorporated other commemorative activities, especially rituals that resemble funeral practices. At many marches, participants observed a moment of silence, often illuminated by candlelight. Women were encouraged to wear black or other colors associated with mourning.[37] Some went further to draw parallels between sexual violence and death. A 1981 event in Rochester, for example, included a "period of silence at a 'graveyard' and a eulogy for women victimized by 'institutional' violence including toxic shock and infant formula starvation."[38] Three years later, a TBTN in Arizona held a vigil for women who had been killed or assaulted. Dramatically, thirteen women dressed in violet shrouds carried a coffin to the state capitol building. "After setting the coffin on the ground, the shrouded women began to keen and wail for women who had been killed," attracting a crowd of onlookers.[39] More recently, students at the University of Pennsylvania incorporated "African libations and drum music as a ceremonial way of remembering those lost" into their TBTN.[40]

Other memorials recognized significant places associated with violence against women. March routes frequently marked sites where attacks on women occurred, such as red-light or pornography districts. In 1986, organizers of the rally in D.C. moved the event from its usual location at Dupont Circle to a park where a woman had been brutally raped.[41] That same year a march at San Diego State University circulated through campus; when it passed sites of recent assaults, "women carrying placards reading 'A Rape Occurred Here' stepped from the procession to mark the spot."[42] Most of these commemorations marking specific sites of violence were temporary, noted either by remarks or observations at the location or by physical signs that were not intended to remain permanently. An exception is the monument in Montreal that commemorates the 1989 massacre of fourteen women engineering students. That site has become a central location for annual TBTN events and commemorations of their murders and the violent deaths of other women.[43] But whether ephemeral or monumental, ritualized or frozen, the act of connecting TBTN to specific sites has become a way that activists inscribed women's history on the landscape, thereby giving a place different meaning.

Likewise, TBTN organizers have used temporary physical memorials to raise awareness. These memorials involve TBTN participants in the act of remembering together; they also speak to an audience of passersby, people who might not participate in TBTN but nonetheless can be moved through their encounter. A 1984 action in Phoenix, for instance, featured twenty-five life-sized silhouettes representing women who had been killed as the result of sexual or domestic violence. Hung throughout the campus of Arizona State University, the posters outlined a woman's figure on which her name, date of murder, and murderer's relationship was inscribed. An organizer explained that the figures were intended to "illustrate graphically, visually, and powerfully the loss of women's lives. These women are like shadows in all women's lives. Their absence speaks tellingly of the brutality we all face."[44] More recently, a 2007 display called Silent Silhouettes commemorated women who were murdered in East Lansing, Michigan. The installation featured women's bodies, cut out of plywood and painted red, with brief biographical information explaining the circumstances of each woman's death. One figure introduced "Heaven LaTalier, 14, Warren, MI," relating how "On November 18,

Heaven LaTalier's body was found in a dumpster behind the apartment building where she lived. Heaven was a freshman in high school. Nathaniel Tyrone Gilbert, a 16 year old boy who lived near her, is charged with sexually assaulting her before strangling her and putting her body into the dumpster."[45] This display resembles one that the TBTN Foundation now encourages organizers to set up to raise awareness. After cutting out life-size paper figures of men and women, the foundation instructs activists to "put a red paper heart on each and then make the heart broken for 1 out of every 4 women and 1 out of every 6/7 men."[46]

Beginning in the mid-1980s and accelerating in the 1990s, new generations of activists generally moved TBTN out of urban parks and streets and onto campuses. Students became primary organizers, with co-sponsorship and planning done by campus groups. University-based women's centers, student-run crisis lines, women's studies departments, and student feminist collectives replaced the coalitions of nonprofits, social service agencies, and women's groups responsible for earlier TBTNs. Bringing TBTN into academic spaces reasserted the links between activism and scholarship at the heart of feminist history. It also addressed a point of persistent conflict over the choice of locations selected by TBTN organizers. By marching through high-crime districts, participants identified areas where attacks occurred but also brought the attention of police and the public to communities already vulnerable to racist stereotyping by law enforcement. For those activists concerned about mitigating crime by eliminating stereotypes and economic inequalities, TBTN thereby signified feminists' insensitivity to and ignorance of such bias. A 1984 critique by Valerie Amos and Pratibha Parmar, for instance, charged that TBTN actually worsened conditions in communities of color: "When women marched through Black inner city areas to 'Reclaim the Night,' they played into the hands of the racist media and the fascist organizations, some of whom immediately formed vigilante groups patrolling the streets 'protecting' innocent white women by beating up black men."[47]

If TBTN's relocation relieved organizers from such criticisms, it also altered TBTN in other ways. Changing the locations of TBTN diminished activists' sense that they risked danger by invading men's sphere. When marching through red-light districts or city avenues, participants often encountered verbal abuse and harsh insults. These hostile reactions confirmed women's sense of the importance of reclaiming public streets and heightened the pride they felt at their collective acts of courage.[48]

In contrast, rather than intruding into male space, marking specific sites of violence, or pressing to change local laws, campus marches generally focused more on creating spaces where people could share their stories with their peers.[49]

Moreover, shifting organizational responsibility to campus groups changed how TBTN addressed violence. Early marches in Boston, D.C., New York, Pittsburgh, and elsewhere articulated an agenda for "reclaiming the night" that included infant and maternal death, death from illegal abortion, inadequate medical and mental health treatment for women, and racially motivated murders of African American men and children. These complex understandings often reflected, and were reflected in, the multi-issue collaborations that organizers built. Sponsors of Boston's first TBTN in 1978, for example, included battered women's shelters and organizations expressly focused on ending sexual violence, in addition to the Combahee River Collective, Prostitutes Union of Massachusetts, Wages for Housework, the Abortion Action Coalition, and the Committee to End Sterilization Abuse. Such coalitions were often tension-filled but found common ground for the purposes of TBTN.[50]

The broader agenda that typified TBTN in the 1970s and 1980s contrasts with more recent efforts focused on survivors' need to feel safe and understand they are not alone. An online history of TBTN in Ann Arbor, Michigan, exemplifies this transformation. It recalled that in 1978, members of the National Organization for Women organized the first local TBTN. Responsibility later shifted to the Ann Arbor Coalition Against Rape and University Women Against Rape. "Today, survivor speakouts are an inseparable part of Take Back the Night," the Ann Arbor website recounted. "Most present-day rallies offer survivors of violence an opportunity to give voice to their experiences and publicly affirm their transition from victim to survivor."[51] Similarly, at Wesleyan College in Connecticut, an organizer of the 2014 march explained that TBTN is "more of a supporting survivors event as opposed to a political rally because there's a community need for that." Whereas pre-march speeches and other parts of the TBTN program still aim to contextualize violence and understand its causes, the sharing of personal memories in a protective space is understood as "a powerful healing ritual for survivors and the men and women who care about them," in the words of organizers.[52]

New forms of collective protest continue to arise alongside TBTN's ritual. The SlutWalk, an international movement begun in Toronto in 2011,

for example, has drawn thousands of participants to march publicly to protest sexual violence and the culture of blame and shame that continues
to support it. More recently, a nationwide protest was sparked by Emma
Sulkowicz. A student at Columbia University, Sulkowicz carried her mattress around campus to publicize her school's inadequate investigation and
response to her 2013 rape. "Mattress Performance (Carry That Weight)"
became Sulkowicz's senior thesis; it also inspired students at schools
throughout the United States to stage similar actions. Like TBTN, these
events make visible the continued objectification of women but they reject
its recent mournful and somber tone, instead emphasizing angry protest. It
remains to be seen, however, whether they will endure.[53]

A USEABLE PAST

TBTN continues as an artifact of an earlier generation's activism and movement culture. As organizers draw from and reproduce a TBTN archive, the
visual images, rituals, and language they use fashion a continuum of wom-
en's history and activism. Repeated graphics including female silhouettes,
raised fists, and crescent moons represent a shared visual vocabulary for
TBTN and, more generally, for contemporary feminism that has changed
little since the 1970s; through this consistency, TBTN links contemporary
activists to their predecessors. Together the promotional materials, visual
representations, and ritualized actions reinforce a call to action. For younger
or newer activists, the forms of remembering help create a connection with
earlier marches and events in other places; for repeat and long-time participants, these activities evoke memories of their own participation. In these
ways, history helps create a sense of solidarity across time and generations
that can inspire activists to get (or stay) involved. The history also reminds
participants of the need for continued effort—despite many years of activism, the problem of violence against women persists. As one organizer from
the University of Toledo, in Ohio, explained: "We are celebrating 20 years of
a collective of women fighting for the end of violence against women. Sadly,
this also means after 20 years, Toledo still has a need for this event, meaning
that violence against women is an issue that has not seen improvement."[54]

Over the past forty years many symbols and rituals of TBTN have been
retained but their meaning and context have changed. In this way TBTN
functions as a form of living history, transforming to suit the present-day

needs of organizers and participants. There may be multiple explanations for why and how TBTN has changed, including shifts in commemorative forms. TBTN still relies on memory but the event also uses history in problematic ways, presenting only a partial truth. The collective memory that now forms the heart of TBTN focuses mostly on individual experience and overlooks more complex narratives of feminism and women's lives. This forgetting includes amnesia about TBTN's shifting focus. The result is a useable past that links TBTN to a history of collective action but might not do enough to mobilize activists to believe in their power to make change.

NOTES

Many thanks to Leslie Brown, Jacki Castledine, and the scholars who attended the Solidarity and Social Justice conference at Rutgers University in the fall of 2013. Their comments and questions gave me incentive to continue this project. My appreciation extends to Nancy Hewitt, also, for her ongoing encouragement and her valuable insights. She remains a constant source of inspiration.

1 "TBTN Hamilton Interviews the Most Excellent Andrea," Sept. 2, 2011, http://takebackthenighthamilton.worpress.com/2011/09/02/tbtn-hamilton-interviews-the-most-excellent-andrea.

2 On feminist waves, see Nancy Hewitt, ed., *No Permanent Waves: Recasting Histories of U.S. Feminism* (New Brunswick, NJ: Rutgers University Press, 2010); Hewitt, "Feminist Frequencies: Regenerating the Wave Metaphor," *Feminist Studies* 38 (Fall 2012): 658–680.

3 On social movement culture see, for example, Verta Taylor and Nancy Whittier, "Analytical Approaches to Social Movement Culture: the Culture of the Women's Movement," in *Social Movements and Culture*, ed. Hank Johnston (Florence, SC: Taylor and Francis, 2013); Eric Hobsbawm and Terence Ranger, eds., *The Invention of Tradition* (Cambridge: Cambridge University Press, 1992).

4 On public history and modern feminism see Nicole Eaton, "Moving History Forward: American Women Activists, the Search for a Useable Past, and the Creation of Public Memory" (PhD diss., Brown University, 2012); Lara Kelland, "Clio's Foot Soldiers: Twentieth-Century U.S. Social Movements and the Uses of Collective Memory" (PhD diss., University of Illinois-Chicago, 2013).

5 Edward S. Casey, "Public Memory in Place and Time," in *Framing Public Memory*, ed. Kendall R. Phillips (Tuscaloosa: University of Alabama Press, 2004), 25.

6 Maria Grever, "The Pantheon of Feminist Culture: Women's Movements and the Organization of Memory," *Gender and History* 9 (Aug. 1997): 370.

7 Hewitt, "Feminist Frequencies," 661; Sara M. Evans, "Feminism as History and Politics," *Minnesota History* 48 (Summer 1983): 235.

8 Laura Mayhall, "Creating the 'Suffragette Spirit': British Feminism and the Historical Imagination," in *Archive Stories: Facts, Fictions, and the Writing of History*, ed. Antoinette Burton (Durham, NC: Duke University Press, 2005), 247.

9 Bold, Knowles, and Leach argue that TBTN's primary emphasis is activism, not memorializing, although when the event occurs within the space of a memorial park, it takes on new meanings. Christine Bold, Ric Knowles, and Belinda Leach, "National Countermemorials: Feminist Memorializing and Cultural Countermemory: The Case of Marianne's Park," *Signs* 28 (Autumn 2002): 125–148.

10 Susan Brownmiller, *Against Our Will: Men, Women, and Rape* (New York: Martin Secker & Warburg, 1975); Ruth Rosen, *The World Split Open: How the Modern Women's Movement Changed America* (New York: Viking, 2000), 184–185; Sara M. Evans, *Tidal Wave: How Women Changed America at Century's End* (New York: Free Press, 2003), 207; Estelle B. Freedman, *No Turning Back: The History of Feminism and the Future of Women* (New York: Ballantine Books, 2002), 286; Maria Bevacqua, *Rape on the Public Agenda: Feminism and the Politics of Sexual Assault* (Boston: Northeastern University Press, 2000).

11 For a global history see Finn Mackay, *Radical Feminism: Feminist Activism in Movement* (London: Palgrave Macmillan, 2015); Finn Mackay, "Mapping the Routes: An Exploration of Charges of Racism Made against the 1970s UK Reclaim the Night Marches," *Women's Studies International Forum* 44 (2014): 46–54.

12 "History: Over Thirty Years of Progress," published Mar. 21, 2012, http://sites.temple.edu/takebackthenight/registration/history/. Others who cite the International Tribunal as the inspiration for the first TBTN include Mackay, *Radical Feminism*, 72–73; Freedman, *No Turning Back*, 286.

13 "Reclaim the Night," *Isis International Bulletin* 12 (Summer 1979): 12; Miriam Frank, "Anti-Rape Protests," *off our backs*, July/Aug. 1977, 9.

14 "Take Back the Night: A Short History," Sept. 1978, Folder 9; and Meeting Minutes, May 8, 1978, Folder 10, The Coalition to Take Back the Night Records, 1978–1991, Northeastern University Archives (hereafter NEU). See also "Preface: Some Background Notes," 1983 Take Back the Night Coalition (NYC), Folder 16, Coalition to Take Back the Night Records, NEU.

15 For example, see "Shining the Spotlight on Take Back the Night," accessed Apr. 24, 2014, http://wesleying.org/2014/04/24/shining-the-spotlight-on-take-back-the-night/#more-119376; Anne Pride, "Women Take Back the Night," *FAAR News*, Nov./Dec. 1977, 18.

16 Laura Lederer, ed., *Take Back the Night: Women on Pornography* (New York: William Morrow, 1980), 19.

17 For example, see "The History of Take Back the Night," *Gay Community News* 6 (1978): 8; "Protest Violence by Men," *New York Amsterdam News*, Oct. 20, 1984, 11; "Shining the Spotlight on Take Back the Night."

18 "Preface: Some Background Notes," 1983 Take Back the Night Coalition (NYC), Folder 16, Coalition to Take Back the Night Records, NEU.

19 "Night Riders," *off our backs*, Apr. 1979, 26. See also the letter from the New Haven Women's Liberation Center to the Boston Coalition soliciting information to help organize a TBTN march in Folder 6, Coalition to Take Back the Night Records, NEU; Mackay, *Feminist Activism*, 74–75.

20 "Take Back the Night Meeting #4—May 8," and "Goals and Principles," May 8, 1978, Folder 10, Coalition to Take Back the Night Records, NEU.

21 "Take Back the Night," Folder 14, The Coalition to Take Back the Night Records, NEU; "March to Stop Violence," *Women: A Journal of Liberation* 6 (1979): 30–31.

22 *Take Back the Night*, Aug. 26, 1978, brochure, Folder 1, The Coalition to Take Back the Night Records, NEU; Pamphlet, Nov. 18, 1978, Folder 9, Box 23, Women's Liberation Collection, Smith College.

23 "Minutes from the meeting of 12/18/89 held at Mt. Holyoke College," Box 1, Folder "Take Back the Night, 1989–90," Women's Resource Center Collection, Smith College.

24 http://takebackthenighthamilton.files.worpress.com/2013/08/mac-tbtn-solidarity -event-poster (accessed Sept. 11, 2013).

25 "The TBTN Event Manual," 24, last modified Apr. 30, 2015, http://www .takebackthenight.org.

26 Kate Eichhorn, *The Archival Turn in Feminism: Outrage in Order* (Philadelphia: Temple University Press, 2013), 3.

27 "Reclaim the Night: Personal Account," Folder 17, Coalition to Take Back the Night Records, NEU.

28 Marie Herbert, "Women March Against Violence," *Fenway News*, Sept. 1978, in Folder 12; and "Violence Against Women Is Not New," flyer, Folder 8, Coalition to Take Back the Night Records, NEU; "Take Back the Night," *off our backs*, Nov. 1981, 9. In some places, TBTN occurs on International Women's Day, March 8. "South Africa: March Against Violence Against Women," *off our backs*, June 1991, 9.

29 Mayhall, "Creating the 'Suffragette Spirit," 246.

30 "Take Back the Night" flyer, Nov. 18, 1978, Folder 9, Box 23, Women's Liberation Collection, Smith College.

31 Pride, "Women Take Back the Night."

32 "Violence Against Women is Not New," flyer, Oct. 31, 1978, Folder 8, Coalition to Take Back the Night Records, NEU.

33 "Dutch Women Take Back the Night," *off our backs*, Nov. 1978, 6; Frank, "Anti-Rape Protests."

34 "Interview with Helen Manning," and "Interview with Krista Warnke," posted Sept. 3, 2011, http://takebackthenighthamilton.wordpress.com/2011/09/03/interview-with -helen-manning/; Allan Lengel, "A Nighttime Rally Against Rape," *Washington Post*, Apr. 5, 1998, B5.

35 Nora Amalia Femenia and Carlos Ariel Gill, "Argentina's Mothers of Plaza de Mayo: The Mourning Process from Junta to Democracy," *Feminist Studies* 13 (Spring 1987): 9–18; Christopher Capozzola, "A Very American Epidemic: Memory Politics and Identity Politics in the AIDS Memorial Quilt, 1985–1993," *Radical History Review* 82 (Winter 2002): 91–109.

36 "History of the Clothesline Project," accessed July 22, 2013, http://www
.clotheslineproject.org/history.htm.

37 "Notes from the Sat., Feb 10 [1990] Meeting," Box 1, Folder "Take Back the Night,
1989–90," Women's Resource Center College, Smith College.

38 Loie Hayes, "More Actions Against Violence and Porn," *off our backs*, Aug./Sept.
1981, 17.

39 Chiquita Rollins, "Phoenix Women Take Back the Night . . . and More," *off our
backs*, Nov. 1984, 5.

40 "Activist Connections—Take Back the Night 2013."

41 Lori Woehrle, "D.C. Take Back the Night," *off our backs*, Oct. 1986, 8.

42 Leonard Bernstein, "Sixth Sexual Attack Reported at SDSU," *Los Angeles Times*, Oct.
22, 1986, 4; "San Diego Students Take Back the Night," *off our backs*, Dec. 1986, 12.

43 Julie Bindel, "The Montreal Massacre: Canada's Feminists Remember," *The
Guardian*, Dec. 3, 2012, http://www.theguardian.com/world/2012/dec/03/montreal
-massacre-canadas-feminists-remember.

44 Rollins, "Phoenix Women Take Back the Night."

45 Silent Silhouettes display, 2007, accessed Oct. 10, 2013, http://www.flickr.com/
photos/lansingtbtn/.

46 "The TBTN Event Manual," 10.

47 Valerie Amos and Pratibha Parmar, "Challenging Imperial Feminism," *Feminist
Review* 17 (Autumn 1984): 14; Mackay, "Mapping the Routes."

48 "Interview with Helen Manning"; Nancy Fithian, "Take Back the Night," *off our
backs*, Nov. 1981, 9.

49 "Shining the Spotlight on Take Back the Night."

50 "Take Back the Night: A Short History," Sept. 1978, Folder 9, Coalition to Take Back
the Night Records, NEU.

51 "Ann Arbor's Take Back the Night: History," accessed July 25, 2013, http://sitemaker
.umich.edu/tbtn/history_of_tbtn.

52 "Take Back the Night March Set for Weds., Oct. 26 at 6 P.M.," accessed July 25, 2013,
http://tulane.edu/socialwork/take-back-the-night.cfm; "Shining the Spotlight on Take
Back the Night"; "Activist Connections—Take Back the Night 2013," posted Apr. 7, 2013,
https://genderandsocs13.wordpress.com/2013/04/07/take-back-the-night-activist
-connections/.

53 Joetta L. Carr, "The SlutWalk Movement: A Study in Transnational Feminist
Activism," *Journal of Feminist Scholarship* 4 (Spring 2013): 24–38; Kate Taylor, "Mat-
tress Protest at Columbia University Continues into Graduation Event," *New York
Times*, May 19, 2015, A23.

54 Aimee Portala, "Take Back the Night Marks 20 Years in Toledo," Apr. 24, 2014,
http://wordpress.utoledo.edu/newsreleases/2014/04/24/take-back-the-night-marks
-20-years-in-toledo/.

SELECTED BIBLIOGRAPHY

Alexander, Michelle. *The New Jim Crow: Mass Incarceration in the Age of Colorblindness.* Rev. ed. New York: The New Press, 2012.

Baxandall, Rosalyn. "Re-Visioning the Women's Liberation Movement's Early Narrative: Early Second Wave African American Feminists." *Feminist Studies* 27, no. 1 (2001): 225–245.

Bevacqua, Maria. *Rape on the Public Agenda: Feminism and the Politics of Sexual Assault.* Boston: Northeastern University Press, 2000.

Bold, Christine, Ric Knowles, and Belinda Leach. "National Countermemorials: Feminist Memorializing and Cultural Countermemory: The Case of Marianne's Park." *Signs* 28 (Autumn 2002): 125–148.

Boyd, Nan Alamilla. "Who Is the Subject? Queer Theory Meets Oral History." *Journal of the History of Sexuality* 17, no. 2 (2008): 177–189.

Brest, Paul, and Ann Vandenberg. "Politics, Feminism, and the Constitution: The Anti-Pornography Movement in Minneapolis." *Stanford Law Review* 39, no. 3 (February 1987): 607–661.

Brinkley, Douglass. *Rosa Parks.* New York: Penguin Press, 2000.

Brown, Elsa Barkley. "What Has Happened Here: The Politics of Difference in Women's History and Feminist Politics." *Feminist Studies* 18 (Summer 1992): 295–312.

Burns, Stewart. *Daybreak of Freedom: The Montgomery Bus Boycott.* Chapel Hill: University of North Carolina Press, 1997.

Butler, Judith. *Undoing Gender.* New York: Routledge, 2007.

Butler, Pamela. "Sex and the Cities: Re-evaluating 1980s Feminist Politics in Minneapolis and St. Paul." In *Queer Twin Cities: Twin Cities GLBT Oral History Project,* edited by Michael David Franklin, Larry Knopp, Kevin P. Murphy, Ryan Patrick Murphy, Jennifer L. Pierce, Jason Ruiz, and Alex T. Urquhart, 203–239. Minneapolis: University of Minnesota Press, 2010.

Capozzola, Christopher. "A Very American Epidemic: Memory Politics and Identity Politics in the AIDS Memorial Quilt, 1985–1993." *Radical History Review* 82 (Winter 2002): 91–109.

Castledine, Jacqueline. *Cold War Progressives: Women's Interracial Organizing for Peace and Freedom.* Champaign: University of Illinois Press, 2012.

Clark-Lewis, Elizabeth. *Living In, Living Out: African American Domestics in Washington, D.C., 1910–1940.* Washington, DC: Smithsonian Institution Press, 1996.

Crenshaw, Kimberlé. "Mapping the Margins: Intersectionality, Identity Politics, and Violence against Women of Color." *Stanford Law Review* 43, no. 6 (1991): 1241–1299.

Curtin, Mary Ellen. "The 'Human World' of Black Women in Alabama Prisons, 1870–1900." In *Hidden Histories of Women in the New South,* edited by Virginia Bernhard,

Betty Brandon, Elizabeth Fox-Genovese, Theda Perdue, and Elizabeth Turner, 11–30. Columbia: University of Missouri Press, 1994.

Davis, Angela. "Joanne Little: The Dialectics of Rape." *Ms.* 3, no. 12 (June 1975): 74–77.

Dinner, Deborah. "The Universal Childcare Debate: Rights Mobilization, Social Policy, and the Dynamics of Feminist Activism, 1966–1974." *Law and History Review* 28, no. 3 (2010): 577–628.

Downs, Donald Alexander. *The New Politics of Pornography.* Chicago: University of Chicago Press, 1989.

Duggan, Lisa, and Nan Hunter, eds. *Sex Wars: Sexual Dissent and Political Culture.* New York: Routledge, 1995.

DuPlessis, Rachel Blau, and Ann Snitow, eds. *The Feminist Memoir Project: Voices from Women's Liberation.* New York: Three Rivers Press, 1998.

Echols, Alice. *Daring to Be Bad: Radical Feminism in America 1967–1975.* Minneapolis: University of Minnesota Press, 1989.

Eichhorn, Kate. *The Archival Turn in Feminism: Outrage in Order.* Philadelphia: Temple University Press, 2013.

Enke, A. Finn. *Finding the Movement: Sexuality, Contested Space, and Feminist Activism.* Durham, NC: Duke University Press, 2007.

Evans, Sara M. "Feminism as History and Politics." *Minnesota History* 48 (Summer 1983): 230–235.

———. *Tidal Wave: How Women Changed America at Century's End.* New York: The Free Press, 2003.

Fergus, Devin. *Liberalism, Black Power, and the Making of American Politics, 1965–1980.* Athens: University of Georgia Press, 2009.

Fischer, Gayle V. *Pantaloons and Power: A Nineteenth-Century Dress Reform in the United States.* Kent, OH: Kent State University Press, 2001.

Freedman, Estelle B. *No Turning Back: The History of Feminism and the Future of Women.* New York: Ballantine Books, 2002.

———. *Redefining Rape: Sexual Violence in the Era of Suffrage and Segregation.* Cambridge, MA: Harvard University Press, 2013.

Gallagher, Julie. *Black Women and Politics in New York City.* Champaign: University of Illinois Press, 2012.

Geary, Daniel. *Beyond Civil Rights: The Moynihan Report and Its Legacy.* Philadelphia: University of Pennsylvania Press, 2015.

Giddings, Paula. *When and Where I Enter: The Impact of Black Women on Race and Sex in America.* New York: Morrow, 1984.

Ginzberg, Lori D. *Untidy Origins: A Story of Woman's Rights in Antebellum New York.* Chapel Hill: University of North Carolina Press, 2005.

Glenn, Evelyn Nakano, Grace Chang, and Linda Rennie Forcey, eds. *Mothering: Ideology, Experience, and Agency.* New York: Routledge, 1993.

Gore, Dayo F. *Radicalism at the Crossroads: African American Women Activists in the Cold War.* New York: New York University Press, 2011.

Grever, Maria. "The Pantheon of Feminist Culture: Women's Movements and the Organization of Memory." *Gender and History* 9 (August 1997): 364–374.

Gross, Kali N. "African American Women, Mass Incarceration, and the Politics of Protection." In "Historians and the Carceral State." Special issue, *Journal of American History* 102, no. 1 (June 2015): 25–33.

———. *Colored Amazons: Crime, Violence, and Black Women in the City of Brotherly Love, 1880–1910*. Durham, NC: Duke University Press, 2006.

Gross, Kali N., and Cheryl D. Hicks. "Introduction—Gendering the Carceral State: African American Women, History, and Criminal Justice." *Journal of African American History* 100, no. 3 (Summer 2015): 357–365.

Haley, Sarah. *No Mercy Here: Gender, Punishment and the Making of Jim Crow Modernity*. Chapel Hill: University of North Carolina Press, 2016.

Hall, Jacquelyn Dowd. "The Mind That Burns in Each Body: Women, Rape, and Racial Violence." In *Powers of Desire: The Politics of Sexuality*, edited by Ann Snitow, Christina Stansell, and Sharon Thompson, 328–349. New York: Monthly Review Press, 1983.

Hamlin, Françoise N. *Crossroads at Clarksdale: The Black Freedom Struggle in the Mississippi Delta after World War II*. Chapel Hill: University of North Carolina Press, 2012.

Harwell, Debbie Z. *Wednesdays in Mississippi: Proper Ladies Working for Radical Change, Freedom Summer 1964*. Jackson: University of Mississippi Press, 2014.

Hewitt, Nancy A. "Beyond the Search for Sisterhood: American Women's History in the 1980s." *Social History* 10, no. 3 (October 1985): 299–321.

———. "The Emma Thread: Communitarian Values, Global Visions." In *Voices of Women Historians: The Personal, the Political, the Professional*, edited by Eileen Boris and Nupur Chaudhiri, 234–246. Bloomington: Indiana University Press, 1999.

———. "Feminist Frequencies: Regenerating the Wave Metaphor." *Feminist Studies* 38 (Fall 2012): 658–680.

———, ed. *No Permanent Waves: Recasting Histories of U.S. Feminism*. New Brunswick, NJ: Rutgers University Press, 2010.

———. *Southern Discomfort: Women's Activism in Tampa, Florida, 1880s–1920s*. Champaign: University of Illinois Press, 2003.

Hickey, Georgina. "The Geography of Pornography: Neighborhood Feminism and the Battle Against 'Dirty Bookstores' in Minneapolis." *Frontiers: A Journal of Women's Studies* 32, no. 1 (2001): 125–151.

Hicks, Cheryl D. *Talk with You Like a Woman: African American Women, Justice, and Reform in New York, 1890–1935*. Chapel Hill: University of North Carolina Press, 2010.

Hine, Darlene Clark. "Rape and the Inner Lives of Black Women in the Middle West." *Signs* 14, no. 4 (Summer 1989): 912–920.

Horowitz, Daniel. *Betty Friedan and the Making of the Feminine Mystique*. Amherst: University of Massachusetts Press, 1998.

Hunter, Tera. *To 'Joy My Freedom: Southern Black Women's Lives and Labors after the Civil War*. Cambridge, MA: Harvard University Press, 1997.

Ignatiev, Noel. *How the Irish Became White*. New York: Routledge, 1995.

Isenberg, Nancy. *Sex and Citizenship in Antebellum America*. Chapel Hill: University of North Carolina Press, 1998.

Jetter, Alexis, Annelise Orleck, and Diana Taylor, eds. *The Politics of Motherhood: Activist Voices from Left to Right*. Hanover, NH: University Press of New England, 1997.

Kaplan, Temma. *Crazy for Democracy: Women in Grassroots Movements*. New York: Routledge, 1997.

Kunzel, Regina. *Criminal Intimacy: Prison and the Uneven History of Modern American Sexuality*. Chicago: University of Chicago Press, 2008.

Ladd-Taylor, Molly. "Toward Defining Maternalism in U.S. History." *Journal of Women's History* 5, no. 2 (1993): 110–113.

Laville, Helen. *Cold War Women: The International Activities of American Women's Organisations*. Manchester, UK: Manchester University Press, 2002.

LeFlouria, Talitha L. *Chained in Silence: Black Women and Convict Labor in the New South*. Chapel Hill: University of North Carolina Press, 2015.

Lerner, Gerda. *Fireweed: A Political Autobiography*. Philadelphia: Temple University Press, 2002.

Logsdon-Conradsen, Susan. "From Maternalism to Activist Mothering." *Journal of the Motherhood Initiative for Research & Community Involvement* 2, no. 1 (2011): 9–36.

Lynch-Brennan, Margaret. *The Irish Bridget: Irish Immigrant Women in Domestic Service in America, 1840–1930*. Syracuse, NY: Syracuse University Press, 2009.

Mackay, Finn. "Mapping the Routes: An Exploration of Charges of Racism Made against the 1970s UK Reclaim the Night Marches." *Women's Studies International Forum* 44 (2014): 46–54.

———. *Radical Feminism: Feminist Activism in Movement*. London: Palgrave Macmillan, 2015.

MacKinnon, Catharine, and Andrea Dworkin, eds. *In Harm's Way: The Pornography Civil Rights Hearings*. Cambridge, MA: Harvard University Press, 1997.

Mattingly, Carol. *Appropriate[ing] Dress: Women's Rhetorical Style in Nineteenth-Century America*. Carbondale: Southern Illinois University Press, 2002.

May, Elaine Tyler. *Homeward Bound: American Families in the Cold War Era*. New York: Basic Books, 1988.

Mayhall, Laura. "Creating the 'Suffragette Spirit': British Feminism and the Historical Imagination." In *Archive Stories: Facts, Fictions, and the Writing of History*, edited by Antoinette Burton, 232–250. Durham, NC: Duke University Press, 2005.

McCaskill, Barbara. *Love, Liberation, and Escaping Slavery: William and Ellen Craft in Cultural Memory*. Athens: University of Georgia Press, 2015.

McDuffie, Erik S. *Sojourning for Freedom: Black Women, American Communism, and the Making of Black Left Feminism*. Durham, NC: Duke University Press, 2011.

McGuire, Danielle L. *At the Dark End of the Street: Black Women, Rape, and Resistance—A New History of the Civil Rights Movement from Rosa Parks to the Rise of Black Power*. New York: Alfred A. Knopf, 2010.

———. "Joan Little and the Triumph of Testimony." In *Freedom Rights: New Perspectives on the Civil Rights Movement*, edited by Danielle McGuire and John Dittmer, 191–221. Lexington: University Press of Kentucky, 2011.

McNeil, Genna Rae. "The Body, Sexuality, and Self-Defense in *State vs Joan Little*, 1974–75." *Journal of African American History* 93, no. 2 (Spring 2008): 235–261.

———. "'Joanne Is You and Joanne Is Me': A Consideration of African American Women and the 'Free Joan Little' Movement, 1974–1975." In *Sisters in the Struggle: African American Women in the Civil Rights–Black Power Movement*, edited by Bettye Collier-Thomas and V. P. Franklin, 259–279. New York: New York University Press, 2001.

Meyerowitz, Joanne, ed. *Not June Cleaver: Women and Gender in Postwar America, 1945–1960*. Philadelphia: Temple University Press, 1994.

Morris, Tiyi. *Womanpower Unlimited and the Black Freedom Struggle in Mississippi*. Athens: University of Georgia Press, 2015.

Muhammad, Khalil Gibran. *The Condemnation of Blackness: Race, Crime, and the Making of Modern Urban America*. Cambridge, MA: Harvard University Press, 2010.

Nadasen, Premilla. *Household Workers Unite: The Untold Story of African American Women Who Built a Movement*. Boston: Beacon Press, 2015.

Ownby, Ted, ed. *The Civil Rights Movement in Mississippi*. Jackson: University Press of Mississippi, 2013.

Polatnick, M. Rivka. "Diversity in Women's Liberation Ideology: How a Black and a White Group of the 1960s Viewed Motherhood." *Signs* 21 no. 3 (1996): 679–706.

Potter, Claire Bond. "Taking Back Times Square: Feminist Repertoires and the Transformation of Urban Space in Late Second Wave Feminism." In "Calling the Law Into Question," edited by Andy Urban and Amy Tyson. Special issue, *Radical History Review* 113 (April 1, 2012): 67–80.

Reger, Jo. "Motherhood and the Construction of Feminist Identities: Variations in a Women's Movement Organization." *Sociological Inquiry* 71 (2001): 85–110.

Rosen, Ruth. *The World Split Open: How the Modern Women's Movement Changed America*. New York: Viking, 2000.

Rzeszutek, Sara. *James and Esther Cooper Jackson: Love and Courage in the Black Freedom Movement*. Lexington: University Press of Kentucky, 2015.

Sears, Clare. *Arresting Dress: Cross-Dressing, Law, and Fascination in Nineteenth-Century San Francisco*. Durham, NC: Duke University Press, 2015.

Silliman, Jael, Marlene Fried, Loretta Ross, and Elena Gutiérrez. *Undivided Rights: Women of Color Organize for Reproductive Justice*. Cambridge, MA: South End Press, 2004.

Snitow, Ann. "Feminism and Motherhood: An American Reading." *Feminist Review* 40 (1992): 32–51.

Springer, Kimberly. *Living for the Revolution: Black Feminist Organizations, 1968–1980*. Durham, NC: Duke University Press, 2005.

Stryker, Susan. *Transgender History*. Berkeley, CA: Seal Press, 2008.

Sze, Julie. *Noxious New York: The Racial Politics of Urban Health and Environmental Justice*. Cambridge, MA: The MIT Press, 2007.

Taylor, Verta, and Nancy Whittier. "Analytical Approaches to Social Movement Culture: The Culture of the Women's Movement." In *Social Movements and Culture*, edited by Hank Johnston, 163–187. Florence, SC: Taylor and Francis, 2013.

Theoharis, Jeanne. *The Rebellious Life of Mrs. Rosa Parks*. New York: Beacon Press, 2013.

Thompson, Heather Ann. "Why Mass Incarceration Matters: Rethinking Crisis, Decline, and Transformation in Postwar American History." *Journal of American History* 97, no. 3 (December 2010): 703–734.

Umansky, Lauri, *Motherhood Reconceived: Feminism and the Legacies of the Sixties*. New York: New York University Press, 1996.

Valk, Anne, and Leslie Brown. *Living with Jim Crow: African American Women and Memories of the Segregated South*. New York: Palgrave Macmillan, 2010.

Van Cleve, Stewart. *Land of Ten Thousand Loves: A History of Queer Minnesota*. Minneapolis: University of Minnesota Press, 2012.

Vapnek, Lara. *Breadwinners: Working Women and Economic Independence, 1865–1920*. Champaign: University of Illinois Press, 2009.

Weigand, Kate. *Red Feminism: American Communism and the Making of Women's Liberation*. Baltimore: Johns Hopkins University Press, 2001.

White, Deborah Gray. *Ar'n't I a Woman?: Female Slaves in the Plantation South*. New York: W. W. Norton, 1985.

———. *Too Heavy a Load: Black Women in Defense of Themselves, 1894–1994*. New York: W. W. Norton, 1999.

NOTES ON CONTRIBUTORS

LESLIE BROWN was a professor in history at Williams College, where she taught courses in race and gender in U.S. history. She completed her BA at Tufts University, and her MA and PhD at Duke University, where she co-coordinated the NEH-supported project "Behind the Veil: Documenting African American Life in the Jim Crow South." She is the author of *Upbuilding Black Durham: Gender, Class, and Black Community Development in the Urban South,* her first book, which won the 2009 Frederick Jackson Turner Prize (Organization of American Historians). With Anne Valk, she co-edited *Living with Jim Crow: African American Women and Memories of the Segregated South,* which won the Oral History Association Biennial Book Award in 2011. In 2014, she published an edited collection, *African American Voices II: From Emancipation to the Present.*

JACQUELINE CASTLEDINE is a core faculty member in the University Without Walls at the University of Massachusetts Amherst, where she also directs program innovation for the College of Humanities and Fine Arts. She is co-editor of *Breaking the Wave: Women, Their Organizations, and Feminism, 1945–1985,* author of *Cold War Progressives: Women's Interracial Organizing for Peace and Justice,* and has published in numerous collections and journals including *Reviews in American History,* the *Journal of Women's History,* and *Women's History Review.*

KIRSTEN DELEGARD is a scholar-in-residence in the history department at Augsburg College, where she runs the Historyapolis Project. The project uses digital tools to make the history of Minneapolis accessible to a broad audience. Augsburg students are deeply involved with Historyapolis, which works to catalyze community dialogue around challenging aspects of local history. Delegard has a PhD in women's history from Duke University. She is the author of *Battling Miss Bolsheviki: The Origins of Female Conservatism in the United States* (2012). She was also the co-editor, with Nancy A. Hewitt, of the textbook *Women, Families, and Communities: Readings in American History* (2008). She was the visual editor of Mary Lethert Wingerd's *North Country: The Making of Minnesota* (2010). Delegard is also at work on a new history of Minneapolis tentatively titled *City of Light and Darkness: The Making of a Progressive Metropolis in Minneapolis.*

ANDREA ESTEPA is a visiting assistant professor of history at the College of William and Mary. She holds a Ph.D. in history from Rutgers University. Her article "Taking the White Gloves Off: Women Strike for Peace and 'the Movement,' 1967-73" appears in *Feminist Coalitions: Historical Perspectives on Second-Wave U.S. Feminism.* She is at work on a book about Women Strike for Peace and its role in the development of the New Left.

PAULA J. GIDDINGS is the Elizabeth A. Woodson 1922 Professor in Africana Studies at Smith College. She is also the editor of *Meridians: feminism, race, transnationalism,* a peer-reviewed scholarly journal supported by Smith College and published by Indiana University Press. She has published four books: *When and Where I Enter: The Impact of Black Women on Race and Sex in America; In Search of Sisterhood: Delta Sigma Theta and the Challenge of the Black Sorority Movement; Burning All Illusions* (editor), an anthology of articles on race published by *The Nation* magazine from 1867 to 2000; and *Ida, A Sword among Lions: Ida B. Wells and the Campaign against Lynching,* winner of the *Los Angeles Times* Prize in Biography (2008), the Letitia Woods Brown Book Award from the Association of Black Women Historians (2008), and deemed one of the most important books of the year by the *Chicago Tribune* and the *Washington Post.*

CHRISTINA GREENE is an associate professor in the Department of Afro-American Studies, and a faculty affiliate in the Departments of History, and Gender & Women's Studies at the University of Wisconsin–Madison. She received her PhD in history from Duke University in 1996. From 1985 to 1994 she was the Project Director at the Duke University/University of North Carolina (Chapel Hill) Center for Research on Women; and from 1988 to 1997 she served on the Board of Directors at the Institute for Southern Studies. She is the author of *Our Separate Ways: Women and the Black Freedom Movement in Durham, North Carolina,* which won the 2005 Julia Cherry Spruill Award for best book in southern women's history from the Southern Association of Women's Historians. She is currently at work on a book-length study of the 1970s Free Joan Little Campaign.

JEN MANION is an associate professor of history at Amherst College. They received a BA from the University of Pennsylvania and a PhD from Rutgers University. Their book *Liberty's Prisoners: Carceral Culture in Early America* is an intersectional social history of the origins of the prison system in the U.S. Manion has published essays in *TSQ: Transgender Studies Quarterly, QED: A Journal in GLBTQ Worldmaking, Signs: Journal of Women in Culture and Society,* and *Radical History Review.* They were awarded a National Endowment for the Humanities Fellowship at the American Antiquarian Society in 2012–2013 to examine gender crossing in the eighteenth and nineteenth centuries. Their new manuscript is tentatively titled, "Born in the Wrong Time: Transgender Archives and the History of Possibility, 1770–1870."

DANIELLE L. McGUIRE is the author of *At the Dark End of the Street: Black Women, Rape, and Resistance—a New History of the Civil Rights Movement from Rosa Parks to the Rise of Black Power,* which won the 2011 Frederick Jackson Turner Award from the Organization of American Historians and the 2011 Lillian Smith Book Award. She is an associate professor in the history department at Wayne State University. Her dissertation on sexualized racial violence and the African American freedom struggle received the 2008 Lerner Scott Prize for best dissertation in women's history. Her essay, "It was Like We Were All Raped: Sexualized Violence, Community Mobilization, and the African American Freedom Struggle," published in the *Journal of American History,* won the A. Elizabeth Taylor Prize for best essay in southern women's history and was reprinted in the *Best Essays in American History 2006.* McGuire is a distinguished lecturer for the Organization of American Historians and has appeared on CNN, MSNBC, National Public Radio, BookTV, and dozens of local radio stations throughout the United States, Europe, Canada, and South America. Her popular essays have appeared online on the *Huffington Post,* TheGrio.com and TheRoot.com, and CNN.com.

DANIELLE PHILLIPS is an assistant professor in the Multicultural Women's and Gender Studies Department at Texas Woman's University. She teaches courses on feminist and womanist theories, the politics of motherhood, and women's labors and migrations. Her work has appeared in *Signs* and *Journal of the Motherhood Initiative for Research and Community Involvement.* Her current book project, "Putting Their Hands on Race: Irish Immigrant and

Southern African American Domestic Workers in New York, 1865–1940," is a comparative study of Irish immigrant and southern African American women who labored as domestic workers after having migrated to New York.

ARIELLA ROTRAMEL is the Vandana Shiva Assistant Professor in Gender and Women's Studies at Connecticut College. Rotramel holds a PhD in Women's and Gender Studies from Rutgers, The State University of New Jersey. Rotramel's research and teaching agenda reflect her interdisciplinary training and commitment to feminist praxis. Her book project, "Pushing Back: Transnational Women of Color Leadership," is an intensive study of two transnational communities of color organizations in New York City seeking to address housing justice, domestic worker's rights, and environmental racism.

REBECCA TUURI received her PhD in history from Rutgers in 2012. She is currently an assistant professor of history at the University of Southern Mississippi, where she teaches African American, civil rights, women's and gender, and world history. Her manuscript, "Careful Crusaders: The National Council of Negro Women in the Black Freedom Struggle," is under advance contract with the University of North Carolina Press in its Justice, Power, and Politics series. She has an article, "'This was the most meaningful thing that I've ever done': The Personal Civil Rights Approach of Wednesdays in Mississippi," forthcoming in the *Journal of Women's History*. She is the recipient of a 2016 National Endowment for the Humanities Summer Stipend and also has presented at several national conferences on the history of Wednesdays in Mississippi, the National Council of Negro Women, and women in the civil rights movement more broadly.

ANNE VALK is the associate director for Public Humanities at Williams College where she works on engaged humanities projects with students, faculty, and community organizations. Since receiving her PhD in history from Duke University in 1996, she has published several books on women's history, including *Radical Sisters: Second-Wave Feminism and Black Liberation in Washington, DC, 1963–1980*, which won the Richard L. Wentworth Illinois Award in American History awarded by the University of Illinois Press. With Leslie Brown, she wrote *Living with Jim Crow: African American Women and Memories of the Segregated South*, winner of the 2011 book award from the Oral History Association. She has also published many book chapters and articles on topics related to feminism, oral history, and public history. From 2014 to 2016 Valk served as vice-president and then president of the Oral History Association.

DEBORAH GRAY WHITE is Board of Governors Distinguished Professor of History at Rutgers University, New Brunswick, New Jersey. She is author of *Ar'n't I a Woman? Female Slaves in the Plantation South*; *Too Heavy a Load: Black Women in Defense of Themselves, 1894–1994*; several K–12 textbooks on U.S. history; and *Let My People Go, African Americans 1804–1860* (1999). In 2008, she published an edited work entitled *Telling Histories: Black Women in the Ivory Tower*, a collection of personal narratives written by African American women historians that chronicle the entry of black women into the historical profession and the development of the field of black women's history. *Freedom On My Mind: A History of African Americans*, a co-authored text, is her most recent publication. As a fellow at the Woodrow Wilson International Center for Scholars in Washington, D.C., and as a John Simon Guggenheim Fellow, White conducted research on her in-press manuscript, "Lost in the USA: Marching for Identity at the Turn of the Millennium." She was recently awarded the Carter G. Woodson Medallion for excellence in African American history, and also received an honorary doctorate from her undergraduate alma mater, Binghamton University.

INDEX

abortion: Abortion Action Coalition, 201; Jane abortion service, 149, 159–161; legal access to, 150, 158–159, 201; and radical feminists, 150, 158–159. *See also* reproductive rights

Action Committee for Decent Daycare (ACDC), 157, 158, 161

Action Fellowships, 35

African American men. *See* Black men

African American women. *See* Black women

AIDS Memorial Quilt, 198

Alexander, Ferris and Edward, 166–167, 171, 172, 175, 177

Alligood, Clarence, 98, 106, 113n1

Alonso, Harriet, 92

Alpert, Jane, 152; "Mother Right," 152

Amnesty International, 109

Amos, Valerie, 200

Anderson, Becky, 173fig.9.1

Anderson, Liz, 173fig.9.1, 174, 176

Andrea (student demonstrator), 186

Ann Arbor Coalition Against Rape, 201

Anthony, Susan B., 129, 140

antipornography feminists, 175–177; and Christian Right, 168, 185n69; reprisals against, 178–179; and "sex-positive" feminists, 168

Barkley-Brown, Elsa, 2; "What Has Happened Here," 2

Barnes, Thelma, 38

Barnett, Etta Moten, 36

Barrett, James R., 26

Batson, Ruth, 34, 36, 46n9

Baxandall, Rosalyn, 151, 158, 163n17

Beaglehole, Ruth, 158

Beal, Frances, 32, 33, 34, 37, 39, 40, 41, 44; "Double Jeopardy," 33

Beecher, Catharine, 131

Benería, Lourdes, 147–148, 149, 157

Benjamin, Jean, 36

Bethea-Shields, Karen, 104, 106, 108, 110, 118n33, 118n35

Bethune, Mary McLeod, 46n12

Blacer, Cathy, 173fig.9.1

Black activists: and civil rights movement, 34; and flexible loyalties, 46n11; and KKK terrorization, 102; as NCNW staff, 36; and networking, 44

Black Codes, 22, 136

Black feminists: Black feminist organizations, 32–34; and motherhood, 151, 152; and reproductive rights, 160

Black freedom movement, 4–5, 39; and Height, 34; and liberalism, 44; NCNW support of, 35, 36; shift to Black separatism, 33. *See also* civil rights movement

Black men: Black women unprotected by, 69; and Irish immigrant men, 28, 28n3; and Joan Little, 106; mobility of enslaved, 136–37; Parks on, 69, 71–72, 79; and TBTN, 200; voting rights of, xix

Black Nationalist movement, 151–52

Blackness: gendered criminalization of, 101; redefining of, 27

Black Panthers, 42, 105

Black Power movement: and criminalization of Blackness, 101; and liberalism, 45n6; and NCNW, 34, 41, 42, 44; origins of, 45n6

Blackwell, Unita, 36, 38, 39, 40, 47n32

Black womanhood: and dress reform, 132,

CPSIA information can be obtained
at www.ICGtesting.com
Printed in the USA
LVOW10s1232301116

515039LV00004B/7/P